AFC Champs
1978, 1980

Steelers!

ONLy 4 Time
SUPER BowL
Winners

SUPER BowL
Wins
IX, X, XIII, XIV

World ChaMPS

1980 SUPER BowL
XIV
F STEELERS 31
RAMS 19

SUPER BowL XIII
STEELERS 35
CowBoys 31

WORLD
CHAMPIONS

SuPer BowL IX
STEELERS 16
ViKings 6

SUPERBowLX
STEELERS 21
CowBoys 17

Steelers!

Team of the Decade
by Lou Sahadi   Foreword by Art Rooney

Times
BOOKS

Photographs courtesy of:
Mickey Palmer—Cover
Mickey Palmer and Mitchell Riebel (Focus On Sports) —
Inside Color
Harry Homa and Bill Amatucci —Black and White
Photography

Published by TIMES BOOKS, a division
of Quadrangle/The New York Times Book Co., Inc.
Three Park Avenue, New York, N.Y. 10016

Published simultaneously in Canada by
Fitzhenry & Whiteside, Ltd., Toronto.

Copyright © 1979 by Lou Sahadi.

Library of Congress Cataloging in Publication Data

Sahadi, Lou.
    Steelers, team of the decade.

    1. Pittsburgh Steelers (Football club)—History.
2. Football players—United States—Biography.
I. Title.
GV956.P57S23 1979   796.33'264'0974886
79-13214
ISBN 0-8129-0843-0

Manufactured in the United States of America.

For
Tina, Michael, Amy, Nina,
Marian, Ronnie,
and Philip . . . Godchildren all.

Contents

Foreword

A lot of people feel that as you grow older you become a center of wisdom. I do not subscribe to such a theory. What really happens is that you make your share of mistakes and, I suppose, the more successful people learn by these errors. Perhaps you could sum this idea up in a word: experience.

And I have had plenty of experience. All my life I have been involved in sports. I have been a player, a football coach, and a baseball manager. I have owned the Pittsburgh Steelers since 1933.

(Editor's note: Rooney and his brother, Father Silas, still hold records in the old Three-I baseball league and both were offered contracts in the major leagues. Rooney's arm went dead, and Father Silas turned down a New York Yankee offer and entered the seminary.)

One thing I learned from experience: You are a genius when you win and plain dumb when you lose. Believe me, a fine line separates the two.

Winning is like making Irish Stew: You must blend the ingredients properly. I have no idea how to make Irish Stew, but in sports you must have a blend of good coaching, good players, and good luck. When things are going right the enemy's punt tumbles into the end zone. When your luck is sour the punt rolls out on the four.

Over the years we have had some great teams in Pittsburgh, but one of the ingredients was always missing. Our alumni include some of the most illustrious athletes ever to play in the league. And we have had some coaches who were candidates for the Hall of Fame.

Perhaps one of the coaches, Buddy Parker, summed it up best. Upon resignation he told newsmen, "This team has been so damned unlucky that when it gets lucky, it will last for a long, long time."

During the not so lucky times a newsman came into my office and said, "I've finally figured out who the black cat is around here."

"Who?" I asked.

"You," he said. "You are the only one who has been around here since the beginning."

All this notwithstanding, the ingredients began to mix in 1969. That was the year my two boys—Dan and Art, both deeply active in the administration of the team—and I began looking for a new coach. We compiled lists, held extensive interviews, and eventually decided on an impressive young man named Chuck Noll. Like so many assistant coaches he was unknown to the public at large but within the football fraternity he owned strong credentials.

In his first year Chuck's team won its opener against the Detroit Lions and then dropped thirteen games in a row. What impressed me most was that despite the adversity Noll never lost control of the team. That old friend experience told me the Steelers had a great coach.

From that time on, the Steelers have compiled one of the most fabled records in the history of the National Football League. That record is well chronicled in this fine book.

Art Rooney

Acknowledgments

The author wishes to express his sincere thanks
to Joe Gordon of the Pittsburgh Steelers and
Fran Connors of the National Football League,
who provided the necessary research towards
the writing of this book, and to Jeannette Auger,
who assisted on the clerical end.

Introduction

Chuck Noll

It was some kind of year. It's been some kind of decade, for that matter. During that period the Pittsburgh Steelers have established themselves among the great teams in the history of professional football. That's saying a lot, but then the Steelers have accomplished a great deal to earn the accolade.

In the last five years the Steelers have appeared in the Super Bowl three times. No other team has done that. Pittsburgh has won all three times. No other team has achieved that, either. All the great teams of the past can be measured against the Steelers. It will take a lot of doing to beat their record.

Yet it was a long time coming. In the first forty-two years of the franchise the Steelers never won anything. That defies belief. But what they have accomplished the last seven years also appears unbelievable. They háve made the playoffs every year since 1972. The famine has become a feast. What better reward for generous owner Art Rooney and his two sons, Dan and Art Jr., who along with faithful Steeler fans waited all those years?

It all began in 1969, when Chuck Noll was named coach. He was picked to lead the Steelers out of the wilderness. They were truly lost. In the previous five seasons Pittsburgh had won only eighteen games. Hardly inspiring. Furthermore, the Steelers had only produced four winning seasons since 1950.

Amazingly, it took Noll only three years to make the Steelers winners. Not only that, he has kept them on top since. In the last seven years the Steelers have produced a 76–23–1 record. That's a winning percentage of 76 percent. Amazing, indeed.

The decade will end with the 1979 season. But the Steelers don't plan to fade after that. After Pittsburgh emerged victorious in Super Bowl XIII, Noll felt that his team hadn't peaked yet. It's awesome to think what will happen next. The next decade should be interesting. . . .

L.S.

Steelers!

The Rooneys

The cigar is always there. It's part of his identity. He's never been much for Gucci shoes or custom clothes or chauffeur-driven limousines. They're definitely not his style. He would be uncomfortable with them. He would much rather sit around puffing on his cigar, talking about the old days, the hard times and the good times. His recall is amazing for someone seventy-eight years old. He doesn't want to forget the smoke-filled hotel rooms or the booze or the daily trips to the race track. They are so much a part of his life, just like the storied hilltop Victorian house he has lived in for over forty-five years. It is as if he didn't want things to change, and while the years have changed around him, Art Rooney hasn't.

In a world of never-ending change Rooney has remained the same generous, compassionate, kind owner amid the organized violence that is professional football. He's been part of its existence since 1933, when he invested $2,500 in securing a franchise for Pittsburgh, a city he has been identified with ever since. For forty-two years his teams never won a championship and usually lost more games than they won. Yet Rooney never wavered. In all those years he never complained or quit hoping for the day his beloved Steelers would win a championship.

In 1975 it was about to happen. Pittsburgh was going to the Super Bowl for the first time. About ten days before the Steelers were scheduled to meet the Minnesota Vikings in Super Bowl IX, Rooney invited some of his players to his 115-year-old house for a quiet dinner.

It was a special moment for him. Franco Harris was there, as were Joe Greene and Dwight White, two of the star defensive players. It was a relaxed evening, Rooney puffing on his ever-present cigar, with very little talk of football. The atmosphere was warm and informal, and Rooney regaled his guests with his stories about horse racing. Aside from the Steelers Rooney's great love is race horses. He has bet on them, owned them, and been the proprietor of several race tracks.

Rooney was telling his players how it had felt when he won his first daily double. Back then, Rooney had been a big horse player. He had won more often than not. In fact, it was with his winnings from one particularly successful day that he had put down the money to purchase the Steelers.

"The horses came into the stretch and I was jumping up and down," related Rooney, smiling. Then in a serious tone of voice he likened the Steelers to that winning horse.

"I believe if we can hold this club together, it will be a strong ball club for five or six years," he remarked. "We might not win every time, but at least we'll have the team that can do it any year."

The players agreed. Then Greene looked at Rooney and said, "I think we'll hold the key for a while."

The Steelers went on to beat the Vikings, 16–6. After forty-two years they finally won a championship. All the world knew that, but nobody knew about a tender postlude in the Pittsburgh dressing room just minutes after the game. Rockey Bleier walked up to Rooney and hugged him. Tears were trickling down Rooney's time-weathered cheeks. This was his moment, better than winning his first daily double.

"Thank you for giving me the chance to play," whispered Bleier.

"Thank you for being part of the championship," murmured Rooney.

The Steelers' joy in winning the game for Rooney was contagious. It gave them an emotional edge they carried onto the field. Winning made it all worth while.

"Art Rooney is the greatest man who ever walked," exclaimed Terry Bradshaw. "Winning this for him was the big thing. He's the kind of man who'll get all of those boxing buddies of his together for a party, and he'll let them take that beautiful trophy out to the back alley to admire it."

NFL commissioner Pete Rozelle presented Rooney with the Super Bowl trophy in a small, crowded dressing room on a makeshift platform. But what Rooney held in his hand seemed more meaningful to him—the game ball. The players had presented their beloved owner with the football from the biggest victory in Pittsburgh's history.

"When they came and told me before the game that I was to go down there and accept the award if we won, I started to get worried," Rooney revealed. "I'm not emotional at football games, but if I go to a wake and people break down I break down right with 'em. I can't help myself, and I was afraid that would happen to me on national television. I didn't want to be embarrassed.

"I told them that I thought they should take Danny [Rooney] down to accept the trophy. He does a much better job than I do in that kind of a situation, but I really had to steel myself up to keep my composure."

He did. Five minutes before the end of the game he made his way to the Steelers' dressing room and waited for his players.

"I just wanted to see if my hair was combed," he said, smiling.

That moment recalled a similar scene just three years before. In the closing minutes of the 1972 AFC championship game against Oakland Rooney left his seat in Three Rivers Stadium and began his descent to the Steeler dressing room. The Raiders had just scored a touchdown with less than a minute to play, apparently to win the game, 7–6. It was the first time that the Steelers had ever reached the playoffs, and Rooney wanted to thank his players personally for what they had accomplished.

Puffing on his cigar, Rooney entered the elevator that would take him down from his private box on the fifty-yard line. On the way down Rooney heard a large roar from the crowd. He looked at the others in the elevator. No one knew what to say. When the elevator stopped at field level Rooney quickly headed to the dressing room.

"What happened?" he asked as he entered.

"We scored a touchdown," shouted an attendant.

Rooney couldn't believe it. The next few minutes caused him a great deal of anxiety.

"I was waiting in the locker room and I couldn't figure out where the players were," remarked Rooney. "Then we heard there was a question about the touchdown. I was dying while we waited to find out. It was the longest wait in my life."

Rooney never got to see Franco Harris' "Immaculate Reception," the catch that gave the Steelers their dramatic last-second victory.

Actually, the Steelers began their stay in Pittsburgh illegally. Rooney made a killing on the horses one weekend in New York. On Saturday he won big at Empire City and then on Monday went up to Saratoga and parlayed it all into winnings somewhere between $200,000 and $400,000. Nobody really knows how much, but it was a lot of money. When Rooney learned about a professional football league he called NFL president Joe Carr to ask him about the possibility of starting a team in Pittsburgh.

For $2,500 Rooney bought himself a football franchise. He called them the Pittsburgh Pirates after the city's baseball team. The trouble was that Pittsburgh had a Blue Law that prohibited the playing of professional sports on Sundays, the day the NFL scheduled its games.

But Rooney's luck was good. An amendment to repeal the law was expected to be passed the week before Pittsburgh's first game, September 20, 1933, against the New York Giants at Forbes Field. The city council became bogged

Art Rooney accepts the first of three Super Bowl trophies from Commissioner Peter Rozelle after Super Bowl IX.
In his left arm he cradles the game ball presented to him by the players.

down that week in other legislation, however, and couldn't approve the appeal. The Blue Law was still effective.

The pro-Blue Law forces had a rallying point. They organized to protest the scheduled game, arranging a demonstration to take place Sunday at Forbes Field. Rooney acted quickly. He hurried down to City Hall to get some answers. First he spoke with Harmar Denny, the director of public safety.

"There are only two people with the authority to stop the game," Denny began. "I'm one of them, but I won't be in town Sunday. I'm going away with my family."

"That's great," Rooney said with a smile. "You need the vacation. Who's the other guy?"

"The other is Franklin McQuade, the superintendent of police," replied Denny.

Rooney thanked him and left. His next stop was McQuade's office. Rooney knew McQuade, too.

"Say, Frank, how would you like to be my personal guest at the game Sunday?" asked Rooney. "You can sit right next to me on the fifty-yard line."

"Thanks, it sounds great," replied McQuade.

Rooney managed to pull it off. Some four thousand fans showed up to see the debut of professional football in Pittsburgh. With Denny out of town and McQuade sitting next to Rooney the anti-sports protestors couldn't find either of the two city officials they were looking for the day of the game. Nonetheless, pro football in Pittsburgh began on a losing note, as the Giants easily defeated the Pirates, 23–2.

"New York won, but our team looked terrible," said Rooney after the game. "The fans didn't get their money's worth today."

In later years Rooney brought a list of colorful characters to Pittsburgh. The first was Johnny "Blood" McNally, a star halfback with the Green Bay Packers. Blood and Packer coach Curly Lambeau had had a heated disagreement. Blood had vowed he would never play for Lambeau again, which was all right with the Packer coach. Rooney moved quickly. He saw Blood as a big box office draw and signed him as player-coach to replace his departed coach, Joe Bach.

"I had no doubt that Johnny would help us as a player," said Rooney. "But I did wonder

Johnny "Blood" McNally

slightly about his ability to control the other men on the team if he was coach."

Blood was a free spirit, so much so that his off-field escapades were legendary around the league. He gave himself his nickname when he spotted a theater marquee advertising the movie *Blood and Sand*. The name appealed to him, and so did a lot of women. He was the Valentino of the gridiron. The fact that Blood also liked the horses didn't go unnoticed by Rooney.

"The truth was, you couldn't depend on

Bill Dudley

Colorado University for the unheard-of sum of $15,800. White was easily the most highly paid player in pro football.

"I thought I would bring a little class to the game," Rooney explained years later. "Anyhow, the fifteen thousand got pro football a lot of publicity. White was an asset to the game, an extremely high class fellow, and he went on to become a Supreme Court Justice."

White played only the 1938 season for Pittsburgh. At the end of it he went to England as a Rhodes Scholar. Blood resigned the following year and the Steelers continued their losing seasons. They were also losing money.

"Only once since we started the team did we make money," admitted Rooney. "Outside of that, we lost. Never any big money, mind you, $15,000 was the worst. But we knew we'd make money if we gave this town a team."

Rooney never stopped trying. It wasn't until 1942 that the Steelers went over .500 for the first time, chiefly on the performance of scrawny rookie running back Bill Dudley. Running from the single wing attack, Dudley led the NFL in rushing. He carried the ball 162 times for 696 yards, an average of 4.3 a run.

"If I had to pick my favorite Steeler of all time, it would be Bill Dudley," confessed Rooney. "He didn't know the meaning of the word 'quit.'"

Dudley starred for three seasons with the Steelers. He constantly fell victim, however, to arguments with head coach Jock Sutherland. He was finally traded to Detroit in a deal that pained Rooney.

"It was like losing one of my own sons," he said.

Pittsburgh kept losing. They even lost out on Johnny Unitas, who went on to become one of the top quarterbacks in NFL history. In 1955 Unitas was a rookie out of Louisville University. That year Pittsburgh had three veteran quarterbacks on the roster, Jim Finks, Ted Marchibroda, and Vic Eaton. Walt Kiesling, the Steeler coach, was not impressed with Unitas at all. Despite the urging of Rooney's sons that Unitas was a great passer, perhaps the best in the league, Unitas was cut. He was later picked up by the Baltimore Colts.

It wasn't until Buddy Parker was named coach in 1957 that Pittsburgh began to gain

Blood all the time," recalled Rooney. "We once played a game in Los Angeles and John missed the train home. The next weekend Johnny was in Chicago watching his old team, the Green Bay Packers. A writer asked him how come he wasn't with the Pirates. Johnny told him that they weren't playing that weekend. A minute later the loudspeaker blared out the Philadelphia-Pittsburgh score."

The next year Rooney shook up the sports world by signing Byron "Whizzer" White of

John Henry Johnson, Pittsburgh's second leading career rusher.
(Left) Bobby Layne calls signals for the Steelers in a game against the New York Giants.

respectability. Parker preferred veteran players to rookies. As a result he traded many draft choices for players who could help him win now.

Quarterback Bobby Layne was one of those players. After Layne came to Pittsburgh from Detroit in 1958, the Steelers had winning seasons in four of the next six years. At the time of the trade Layne was thirty-one years old, but Parker had coached him at Detroit and knew Layne's value.

"Bobby Layne is the greatest leader I've ever been associated with," declared Parker. "He'll set the pace for the rest of our players."

He did. Layne took charge like General Patton on the field and off it as well. It wouldn't be unusual for Layne, while quaffing a few beers, to call a meeting of those around him and start talking strategy. Layne was famous for his late night escapades. With Layne's leadership and passing and the running of Tom Tracy, John Henry Johnson, and Dick Hoak the Steelers produced their best record ever in 1962, 9–5.

The new look didn't last long. In 1963 the Steelers had their last winning season for several years. The 1963 season also marked the retirement of such Steeler stars as wide receiver Buddy Dial, who led the team with sixty receptions for a club record of 1,295 yards; kicker Lou Michaels, who booted the longest field goal in Steeler history, fifty-one yards, that season; and Hall of Fame defensive tackle Ernie Stautner, who had played fourteen years with Pittsburgh.

Johnson, who gained 1,141 yards in 1962, went on to gain 1,048 in 1964 before retiring the following year. Hoak lasted ten years, retiring in 1970 after recording his best year in 1968, when he rushed for 848 yards. Although Roy Jefferson played only five years with Pittsburgh, he holds club records for the most passes caught in one season, sixty-seven in 1969, and

Dick Hoak (42), the only former Steeler player currently on the coaching staff.

Hall of Famer Ernie Stautner.

the most touchdown passes in a single game, four in 1968.

It wasn't until 1969 that a new era in Pittsburgh began. In that year Chuck Noll was named coach, and Dan Rooney, Art's older son, played the major role in operating the club. It was time he did. Dan and his brother, Art Jr., had gained administrative experience all through the years working under their father. Art Jr. was in charge of the scouting area. Both sons were low-keyed but efficient administrators.

"Chuck and I hit it off the first day we met," disclosed Art Jr. "We had an argument."

The dispute wasn't over the draft system, by any means. Both Noll and Art Jr. advocated the draft as the only way to build the Steelers.

Both agreed that the Steelers should draft the best available athlete, not necessarily by position. Noll just wasn't sold on the merits of a scouting combine. The Steelers were members of BLESTO, the Bears-Lions-Eagles-Steelers Talent Organization.

"Buddy Parker was a great coach with a lot of expertise," Art Jr. continued. "But he had a philosophy that the way to win was with veterans who didn't make mistakes. He was the George Allen of his day. I think George may have copied Buddy's approach when he went to the Redskins. I'm sure George is an admirer of Buddy's.

"Our drafts in those days were like the Redskins'. There was a lot of sitting around in the

Art Rooney with his two sons, Dan (left) and Art, Jr.

Steelers' office on draft day. We'd look up at the board and see all those beautiful names and there was nothing we could do about them. I finally started going on scouting trips in 1964, Buddy's last year as coach. The guy who had the most influence on me was Jack Butler, a former Steeler player who had done some scouting for us. We would take trips around the country and we'd sit in the car and figure out what the good teams were doing and what we could do. He finally came up with the BLESTO idea, the idea that we couldn't get the coverage of college players unless we joined together with other teams and pooled our information.

"The irony of the BLESTO thing was that Buddy Parker was the guy who pushed the idea. He convinced my father. Buddy was so anti-draft, but he was the guy who got BLESTO off the ground. He told my dad, 'You should be able to afford this because you'll get the coverage that will allow you to compete with the good drafting teams like Los Angeles and Dallas.'

"We did not want instant respectability. We wanted world championships. We had traded away too many draft choices and too many quarterbacks over the years only to see them come back and haunt us. We were convinced that the draft was the best way to go. The number one pick is so important. You look for different types of players in the draft. That first pick you're looking for a guy who can be a starter and so on, a guy who can contribute to your team, a guy who can make your team, and a guy who's just a prospect.

"Our method of scouting players is not unique. I'm sure the other clubs have the same ideas we do. I'd love to tell you that we're all geniuses here, but I don't believe that. When you look for players, you're looking for critical factors: quickness, control, strength potential, athletic skills, and the normal height-speed ratio. Then what you have to do is figure out their toughness and football intelligence.

"This is especially true when you're looking for free agents. We really rely on the computer on free agents. After you've gone over all the written reports you go to the computer."

The Rooneys prefer to stay behind the scenes. There is no biographical information in the

Steelers' media guide on any of them. And they favor a very informal office atmosphere, somewhat like a family environment.

"All this you see around you, this whole organization, my father really made all this possible for us," said Dan, the team's chief executive officer. "But I realize I'm going a different route from him. I really never felt I was the same as him. Maybe I never had the same desires or approach. I wanted to make my contribution differently.

"My father is a 'people' man. He's a politician. His first reaction is, 'What will people think?' My philosophy is that you have to do what is right and logical, even if it's unpopular, like raising ticket prices. I believe in being business-

like. I think a person has to do his job, hold up his own end. My father worried about everyone's feelings constantly. Sometimes it infuriated me, but that's just the type of person he is. He really worries about people.

"For instance, I'll tell the ground crew that I want the field ready by game time whether it snows or rains. He'll say, 'It's too bad it wasn't ready; they worked hard.' I'll say, 'Get the job done and don't tell me about the problems.' But, you know, he's tougher than people think. He's not above bawling somebody out."

Dan was elevated to president after the Steelers won their first Super Bowl. There wasn't any press conference or even a press release to announce the move. Art Rooney just did it

Art Rooney, Jr.

Dan Rooney

quietly one day in the spring, with the help of the Steelers' publicity director Joe Gordon.

"You know that thing you put out?" Rooney pointed toward the Steeler media guide. "I want you to make Danny the president."

"What are you going to be?" asked Gordon.

"What's that thing they use?" inquired Rooney.

"You mean chairman of the board?" replied Gordon.

"That's it," answered Rooney as he turned and walked out of the office.

So officially Dan has been in the post for five years, and he's comfortable remaining in the background. He is probably the least-known executive in sports. He gets things done

quietly but firmly, and the Steeler organization is looked upon as the most successful in pro football during that time.

"I stay in the background," admits Dan. "A lot of owners in football think they have to say something profound, particularly to explain a win or loss. I think the less you say the better off you are. My job here is to make everyone else's easier. The Steeler players get the recognition and that's the way it should be. That's better than having Chuck Noll or Dan Rooney get it. The players are the characters, if you look at football in the entertainment sense. Just as important as drafting is the development of the players. I really think that's where Noll's genius comes into play. He gives

15

every football player a chance to prove he can't do the job.

"Everybody in the organization feels the freedom to talk to everybody else if they want to. My door is always open. It's a very, very personal thing. There's an open feeling that comes from my father. He created this. It establishes a closeness. Our low-key atmosphere draws everybody together. We've had our differences, but I listen to what my father has to say."

Dan listened to his father several weeks before the 1970 draft. Pittsburgh had finished the 1969 season with a 1–13 record and was assured the number one pick of the entire draft. The Steelers were getting offers from a number of pro teams. They all asked whether the Steelers wanted to trade their number one choice for proven veterans. The offers were tempting. Finally the elder Rooney made a point.

"All I'm going to tell you is this," he said emphatically to his sons. "If we trade the guy, if we give away a guy who turns out to be great, just make sure we get front-line players. We're expert on quarterbacks. We've had Sid Luckman, Johnny Unitas, Len Dawson, Jack Kemp, Earl Morrall, and Bill Nelsen, and we got rid of them all, every one of them."

Rooney's argument was convincing. The Steelers decided to keep their choice and selected Terry Bradshaw. The year before they had picked Joe Greene. The Steelers began to rebuild with top-quality youngsters. That was the strategy they had decided upon the year before. All the time they had kept their choice a secret, even when others outside the organization hinted at the possibility of taking Bradshaw.

"I don't know if getting a lot of publicity is good for an organization," Dan pointed out. "You might be better off creating something of a mystique. Let all the others say they're better, they're super. That's fine. I think that publicity has a tendency to corrupt. I think it really hurts you. It's hard to operate in a fishbowl. It is a problem not getting carried away with your own publicity. Let's face it, if something is written about you, you read it.

"The people in the league respected me pretty early. It was never a problem there, although it may have been in some other places."

Pittsburgh is the only place that counts.

Chuck Noll

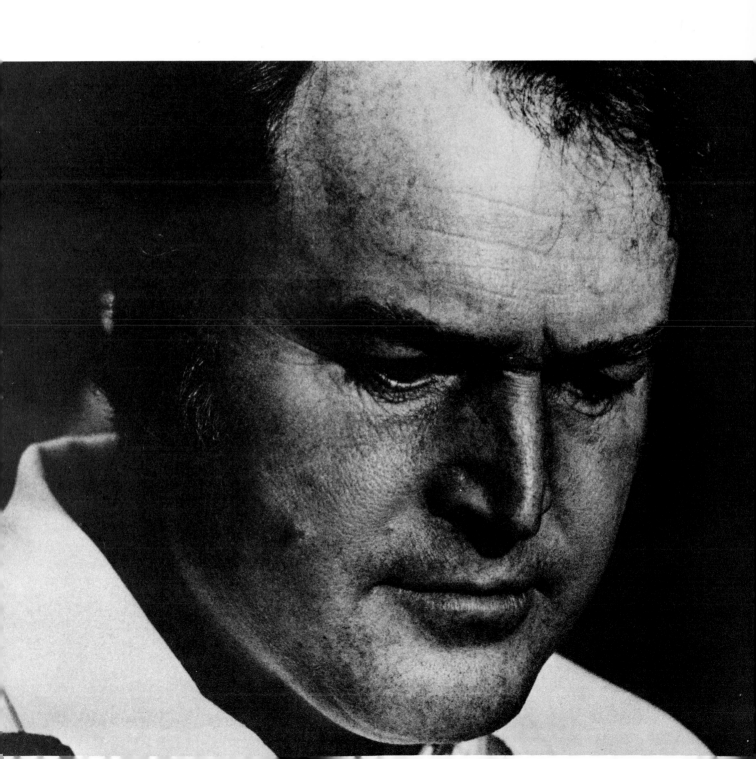

Chuck Noll was fifteen minutes late for his press conference the morning after the Steelers became the first team in history to win three Super Bowls. It was almost as if he hadn't wanted to be there. Public speaking has never held much appeal for him. He is low-keyed, so much so that others have made him out to be complex, which is unfair. He simply abhors the limelight. Even on the field he remains stoic, unemotional. Victory, however, is an achievement he shares with his players, but then he always puts the players first. Anyone who has ever played for him will acknowledge that.

The night before the conference, Noll had savored the victory with his players. Now he walked into a hotel ballroom on the sands of Miami Beach to face the media. There would be questions, hundreds of them. There always were. Questions were something Noll was not exactly comfortable with, so he smiled and apologized for being tardy, revealed that he was looking forward to taking a few days off, and waited for the questions to begin.

"What are you going to do on the days you're taking off?" was the first one.

"Hide," beamed Noll.

It was pure Noll. He is a very private person. He does not look for headlines. Rather, he shuns them. Whatever headlines there may be he's content to let his players have. That's what it's all about for Noll. He has never let his ego temper his emotions or prejudice his thinking. In this era of bravura he is refreshing.

Noll's first job was as a defensive assistant with the Los Angeles Chargers (later the San Diego Chargers) in the old American Football League. In his six years there the Chargers won five divisional titles and two championships. Noll had an opportunity to apply for a head coaching job elsewhere in the league but didn't.

"I had seen guys like Al Davis and Jack Faulkner go from our staff to head coaching jobs with Oakland and Denver, and I didn't think that was fair to San Diego," recalled Noll. "It was a small league with only four teams in a division, and Davis and Faulkner simply knew too much about the Chargers that the Chargers didn't know about their teams.

"That's why I decided to make the move to Baltimore in 1966. The merger [between leagues] was only wishful thinking at the time,

and I knew that if I wanted to be a head coach in the NFL they weren't going to take me from an AFL team."

In the three years Noll spent at Baltimore the Colts lost only seven games. In 1968 they were the NFL champions, losing, however, to the New York Jets, 16–7, in Super Bowl III. The day after the game Dan Rooney met with Noll to offer him the head coaching position with the Steelers.

"Coming off the Super Bowl upset, Chuck had a reason to be bitter and disappointed," Rooney remembered. "But he never lost his poise. I liked his attitude. I also liked the way he evaluated our team. Everything he told me about our personnel was right on target."

Yet Noll didn't know whether he would like going to the Steelers. He didn't like what he had heard about them, about their not caring to become winners. At the time he was also mulling over two other offers he had received. He approached the Steelers clinically.

"When you go for a job interview *you* are being interviewed," remarked Noll. "But in this case I was interviewing them. I didn't want to take just any head coaching job. I wanted to know what management was like. I had heard that the Steelers didn't want to spend any money and that's why they never had a winner.

"But Dan Rooney was willing to give me whatever I needed and he's never gone back on that. There were a lot of negatives there, though. The offices were in a rundown hotel. They were just horrible. The practice facilities were bad, but the Steelers were going to move into Three Rivers Stadium the next year. These things are important. You can't win a championship from a rundown office. Not these days, anyway. You've got to have a first class operation in every respect. When you treat players first class they'll start to believe they are first class."

When Noll took over in 1969 the Steelers were anything but first class. In the season that had just ended they had finished 2–11–1. In the last five years the Steelers had won a total of eighteen games. In the nineteen years before they had had only four winning seasons. It was hardly a record to get excited about.

There were two ways Noll could rebuild the team, either immediately through trades or through the draft system. He quickly decided

Noll discusses the next offensive series with quarterback Terry Bradshaw.

Jubilant Pittsburgh players carry Noll off the field after beating San Diego
for their first division championship in 1972.

to build through the draft. He was concerned not about the immediate results but about the long-range effect. The Steelers had promised him time.

Noll arrived in Pittsburgh just before the 1969 draft. "I got there the day before," he remarked. "But I knew that anyone we drafted had to be a help."

There was strong sentiment for the Steelers to pick Terry Hanratty as their first choice. After all, he had the credentials—a quarterback at Notre Dame and practically a local boy, besides. Everybody agreed that the Steelers needed a quarterback, but then they needed just about everything. Noll conferred with Art Rooney, Jr., who was in charge of the college scouting area, and they both agreed to pick big 6′ 4″, 270-pound Joe Greene first. They got Hanratty on the second round and then L. C. Greenwood and Jon Kolb.

At thirty-seven Noll was the youngest head coach in the NFL. He didn't have to wait long for his first victory; he won it in the opening game of the season. He never got a second one that year, however, because the Steelers lost their remaining thirteen games.

"It got harder to take as the year went along," Noll said with a sigh. "But I felt we were showing some signs of progress. We weren't getting blown off the field. We were losing because we were making mistakes. I could see that there were some players we'd have to get rid of. These were the guys whose goal was just to make the team and collect their paychecks.

"If you mentioned championship to them they wouldn't understand what you were talking about. People talk about coaches motivating players, but that's a bunch of bull. Players motivate themselves. What you have to do is try to get players who have this inner motivation. This is the hard thing because there's no way to measure it.

"You always end up taking somebody else's word for it. What you try to do is look at a player's physical abilities and see if his performance has measured up to it. There are some players, like Brian Piccolo, whose performance goes far beyond their abilities."

With Greene and Greenwood, Noll began to build the defense first. After all, he had earned his reputation there and the defensive players

fit into the puzzle more quickly. In 1970 the Steelers drafted Mel Blount and in 1971 Jack Ham, Ernie Holmes, Dwight White, and Mike Wagner. By 1971 Noll had drafted seven of the Steelers' starting defensive eleven for Super Bowl IX.

"I didn't consciously set out to build the defense before the offense," explained Noll. "It just happened that way, even though I do believe that the teams that win championships are the teams with outstanding defenses. I also believe

that before you learn to win you have to learn how not to lose."

In 1970 the Steelers' record improved to 5–9. They kept on improving the next year, to 6–8, but Noll felt they should have done better. He believed that the Steelers should have turned themselves around in 1971.

"That was a season when we were 6–8 but could have been 9–5 with very little change in our play," Noll said. "That's why when we went 11–3 the next year and everyone else was surprised I wasn't surprised at all. I thought we should have been winners earlier."

Starting with the 1971 season, Noll has produced a 76–24 record, a winning percentage of seventy-six percent. It is the best percentage of any coach in the NFL. He's led his team to the playoffs every year. No other coach has been in the playoffs seven consecutive years. He has also won eleven postseason games, more than anyone else, while losing only four. And who else can say that his team has won three Super Bowls?

Noll's aim has always been toward excellence. He maintains that it begins with the individual, both on and off the football field. The key is discipline. It is an attitude Noll has found through religion.

"One of the most important influences in my life has been the Catholic Church, my religion," disclosed Noll. "I always have been impressed with the Church's attitude toward the individual. I think there has been a concern for individuals in the Catholic Church that has been exhibited in few other places. You know, I think that if you can mold and motivate individuals you can mold and motivate societies. And that's really what a team is, a little society. But if you ignore people's individuality, if you have no concern for them as individuals, you have chaos. And I think that maybe we're beginning to lose our feel for people.

"On this team we base our training on the philosophy that we do all we can to help the individual player, help him make himself the best football player he can be. I emphasize fundamentals. With a solid foundation on the basics the team and the players on the team can take care of themselves."

It's a simple thing, basics, fundamentals. But then again, that's Noll, that's his approach to football. He makes the game simple, while others try to weave a web of complexities. That is why he gives simple, short answers to questions. And yet others can't understand his directness and see him as complex. They are merely looking for something that isn't there.

What is vital for Noll is hard work, plenty of it. Through practice he trains his players in basics to achieve success. It is a tiring job, unappreciated by many. It is the self-discipline Noll advocates that plays a vital part in his team's success. He has certainly demonstrated its value.

"You have to work at it," emphasized Noll. "You have to want to be the best there is and work for it. And I think the working, the striving for excellence, is just as important, and maybe more so, as achieving it.

"A lot of people are saying there's too much pressure these days, too much competition. They're saying that excellence takes too heavy a toll, that it's not worth the strain. There's talk of mediocrity and not of excellence. So many want to aim for the lowest common denominator.

"But I don't think that's what life is all about. You can't be much in life, you can't get much out of life, by being mediocre. And unless you're committed to working toward excellence you're committed to mediocrity, to just getting along. I don't think that's what God has in mind for us."

His dedication to excellence and achieving is unmistakable. One day in training camp it rained, not just a light rain but a heavy downpour. There were puddles everywhere on the training field. Noll looked out the window of his office. He was satisfied.

"You know, we all would have been a lot more comfortable sitting inside today, taking things easy for a change," he remarked. "We all got pretty well soaked out there. What were we trying to prove, running around in the rain? What was the point of it all?

"I'll tell you what we were doing. We were working to improve our game. In football you've got to be quick and alert, and you can't be these things unless you've disciplined yourself with all this practice. You can't let up. You've got to develop that something inside you that's going to help you produce when the crucial time comes that you must produce or fall on your face. That's what this game is all about and I think that's what life is all about.

"If you are prepared properly you can handle things as they come, whether on the field or in your life. That's what self-discipline is all about, and that's what religion is all about, too. Maybe that's why religion is referred to as a discipline. It helps you prepare yourself. It gives you standards by which you can judge how well you're doing. It's a measurement for life, just as the game is a measurement of how well you've practiced."

It is this quiet yet sincere belief that has shaped Noll's view of football and of life itself.

He would prefer to toil under a cloak of anonymity. Yet, he relentlessly strives for excellence. He doesn't look for the glamor that goes with winning, especially the high profile that accompanies winning the Super Bowl.

"I'm not an image guy," Noll admits. "I don't like publicity. I don't need it to survive. You can't play football without emotion, but that doesn't mean you have to wear it on your sleeve."

Only on rare occasions has he been vocal on the sidelines. That's not his style. He discusses crucial situations calmly with his players. The emotion remains inside, yet the intensity is there. His players recognize it.

"He approaches everything he does with tremendous intensity," explains Rocky Bleier. "He is a student of football. He approaches the game as a teacher. His basic premise is that he is not a rah-rah man, not a motivator. It's not up to him to motivate people but to take self-motivated people and give them direction."

It's simple. It's not hard to understand. That's what Chuck Noll has maintained all along. Maybe someday people will believe him.

Terry Bradshaw

He stood on a platform answering one question after another. He was shivering. His pale face was even whiter than usual. There were dark circles around his eyes. The emotion of the game and the flu had visibly exhausted him. He had just finished playing the season's biggest game in wretched weather. He was cold. When he spoke the words quivered. He couldn't wait to leave the interview for the soothing warmth of the sauna. Yet he seemed to savor those precious minutes after the AFC championship game. It was as if he hadn't wanted the season to end. Understandably so. He had just climaxed the greatest season of his nine-year career.

Terry Bradshaw is a paradox. He was perhaps the most maligned quarterback of the past decade. He was ridiculed, misunderstood, even ignored. The favorite rap was that he was dumb. That hurt. It was a heavy burden to carry out to to the football field, where the intelligence of a quarterback reigns supreme. Yet Bradshaw heard them all, the cries and the whispers. It was hellish, as if his entire career was being judged from game to game. Nobody but nobody else in the history of professional football has played under such a heavy handicap. It was unfair.

Even after he won two Super Bowls Bradshaw never got the recognition reserved for winning quarterbacks. Yet without Bradshaw's clutch plays, maybe, just maybe, the Steelers wouldn't have won those Super Bowls. In Super Bowl IX he fired a third-down touchdown pass to Larry Brown to seal the Steelers' 16–6 triumph over the Minnesota Vikings. The following year, in

Super Bowl X, Bradshaw threw the most dramatic pass in Super Bowl history. On a third down play with only 3:02 left in the game Bradshaw was under a double blitz by the Dallas Cowboys. Yet, he took his shots and fired a 64-yard touchdown pass to Lynn Swann that gave the Steelers a 21–17 victory. It was a pass Bradshaw never saw. He was knocked unconscious on the play and removed from the game. Only after his jubilant teammates entered the locker room did Bradshaw learn what had happened.

These knocks Bradshaw accepts. He realizes they are part of the game of football. What he can't understand is why so many people have questioned his intelligence. It cuts Bradshaw, cuts him so deeply that he refuses to discuss the subject. Justifiably so. Nine years was enough. Wasn't it enough that he helped win two Super Bowls? Shouldn't that alone have earned him the accolades he deserved? Why shouldn't Terry Bradshaw have been known as a winner?

In 1978 it all changed. Suddenly, after nine years, Bradshaw attracted a mantle of recognition. It was there for everybody to see. Even the fickle fans and his most serious detractors among the pro football intelligentsia saw it. Bradshaw was recognized for what he was, a smart, winning quarterback. Overnight his image changed: The Steelers won because of Bradshaw. That change was very important to Bradshaw himself. It brought him inner peace. He was satisfied.

The evolution of Chuck Noll's football philosophy brought about the change. The Steeler teams of the past six years had relied on a strong defense and controlling the ball with the run. The opposition's theory had been that if you stopped Franco Harris you stopped the Pittsburgh offense. Noll changed all that in 1978. He emphasized the pass more in his game plans. It became Bradshaw's game and Bradshaw delivered.

Statistically, 1978 was Bradshaw's best season ever. He led the AFC in passing with an 84.8 rating compiled by the NFL statisticians. He led the entire NFL in touchdown passes with twenty-eight and in average yards gained per pass with 7.92. Only Roger Staubach of the Dallas Cowboys finished with a higher rating— just barely—with 84.9, having thrown forty-

five more passes. Bradshaw was voted the most valuable player in the AFC by a wide margin. More importantly, the Steelers won. Bradshaw led them to a 14–2 season, through the playoffs, and into the Super Bowl. Emotionally, he was fulfilled. That was important, too.

"I was more relaxed this year," reflected Bradshaw. "I decided to have fun, just go out and play football without putting all those pressures on myself. I enjoyed playing. I had a ball. No doubt being successful has helped me. Being in so many big games, you kind of get an overall education. It sets you up for the rest of your career. It's like I'm not in a big hurry anymore. I know what I'm doing. Joe Namath once said that you walk up there and suddenly you see a clear picture of what it's all about. I don't know how it happened. It just came.

"It's a great feeling when I'm out there. I have complete control of the offense. I've always called all of my own plays, but now I feel as if I have more command of the offense. If I want to throw ten times in a row I can do it and nobody will ask me why. It's a question of confidence. Obviously I have matured. I'm a little wiser, a little smarter. I used to put too much pressure on myself. When I threw an interception I wanted to run up into the stands and apologize to everybody. I didn't have the confidence. I look back on those days now and shudder. In the past I would get so uptight I couldn't come back from a poor game.

"Look, you're never going to please everybody. I have a few more years left to play. There are going to be times when I'm going to be absolutely horrible. I'm ready for it, and I expect the fans to respond to the way I play. It's part of the game, and I'm resigned to it. I'm mentally prepared now to handle that pressure as compared to the past."

It wasn't always so easy for Bradshaw. There were moments early in his career when he felt alone, apart from the team. At one point his relationship with Noll deteriorated. He felt unsure of himself, lost his confidence, so much so that he wanted to quit. A broken marriage affected him emotionally for a year. He was benched because the Steelers weren't winning enough. The torment of pressure almost destroyed Bradshaw.

Much of that pressure he put on himself.

An all-Pro combination:
Bradshaw hands off to Franco Harris.

30

When he first joined the Steelers as their number one draft choice in 1970 he was looked upon as their savior. Bradshaw wanted to make them winners overnight. But he was young and anxious, and the pressure he inflicted on himself almost overwhelmed him.

It was understandable for Bradshaw to feel this way. He was the first player selected in the draft. He had played at Louisiana Tech, a small college with no big football reputation. By his own admission he was a country boy. Going to a large city like Pittsburgh could excite someone quite easily. The excitement showed.

"I'm looking forward to going to Pittsburgh because the team is a loser," Bradshaw remarked at the time. "I'm not going up there with the idea that I'm going to play for a loser. If I thought that I'd be like anyone else who's a leader. I wouldn't want to go. Since I'm a leader, I'm looking forward to it as a great challenge. I'm going to strive to make giant strides to justify their faith in making me the number one choice and to make everything the opposite of what it is now.

"Just because a team never has played for a championship doesn't mean it doesn't have players of championship caliber. I've always believed that one player can change the thinking of an entire organization."

Because of the past history of Steeler number-one draft choices many wondered whether Bradshaw could take the pressure to produce. They also pointed out that with a young team Bradshaw would be facing even more pressure to

Bradshaw was the first player chosen in the 1970 draft.

lead the Steelers out of the wilderness. Nevertheless Bradshaw felt he was ready. That remained to be proven.

Maxie Lambright, the head coach at Louisiana Tech, was aware of the dangers that Bradshaw would face in pro ball. Although Lambright thought Bradshaw's chances of making it big with the Steelers were good, he realized that it wouldn't be easy. He hoped everyone would give Bradshaw time to develop.

"Terry is a strong, natural passer and an athlete with a lot of courage," Lambright said, "but he's facing a great change. He's always been a very physical player, one who never minded tucking the ball under his arm and running. Well, he'll have to be more careful about that now. Some of those 260-pound linemen would love to tear into a quarterback rolling out there unprotected.

"Bradshaw has a quick, accurate arm. He can really drill the ball to a receiver, even when he's throwing off-balance. He is going to have to learn not to turn the ball loose without recognizing what the defense is doing. In college football he may have seen three varieties of defense. In pro ball he may see ten varieties. There will be a much greater burden on him and I hope everyone realizes that he will need some time to adjust to it, that's all."

A false sense of success enveloped Pittsburgh. After the Steelers dropped their first preseason game, Bradshaw, looking good in relief, was given the starting position. He started the next four games and the Steelers won them all. No one could remember when Pittsburgh had last won four straight. Steeler fans were cheering and everything looked very promising.

"I was on cloud nine," exclaimed Bradshaw. "Everything was great. As a quarterback I didn't have a great preseason. But we won; the team did. That was the important thing. The guys played great defense. We had a great running attack, and everybody felt like this was going to be our year."

It didn't work out that way. Once the regular season began Bradshaw appeared confused. In his first three games, which the Steelers lost, Bradshaw was thrown for a couple of safeties. It wasn't until the fifth game of the season, against the Houston Oilers, that he threw his first touchdown pass. Two weeks later Brad-

shaw was benched in favor of second-year pro Terry Hanratty, who proceeded to lead the Steelers to a 21–10 victory over the Cincinnati Bengals.

The benching shocked Bradshaw. He was confused, discouraged, and hurt. He felt his whole world had fallen apart. He expressed his disappointment in the dressing room after the Cincinnati game.

"I don't want to play second fiddle to Hanratty," snapped Bradshaw. "I don't mind playing behind somebody older, someone ready to retire, but I surely won't play behind someone my age. If the Steelers are going to do that they'd better trade me."

It was a statement Bradshaw shouldn't have made. Publicly, it didn't help his image. Privately, among his teammates, he didn't win many friends. Noll, however, looked upon Bradshaw's remarks in a fatherly way. He sensed Bradshaw's frustrations.

"Terry has a lot of growing up to do, both on the field and off it," emphasized Noll.

As the season progressed Bradshaw realized that he had a lot to learn. Enthusiasm and ability was one thing, but experience was another. While going through this learning stage he grew dejected. He got down on himself. His depression affected his performance on the field. He would become unnerved by a heavy rush and throw the ball wildly. When the season finally ended he had been intercepted twenty-four times and sacked thirty-five times. It had been a nightmare.

"The longer the season went on, the more I was losing my confidence," admitted Bradshaw. "It wasn't the team. Everybody was doing his job. It was just that I wasn't doing mine."

The Steelers finished with a 5–9 record. Bradshaw couldn't wait to go back home to Shreveport, Louisiana. He went to his apartment, packed his bags, and was on a plane within hours after the final game. Some sportswriters called him a tremendous flop. They compared him to the other Steeler first round failures of the past. Pittsburgh fans felt the same way, and Bradshaw went home a very depressed young man. His feelings were hurt. He wanted to escape from the bad memories. It was indeed a different world from that of his college days.

"By the time the season ended I just wanted

to get away from Pittsburgh," said Bradshaw. "All I wanted was to go home. I wanted to be away from sports, football particularly. I wanted to relax and get football out of my mind. The way I felt back then, I didn't know if I wanted to play football any more."

Bradshaw returned to Shreveport a somewhat fallen hero. During the off-season he did a lot of thinking. "I felt my confidence oozing away my first year," he remembered. "It was terrible because I knew that was the one thing I needed most. Because I felt I was losing it, I started pressing. I pressed awfully hard to get the one big play, trying to get ahead.

"Yet I learned a lot in the off-season. I learned a lot without even touching a football. First of all I learned that I had a lot of growing up to do, on the field and off. I decided there'd have to be a lot of studying, adjustments to be made, pressures to overcome. It takes years of professional football to completely understand a certain situation and then get a play to fit into it. I had to learn to control the ball, then cut down on my interceptions. I was definitely not satisfied with my first year at all."

Bradshaw displayed a different attitude his second year. He felt even more secure when Noll told him privately that he was the number-one quarterback. Bradshaw's confidence shot up.

"Noll told me that I was the team's quarterback, period," disclosed Bradshaw. "He told me not to worry if I have a bad game; I'm the quarterback, and I'm going to play. He wasn't going to pull me just because I had a bad game. He told me to just relax and play the kind of football I was capable of playing. What a difference that made to me. I settled down, quit worrying about somebody getting my job, and started to throw the ball well for the first time since my days in college.

"I had to stay in control. It starts when you drop back. You've got to keep your poise, keep your cool. I didn't do that my rookie year. Everything I did was in a rush, hurrying my passes, forcing my handoffs, quick with my fakes. But I was a long way from being a quarterback. I came into the league and read about myself being the star of the future. You can't let stuff like that run around in your mind. You think you're big stuff. But you find out differently pretty fast.

"I tried to push it, but I found out that there are ten other guys on the team. It wasn't me alone. I had to learn not to get upset. I mean, if I was intercepted, we'd get the ball back. You have to keep your cool, stay relaxed out there."

Bradshaw's improvement was seen in his statistics. He managed to complete fifty-four percent of his passes, compared to thirty-eight percent his first year. He also had thirteen touchdown passes, seven more than his rookie season. But, he still had too many interceptions, twenty-two, only two less than the year before; he still had to cut down on them. Even though he was still learning, however, the Steelers' record improved to 6–8, and their future looked brighter.

In 1972 the young quarterback began to put it together and led the squad to an 11–3 record, the best in their history. "I've had three years now, one of frustration, one where I've learned to pass, and one of learning how to run the ball," explained Bradshaw after the 1972 season. "Maybe next year I can learn to do them all together, and then I'll be able to drive them all crazy.

"I think the main thing was that I had to settle down and learn the game. I was in awe of it. Last year I learned how to pass, but I still wasn't attacking a team the way I should be able to. Now I understand the running attack. I've learned how to use my runners, how to mix up the defense."

In 1972 Bradshaw threw 308 passes and completed 147 for a percentage of 47.7, down somewhat from the year before. The most encouraging sign, however, was that he cut his interceptions practically in half, to twelve. He was learning to read defenses and not to force the ball as much.

Even Noll was pleased with Bradshaw's improvement. "Bradshaw has great confidence in himself, but he's not cocky," offered Noll. "We are impressed with his attitude and leadership abilities. He still has things to learn, but we have confidence in Bradshaw's ability to handle pressure. His performance for us in 1972 indicates that he plays best when the pressure is greatest."

During the 1973 season Bradshaw suffered an injury that hurt the Steelers' chances. The year began with hope and promise, and the Steelers were winning. Then, in the seventh

Bradshaw holds almost all Steeler career passing marks.

game of the season, Bradshaw suffered a shoulder separation against the Cincinnati Bengals. Looking to pass, Bradshaw was hit hard, fell to the ground in pain, and was removed from the game. Strangely enough, the fans in Pittsburgh booed Bradshaw. He left the field hurt and confused.

"It was the most disgusting thing I ever saw," said tackle Joe Greene after the game.

Later that night, with his right arm in a sling, Bradshaw stopped for gas on his way home. A couple of teenagers spotted him. Instead of offering him support they jeered at him, which hurt Bradshaw more than the pain he felt in his shoulder.

The Steelers felt Bradshaw's absence sorely. In the first seven games Bradshaw played, the Steelers won six of them. In the month he was on the sidelines the Steelers won two games and lost two and gave up their hold on first place in

hearts, even though he had led the team to eight victories in the nine games he had started. "I've got a bad image created by some people here in Pittsburgh which is uncalled-for," snapped Bradshaw. "But once an image, always an image. They call me dumb and that's what I regret the most.

"I'm open, but I'm working on shutting that up because of misquotes and misinterpretations. I'm at the point where I don't even read the papers any more."

Ironically, Bradshaw didn't start the 1974 season as the Steelers' number one quarterback. Joe Gilliam, another strong-armed thrower who was listed as the team's number three quarterback, did. Gilliam had a fantastic exhibition season. He connected on sixty-five percent of his passes and threw for twelve touchdowns in six games. Noll decided to go with the hot hand and open the season with Gilliam. Although he preferred a balanced attack, he felt that throwing the ball more might work.

It did. After the first six games the Steelers were 4–1–1. Gilliam relied heavily on the pass. In one game he threw fifty passes, a team record. In those six games, in which he started, Gilliam threw 198 passes. During that time Bradshaw played briefly in only one game and threw just two passes. Suddenly Bradshaw seemed forgotten. He decided to talk to Noll.

"I can't understand why he's doing this," said Bradshaw. "Joe has looked good throwing and we've been winning. But you can't make it just on passing. You have to use your running game."

After meeting with Noll, Bradshaw began to realize that the coach was doing what he thought was best for the team. The Steelers were winning, and that was what counted. In the sixth game, however, Gilliam began to cool off and didn't look as good as he had. As a result Noll decided to start Bradshaw in the seventh game.

"I never lost my job," stressed Bradshaw. "There was just another guy who showed up with a hot hand. Noll never gave up on me. He just had to go with the guy who had the hot hand. I accepted that. I'm pleased I handled it as well as I did. I don't say I liked it, but I accepted it."

The turning point in the season for Bradshaw and the Steelers came in a Monday night

the Central Division. Bradshaw returned in the twelfth game and almost rallied his team to a win over Miami before losing, 30–26.

With Bradshaw in the lineup, however, the Steelers won their final two games of the season to finish with a 10–4 record. They gained a spot in the playoffs and faced the Oakland Raiders in Oakland. Any hopes for a championship quickly ended as the Raiders won easily, 33–14.

Bradshaw still didn't win the Steeler fans'

game against the New Orleans Saints in New Orleans. The Steelers won, 28–7, to push their record to 8–2–1. Actually, Bradshaw gained more yards running than he did passing, but it was the way he handled the team that made the difference. The other players felt it, too.

"You could see the transformation of Terry after that game," explained center Ray Mansfield. "It's like anything else. If you've got confidence in what someone else can do you're going to have confidence in what you are doing. Terry picked up something against the Saints, and we could feel it.

"If I had to pinpoint a time and a place when I began to fully appreciate Terry's leadership, it was the New England game two weeks later. We had overlooked Houston and lost the week after the Saints game, yet Noll stuck with Terry for the New England game. Terry really came of age in that game . . . just things he said and did. He had complete control of the game, and he knew it and we knew it.

"He really was something. He came into the huddle and he was in complete charge. He's been that way ever since. He's struggled along at times. There were times he wasn't quite so sure of himself out there, but that's not the case anymore. He's changed completely."

Bradshaw was practically a new person. He had newly found confidence and became the leader the team needed. The Steelers finished the season with a 10–3–1 record and won the Central Division championship. Because of Bradshaw's strong performance many felt that the Steelers had a good chance to win their first NFL championship.

In the opening playoff game against the Buffalo Bills Bradshaw played one of the finest games of his pro career. He hit on twelve of nineteen pass attempts for 203 yards and a touchdown in the 32–14 victory. He was in such control throughout the game that he threw only five passes in the second half.

The following week, in the AFC championship game against Oakland, Bradshaw played another outstanding game. He brought his team from behind to beat the Raiders in Oakland, which doesn't happen often. With the Steelers trailing 10–3 in the fourth quarter, Bradshaw sparked his team to three touchdowns and a 24–13 victory. It was obvious now that Bradshaw was the leader.

"I felt terrible after the Houston loss," recalled Bradshaw. "I figured I had blown the job again. But Noll called me into his office and said he was going to give me another shot against New England.

"The big thing was in knowing the coach had confidence in me. Once he questions what I'm doing, I'm the type person who's going to be bothered by that doubt. A quarterback needs to know a coach is behind him. I think I've grown up a lot this season, and I think I'm getting better and better."

Despite their strong showing in the playoffs the Steelers were rated as underdogs against the Minnesota Vikings in the 1975 Super Bowl. The Vikings had appeared in two previous Super Bowls and lost both of them. The experts now picked the Vikings to win.

In a game Pittsburgh dominated from the beginning with a steady offense and a solid defense, the Steelers won their first NFL championship, 16–6. Bradshaw relied heavily on his ground game and threw only fourteen passes, completing nine for ninety-six yards and a touchdown. He handed the ball regularly to Franco Harris and the big fullback carried thirty-four times for 158 yards, both Super Bowl records. At the same time the strong Steeler defense held the Vikings to only nine first downs and seventeen yards rushing.

When the 1975 season began Bradshaw was solidly established as the team's number-one quarterback for the first time. He had led the Steelers to their first championship, and the greatness that was expected of him had begun to come through. Yet Bradshaw wasn't quite satisfied. There was an unfair rap hanging over his head that he was a "dumb quarterback." It annoyed him and he felt it was unjustified.

"It's been on my back for five seasons," he complained. "I'm sick of talking about it. Every writer wants to discuss it. If I'm so stupid how did Pittsburgh ever make it to the Super Bowl with me at quarterback?

"Some Pittsburgh writer hung the dumb rap on me. When I came up to the club the first year, I was just a little old country boy and I had a Southern accent. I called everybody 'sir' and said things like 'no, sir' and 'thank you, ma'am.' If you're clean-cut and square and like country

music and come from the South, some people think you're stupid."

Bradshaw was indeed growing up. He matured to the point where he earned the respect of his coaches and teammates. When Bradshaw took the Steelers to the 1976 Super Bowl he gained more support.

"A good quarterback is one who complements your offense," explained linebacker Jack Ham. "Terry has been great since 1974. It's just that people think that because he's thrown the ball more in 1978 he's doing better. We have a more balanced football team now. Our offense played super football and that made it easier for the defense. In fact, our offense was the key; it has been Bradshaw's year, especially."

The crowning glory came in Super Bowl XIII. Bradshaw carried the Steelers to an exciting 35–31 victory over the Dallas Cowboys. He threw four touchdown passes and gained 318 yards. Nobody had ever done that in a Super Bowl before. Even so, he didn't forget how hard it had been at the beginning.

"I wanted so bad to make the Steelers a winner so they'd be proud of me," remarked Bradshaw. "Maybe I wanted it too much, put too much pressure on myself. I made mistakes, plenty of mistakes, and some of them were stupid. From stupid it went to dumb, and that's the image I was stuck with.

"Back then the guys here saw me as a hillbilly and didn't even try to understand me. At the same time I kept looking for someone to pat me on the back, instead of realizing that I had to earn it. The talk about being too country, too dumb, hurt. The hardest thing was to be myself, so I withdrew. Now I'm me, and I'm happy."

So are the Steelers.

Bradshaw excels in postseason play. He had the best game of his career, throwing for over 300 yards and four touchdowns, in Super Bowl XIII.

The Offense

Teammates mob Bennie Cunningham (89) and Terry Bradshaw (hidden) after touchdown pass that won the first 1978 Cleveland game in overtime.

For the six years up to 1978 the Steeler offense relied on the run, and for a very good reason: Franco Harris. Harris would control the offense with his long-striding runs either inside or outside. Simple power football: a strong defense on one side of the ledger and Harris on the other. It worked. Twice during those years, 1975 and 1976, the Steelers won Super Bowls. It looked as if their reign would go on forever, but it didn't.

The years in which the Steelers didn't win troubled Noll. He did a great deal of thinking and talking and analyzing long before the 1978 season began, long before the players ever reported to training camp. Noll concluded that Pittsburgh would have to change its offensive philosophy. After hours of studying game films he realized that other teams were unmistakably stacking their defenses to stop Harris. If you stopped Harris, they believed, you stopped the Steelers.

Fine. So Noll simply decided that the Steelers would pass more. If their opponents were still intent on stopping Harris then the passing game would become more effective. The defense was still strong. It was just a matter of changing the emphasis on offense. And if the offense had to move the ball through the air, what difference did that make if the end result was the same?

Noll also had an instinct. He felt strongly that Bradshaw was ready to break out. Bradshaw had matured over the years, and Noll felt that he was ready to take charge. Instead of passing off the run, Bradshaw would now be free to pass as often as he liked, even on first down.

Nobody appreciated the feeling more than Bradshaw. "I didn't feel anymore like a guy who was just asked not to screw things up," he exclaimed. "I felt like a guy who could go out and throw thirty passes if that's what I thought it would take to win.

"In my mind, I compete with every quarterback in the NFL. I want to be right up there with them because if I am my team will be right up there, too. That's the motivation for me now, to be the best. I'm confident now. I don't get rattled any more. I enjoy tight situations now. I used to get nervous and everything. I was torn between running and passing, afraid something bad was going to happen. Time seems to change those feelings.

"The secret to playing well, to reading defenses well, and calling a good game is simple—be relaxed. You have to have confidence in yourself so you can use your ability to the fullest. Maturity plays a great part in anybody's career. I have a good feeling about being ready to play now. I know what I'm going to do."

So did Noll. He was going to open up the offense more. Not that Harris would figure any less in his offensive game plan. In fact, Harris was to be every bit as valuable as he had been

ever since he joined the Steelers in 1972. In five of his first six years Harris had run for over 1,000 yards. (Injuries his second year had prevented him from making it six straight.) With his speed, power, and balance Harris had established himself as the most consistent runner in the NFL. It was no wonder that defenses keyed on him in an effort to stop him. He was the Steeler offense. The combination of Harris and good defense had given Pittsburgh its first world championship in Super Bowl IX, a methodical 16–6 victory over the Minnesota Vikings.

No one will ever forget Harris' performance on that bleak, cold day in New Orleans. He set a Super Bowl record by rushing for 158 yards against a strong Viking defense. It's a record that may never be broken, certainly not for a long time, anyway. Harris couldn't believe he had gained so many yards.

"I gained 158 yards?" he exclaimed after the game, when informed he had set a new Super Bowl record. "You have to be kidding me. Really, 158 yards? I can't believe it. I never thought it could be that high. I'm surprised that I set a new record."

What Franco achieved seemed even more remarkable when he revealed that he hadn't felt so well before the game. During most of the week-long preparations for the Super Bowl, Harris had been bothered by a nagging head cold. It had made him feel weak and affected his breathing.

"Winning the Super Bowl was very important to me and to all of the team," he said, "because it means you're number one and that's what it's all about. It was quite a year. The most significant things that can happen to a running back are to gain 1,000 yards in a season, to contribute to winning a title, and to get a Super Bowl victory. Since all of that happened, I would have to say that it was the most significant year of my life."

And yet it didn't start out that way. In the third game of the season, after carrying the ball once against the Oakland Raiders, Harris hurt his ankle. He was sidelined for the next two weeks. In his first three games Harris gained only 125 yards. When he returned to action nobody gave him much of a chance to gain 1,000 yards.

"When the season opened I felt ready," said

Harris. "Then all of a sudden, boom! I missed three games. I didn't want to miss any at all. I hate to lose that much time. The injury was frustrating, but I tried not to let it get me down. I told myself to just forget it, not to favor the ankle. I figured if it was good enough, fine. If it wasn't I wasn't going to hurt the team. More than anything I was worried about my cutting, but I told myself to just put it out of my mind."

He did, too. Harris ended the season with a strong performance. He gained 881 yards in the Steelers' last nine games to finish with 1,006 yards. For the second time in his three-year career he gained over 1,000 yards. Harris went over the magic figure in the final game of the season against the Cincinnati Bengals. It was personally satisfying to him, and he didn't forget the moment.

"In the huddle, just before the play in which I got it, the look on the linemen's faces told me I was going to get it right then and there," recalled Harris. "If not on that particular play then certainly on the next one.

"That was a tremendous thrill, knowing that they could all share in my accomplishments. After all, the linemen open the holes. Without the holes no back could do anything. Our line was outstanding, and they've gotten better and better, too.

"Running is like anything else. You try to find a good groove. When you find that groove, well, you don't want anything to mess it up. When I get going good I want the ball as often as possible. I don't mind the heavy workload. I don't even think of it in those terms at all."

The 1974 season was a key one for Harris. In 1972, his rookie year, Harris had gained 1,055 yards and had been voted the AFC's Rookie of the Year. But in 1973 he had suffered several injuries, hadn't played much, and gained only 698 yards. Before the 1974 season began he had felt that he had to prove himself all over again.

"Having a good season in 1974 meant a lot to me," Harris disclosed. "A lot of people were down on me when I came to the Steelers from Penn State. It always seems like I have a lot to prove with people. I think that goes back to when I played with Penn State. A lot of people doubted my ability then."

It was true. Before the 1972 college draft

Franco Harris vaults over a teammate on the way to his sixth 1,000-yard season. Franco has been named to the Pro Bowl seven straight times.

the Steelers were deeply concerned about whom to select as their number one choice. One thing was certain: Their prime need was a running back. They narrowed their choices to three: Robert Newhouse of the University of Houston and Lydell Mitchell and Franco Harris, both of Penn State.

Before deciding on Harris, whom the Steelers preferred because of his size, Art Rooney Jr. made a telephone call to Penn State's head coach Joe Paterno, who had been a friend of the Rooney family for years. Paterno spoke to Rooney confidentially.

"Not many people are aware of it, but Harris can run the forty in 4.5 seconds," Paterno revealed. "That's terrific speed for a big man."

As soon as the Steelers selected Harris the critics began to argue that they had made a mistake. Many felt the Steelers should have

Harris became the fifth leading rusher of all time during the 1978 season.

taken Mitchell instead. After all, he was the all-American at Penn State, not Harris.

Their arguments looked even stronger after the 1972 College All-Star game in Chicago. Harris didn't even start the game. Instead, Jeff Kinney of Nebraska did, and Harris didn't do anything in the game to distinguish himself. Many around Pittsburgh believed that Harris would flop as had other Steeler runners taken on the first round in recent years, namely Dick Leftridge, Paul Martha, and Bob Ferguson.

Harris himself wasn't excited at being picked by the Steelers. "I never wanted to come to Pittsburgh," he admitted. "They always had lousy teams and I thought it was a bad city. From what I heard the Steelers didn't have a great image. I'd heard about things being thrown on the field at the players, but I really didn't know because I never followed them. I never followed any professional team for that matter."

In the preseason Harris wasn't exactly a star. Still, the Steelers were winning and he was getting the feel of things. He felt he was making progress. By the time the regular season opened Harris had earned a starting berth, although he had some misgivings.

"I thought I was doing all right, but I heard that the coaches didn't think so," revealed Harris. "They didn't think I was very hungry to make the team. They thought I should go all out, more than I showed.

"But I knew I could play. It's just that I can't get enthusiastic about practice. I use it to get myself in shape, get myself together so when the game starts I'm ready. I don't like it when we scrimmage. I don't like getting hit when it doesn't count."

Things seemed to come apart for Harris. He certainly didn't look like a number one draft choice during the early part of the season. Once again the critics were taking a long look at him. It was a very trying period for him.

In the opening game against Oakland, Franco carried the ball ten times and gained only twenty-eight yards. In the second game against Cincinnati he didn't do much better. He carried the ball thirteen times and could gain only thirty-five yards. The start wasn't promising, to say the least, and it bothered him.

"I played what I considered my worst game ever against the Bengals," admitted Harris. "We lost, 15–10, and I didn't do anything right. I was terrible.

"I went to see Noll and talked to him about it. I felt that he and the team lost faith in me. I was really down on myself. I felt like chucking the whole thing. My mental attitude was as low as it could be.

"The next game against St. Louis I didn't get any action at all. We won, 25–19, without me. The next time against Dallas, I ran the ball three times and gained sixteen yards in a 17–13 loss. In four games I carried the ball exactly twenty-six times for a grand total of seventy-nine yards and I hadn't scored a touchdown. I felt low.

"Then we played Houston in the fifth game. I didn't get a chance to play until the second half. I kept telling myself, 'Give it everything you've got on every play, no matter what.' And you know what happened? I carried thirteen times and gained 115 yards and scored my first touchdown. Boy, was I happy."

Still, he hadn't quite put it all together. In the very next game, against the New England Patriots, Harris carried the ball eleven times and could gain only twenty-seven yards. After six games of his rookie season he had run for a total of 221 yards. No one ever expected that Franco would finish the season with 1,000 yards. He wasn't even thinking along those lines.

But Harris was something else in his next six games. He ran for over 100 yards in each. In the next to last game of the season, against the Oilers, he went over the magic number with sixty-one yards. He added thirty-one more in his final game against the San Diego Chargers to finish with 1,055 yards. He was only the fifth player in pro history to gain over 1,000 yards as a rookie and only the second Steeler ever to reach that figure.

Harris' strong finish helped the Steelers get into the championship playoffs for the first time in the forty-year history of the franchise. They finished with an 11–3 record, their finest showing ever.

In the opening game of the 1972 playoffs the Steelers faced the powerful Oakland Raiders. Despite their record and their home-field advantage the Steelers were the underdogs. From the opening kickoff the game was fiercely contested. Both defenses excelled. Neither Pittsburgh nor Oakland could move the ball consistently on offense. After three quarters the Steelers led 6–0 on a pair of field goals by Roy Gerela.

The Steelers appeared headed toward a victory. With only 1:13 remaining in the game Oakland had the ball on the Steelers' 30-yard line. They were in field goal range, but they needed a touchdown. The Steelers knew it and went into a pass-prevent defense. Oakland's quarterback Ken Stabler dropped back to pass. He looked all around for an open receiver but couldn't find one. So he tucked the ball under his arm and took off down the left sideline. Running practically on a straight line, Stabler raced into the end zone for a touchdown that put the Raiders ahead, 7–6.

Pittsburgh fans groaned. It appeared they would surely lose. Time was against them. The Steelers' strategy was to try to get the ball into field goal range so Gerela would have a chance to kick his third one and win the game.

Oakland anticipated the pass. Only three linemen charged at Bradshaw; the other eight players dropped back to prevent the pass. Bradshaw had no other choice but to put the ball up. He had to get the Steelers downfield in a hurry before time ran out.

His first three passes failed. Things certainly didn't look good for the Steelers. They had a fourth down on their 40-yard line with only twenty-two seconds remaining to play. Once more the Raiders played the pass.

Bradshaw dropped back. He had time but couldn't find someone to throw to. He looked down one side and then the other. Finally his protection broke down. To avoid being tackled, Bradshaw scrambled around in his backfield, hoping for someone to get open.

He avoided one tackler and then another. Then he set and looked straight downfield. He saw running back Frenchy Fuqua trying to get free on Oakland's 37-yard line. Bradshaw instinctively threw the ball in Fuqua's direction, hoping he would make a game-saving catch. Oakland's safety Jack Tatum rushed over to defend. He succeeded in knocking the ball in

(Right) Sam Davis (57) has been with the team longer than any other active player.

Rocky Bleier lands in the end zone during Super Bowl XIII.

the air before it reached Fuqua. Steeler fans moaned. Tatum appeared to have saved the game for the Raiders.

But the ball was still alive. Before it hit the ground Harris grabbed the ball at his shoe tops on the Oakland 40-yard line. He kept his balance as he lunged to catch the ball and began running at top speed for the Oakland goal line. Everyone watched in disbelief as Harris headed down the sideline.

On the 10-yard line it looked for a split second as if Franco would be caught. Oakland defensive back Jimmy Warren, racing over to stop him, tried desperately to shove him out of bounds. But Harris, running at full speed, never broke his stride and went across the goal line standing up. It was the most dramatic game-winning touchdown in Pittsburgh's history and gave the Steelers an unbelievable 13–7 victory. The catch was called the "Immaculate Reception."

"I ran downfield to block for the receiver," explained Harris in the jubilant Pittsburgh dressing room. "Then when the play got messed up I was running toward Fuqua and Tatum, hoping that French would get the ball and that I could block for him. I saw the ball bounce off Tatum and it came right to me at shoetop height. I grabbed it and set sail for the end zone. Then the coaches ran out on the field and all the officials were talking and the referee went over to check the television replay. Well, they don't always call them right, and I was afraid the play would be called back.

"We won. Fate put me in the right spot at the right time, but I was mentally ready, and it paid off. Sure, it was a lucky play, but all that mattered was that we won. It taught me one important thing: Don't ever give up. Always give a little bit more, a little extra. I know from now on that is the way I'm going to play the game."

He certainly has, and so has Franco's running mate Rocky Bleier. Perhaps he epitomizes the spirit of the Steelers. The self-sacrificing Bleier is Harris' lead blocker out of the backfield and is considered one of the premier blocking backs in the NFL. Apart from guard Sam Davis he is the only remaining member of the Steelers to have survived Noll's rebuilding program.

Actually, Noll didn't think much of Bleier's chances when he sat down to reshape the

Steelers in 1969. As a sixteenth-round draft choice from Notre Dame in 1968 Bleier's chances of making the team weren't very good to begin with. But he worked hard, made the team, and saw most of his action on the special teams covering punts and kickoffs. He carried the ball only fourteen times his rookie year and managed to gain only fifty-three yards. His statistics weren't very impressive.

During Bleier's first year with Pittsburgh Noll was still an assistant coach with Baltimore. When he arrived in Pittsburgh before the 1969 season, Bleier was gone. He had had to report for Army duty as an officer and had been sent to Vietnam. Nobody missed Bleier much.

"I was still looking ahead to playing with the Steelers when I got back home," recalled Bleier. "I thought about that as much as I ever thought about anything when I first arrived in Vietnam. I never questioned why I went over there or why our country was involved.

"I never thought about being killed or getting shot or shooting someone. If I had thought about those things I would have ruined myself mentally. I saw guys who went through this and watched the great emotional changes that took them to drugs and alcohol as an escape."

Bleier didn't escape the pains of war. He was on patrol in the jungle with his squad, heading for a clearing where they would be picked up by a helicopter. Upon leaving the jungle they came across a rice paddy. Suddenly machine-gun fire broke out around them. The soldier next to Bleier was hit and died immediately, while everyone else jumped into the paddy to escape the shooting.

Heavy machine-gun fire pinned down the squad. A few minutes later Bleier discovered where the enemy fire was coming from. He began to crawl toward it, hoping to knock it out with a rifle grenade. Just before Bleier fired his rifle a bullet hit him in the leg. It ripped through his left thigh, taking out a large piece of flesh.

"I was about to fire when someone yelled 'Rocky,' and I felt a twinge in my leg as if someone threw a rock and hit me. At first I thought that's what happened until I looked down and saw the blood. I thought right then and there that I would never play football again."

Slowly the squad tried to make its way toward the clearing with the hope of being rescued. Before they got there they were attacked again. As Bleier lay on the ground a grenade landed only a few feet away. His face turned white.

"I was lying on my side and saw it as it bounced in my direction," said Bleier. "I wondered, 'Do I jump with the roll of the grenade or go the opposite way?' I wanted to get rid of it, but before I could grab it the thing exploded."

Bleier took the force of the grenade's explosion on his foot. He blacked out. For the next four hours Bleier and the rest of the squad were pinned down under fire. It wasn't until early evening that they were rescued by helicopters.

For his heroism, Bleier would later be awarded the Bronze Star and the Purple Heart. Yet it was nearly midnight when he received proper medical attention, almost twelve hours since part of his foot and a piece of his leg had been shot off. Infection had begun to set in around his toes and was moving up his calf. His injuries were so bad that the doctors seriously considered amputating part of his right leg.

When Bleier returned to the Steelers in 1970 he couldn't make it through training camp. He couldn't run without experiencing pain. He was only a shadow of the player he had been before he was wounded. Bleier had to have additional surgery to repair the damage to his leg. He returned to the active roster for the final game, but nobody thought he had a chance to stay with the team the following season. Bleier needed a second operation. The Steelers didn't cut him, but placed him on injured reserve. He spent three weeks in the hospital recovering. When he got out he had to start all over again.

"The club gave me an opportunity to correct my foot problems, but I also had to prove that I could be part of the team," said Bleier. "It was a two-way deal, and no matter what happened I had made my mind up that I didn't want to feel obligated or feel like I was being kept around because somebody felt sorry for me."

Bleier earned a spot on the roster for the 1971 season. Although he never ran with the ball, he played six games on the special teams. The following year Bleier's career almost came to an end. Early in the 1972 season he suffered a severe hamstring injury. He carried the ball only

once from scrimmage, and his future looked grim.

Still, Bleier wouldn't quit. He worked hard conditioning his leg and made the special teams in 1973. But it wasn't until 1974 that he completed his amazing comeback. He won a starting job for the first time in his career in the fifth game of the season and has been running alongside Harris ever since. In 1976 he ran his best, 1,036 yards, and joined John Henry Johnson and Franco Harris as the only Steelers to gain 1,000 yards rushing in a single season.

The Pittsburgh running game was solid. It represented half of the Steelers' powerful one-two offensive punch. The remaining half rested with Bradshaw and his gifted receivers. Some think there is no finer wide receiver in football than Lynn Swann, none with the moves and speed that are so well orchestrated with pre-cision leaping and timing. Nobody draws more double coverage than the nimble receiver, and nobody makes bigger clutch plays than Swann.

He has demonstrated this talent on a number of occasions. The latest was in Super Bowl XIII. He slipped through the Dallas secondary midway in the fourth quarter and reached up for a fingertip grab of an 18-yard touchdown pass from Bradshaw. It was the clinching touchdown in the Steelers' 35–31 victory. He finished the day with seven catches for 124 yards.

Swann's electrifying catch brought back memories of the one he made in Super Bowl X against the same Cowboys. That one was perhaps even bigger because no one knew for certain whether Swann would play that day. Even Swann himself had doubts.

Ten days before the game Swann was released from a Pittsburgh hospital after spending forty-

(Right) Tight coverage didn't prevent Swann from grabbing eleven TD passes.

Lynn Swann caught sixty-one passes during the regular season and thirteen during postseason play for his best season ever.

eight hours in bed with a concussion. He had suffered the injury in the AFC championship game against the Oakland Raiders. His head ached. Constant pain dulled his whole body.

As Swann left the hospital he was told to rest. He was ordered to stay away from football. It was a strong possibility that Swann wouldn't be able to play in the Super Bowl. It's not easy to come back from a concussion. Another blow to the head could end his career and receivers in an open field are easy targets for such a blow.

As the Super Bowl approached Swann still hadn't worked out with the team. He wasn't feeling that healthy and was examined daily by a doctor. He now had post-concussion syndrome, blurred vision, dizziness, and even blackouts. It was a frightful feeling, to say the least. Yet the doctors left the decision to play up to Swann. They warned him about some built-in dangers. Another hard shot, for instance, could easily cause more damage.

A few days before the game Swann did some light workouts. No contact—he just ran some pass patterns and worked on his timing. He wasn't taking any chances. Yet something was wrong. Swann didn't seem confident.

"In the workouts I was worried," Swann admitted. "My timing was off. I didn't get dizzy, but I just didn't feel right. I dropped a lot of passes. I had to decide whether it would hurt the team or help the team if I played. I said to myself, 'To hell with it. I'm going out there to play 100 percent.' Sure, I thought about being reinjured, but the doctors left it up to me whether I wanted to play or not. I decided to play."

Did he ever. With only 3:02 left in the game Pittsburgh was clinging to a 15–10 lead. They had a third down and six to go on their own 36–yard line. Dallas played for the pass, figuring Bradshaw would throw short to get an important first down. The pressure was on Bradshaw, who realized that the Cowboys would be coming after him.

Bradshaw called perhaps the most important play in his six-year professional career, "69 Maximum Flanker Post." It was Swann's play. At the snap of the ball Dallas blitzed from the right side. It was not only a blitz but a double blitz of the linebacker and safety. However, Bradshaw got the ball off. Swann sped downfield, covered tightly by cornerback Mark Washington who

ran with him step for step. At the last split second Swann put on a burst of speed, reached out, and caught Bradshaw's pass on his fingertips on the 5-yard line without breaking stride. It was a picture play, and it gave Pittsburgh its second straight world championship, 21–17.

Swann's catch was his fourth of that game. He had had two other remarkable catches earlier. One was a leaping 32-yard catch in the first quarter on the Dallas 16-yard line. The other was a 53-yard grab for which he had outjumped Washington on the Dallas 47-yard line. (The third catch was a beauty, too. Swann had made a 12-yard reception by diving for an underthrown pass on the Cowboys' five-yard line.) Swann set a Super Bowl record with 161 total yards.

Swann suffered another concussion in the opening game of the 1976 season. Again he was playing against Oakland, and again it was George Atkinson who did the damage.

"What happened only intensified my feelings of football getting out of control," emphasized Swann. "When I'm home and I'm talking to friends, I'm wondering why I'm still going out there. Am I really in love with the game? Do I enjoy it that much or is the money that good that I want to keep exposing myself to these dangers when nothing significant has been done to protect people? Maybe I shouldn't be out there, because another concussion could cause serious and permanent damage."

Yet all Swann did in 1978 was run past defensive backs. Despite being double-teamed practically every game Swann had his best season ever. He caught the most passes in his five-year career, sixty-one, gained the most yards, 880, and scored eleven touchdowns, which equaled his 1975 output.

It was no wonder the Steelers went to the passing game more. The other reason was Swann's buddy at the other wide receiver spot, John Stallworth. Like Swann he was drafted in 1974 from little Alabama A&M. In Stallworth's first three years with the club, however, he was slowed by injuries. He caught only forty-five passes, and nobody really knew how good he was.

But in 1977 Stallworth avoided injuries. So much so that he almost surpassed his previous three-year production in one season. He caught

forty-four passes for 784 yards and seven touchdowns, averaging 17.8 yards a catch. Besides speed, concentration, and excellent hands, Stallworth showed the Steelers another quality, consistency. It was no wonder that Noll opened up the passing attack.

Normally, Stallworth lines up on the left side and Swann on the right. They complement each other so well that, as a tandem, they are perhaps the best in the NFL.

"I was in Lynn's shadow for a long time," remarked Stallworth. "But I felt I had as much ability as he did. The good thing about it was we came in as sort of a team and we've stayed that way. Swannie's maybe a little more flashy and had the early success, but I think we both know how close we are, talent-wise.

"All Lynn's publicity was justly earned. He hit it big right off the bat. Me? I was a slow starter. I wasted a couple of seasons with a bunch of nagging injuries, sprains, muscle pulls, things like that. I used to get muscle pulls all the time, but that's because I went at everything hard. I can remember back when I was a rookie I used to run everywhere during camp, and if we were practicing our stance I'd practice that hard. Now I know better. I've learned to take care of my body more. I've learned to avoid pulled hamstrings and the like. The key for me is to stay healthy.

"In 1977 things started happening. I was healthy, and I got to play regularly. Bradshaw got confidence in me. Now he's going to get me the ball, and I'm going to make catches. My time has come."

It almost didn't. As a child Stallworth was frail. He was a thin youngster who seemed to be constantly ill. At one point it was feared he had polio. He was paralyzed on his left side for ten days. Stallworth wasn't exactly a highly sought-after college prospect. Even the University of Alabama looked past him, though he lived a couple of blocks away.

"My mom never did want me to play football," disclosed Stallworth. "Mom's still not happy about it. She sees the size of the people I have to play against, and she worries every game."

Once during the 1977 season she really had reason to worry. Stallworth was hit by a vicious forearm smash delivered by Cincinnati's Mel

Morgan. The force of the blow gave Stallworth a concussion. NFL Commissioner Pete Rozelle didn't like what he saw in the game films and suspended Morgan for a game.

"You know, I never fully realized what had happened to Swannie in the past until I got hit in that game," said Stallworth. "Sure, I used to think about it, but I never worried until after that. It goes with the territory, but maybe that's why I started sliding when I went to catch low passes, to make sure I wouldn't get hit in the face again. It's my own invention. I don't know why I started to do it. It just sort of happened after the injury. Anyway, it worked out pretty well."

What has worked out even better is the efficiency demonstrated by Bradshaw, Swann, and Stallworth. It has created serious problems for opposing teams. They have learned how fatal it is to double up on one and leave the other to single coverage. There's too much speed to cover. Stallworth finished the 1978 season with forty-one receptions for 798 yards and nine touchdowns, averaging 19.5 yards a catch.

"We're each about as quick as the other," declared Stallworth, "and I guess we can both jump as high, though Lynn starts a little closer to the ground than I do. But we catch the ball differently. Lynn always tries to take it against his body, to cushion it during the catch. I have more of a tendency to catch with my hands. Lynn usually lines up on the strong side, whereas I got to the weak side. But we can flip-flop, and we also sometimes line up on the same side. It depends on the defensive setup."

"Strong side or weak side, it doesn't make much difference," added Swann. "John and I are both moving targets. It's just up to Terry to hit us. What's happened is that we developed a remarkable, almost undefinable rapport among the three of us.

"The art of any pass route is what happens during the last few moments of it, the last five yards or less. John and I are concentrating all the way out, taking the chuck or avoiding it, letting the route develop along the lines we've planned, practiced over and over, yet trying to make it seem like something it isn't. You have to do it to know what I mean. You don't know where all the defenders are, you only sort of sense them. But you know that Terry, if he's

John Stallworth capped a superb season with fourteen receptions and four touchdowns in postseason play. Always a deep threat, Stallworth gathered in nine touchdown passes in 1978.

getting the pass blocking he should be getting, is seeing it all."

That was clearly demonstrated in Super Bowl XIII. Stallworth had a fantastic first half. Bradshaw got the protection he needed, and Stallworth displayed how dangerous he was in the open field. He caught three passes for 115 yards, two of which he turned into touchdowns. One went for twenty-eight yards, and the other, which electrified the crowd, covered seventy-five yards. Stallworth might have bettered Swann's Super Bowl record if he had played the second half, but severe cramps kept him on the sidelines.

"Quite a few people mentioned it to me that they thought I would have been the MVP," said Stallworth. "I tried not to dwell on it too much. I had a good first half, made the two scores. Hopefully, we'll get there again and maybe I'll have another chance at it.

"I think Noll was totally right about the fact that the club hasn't peaked yet. I think Bradshaw's best years are ahead of him. We have a lot of running backs coming that are all going to be super, and our receivers, I think, are just great."

He's right. Before tight end Bennie Cunning-

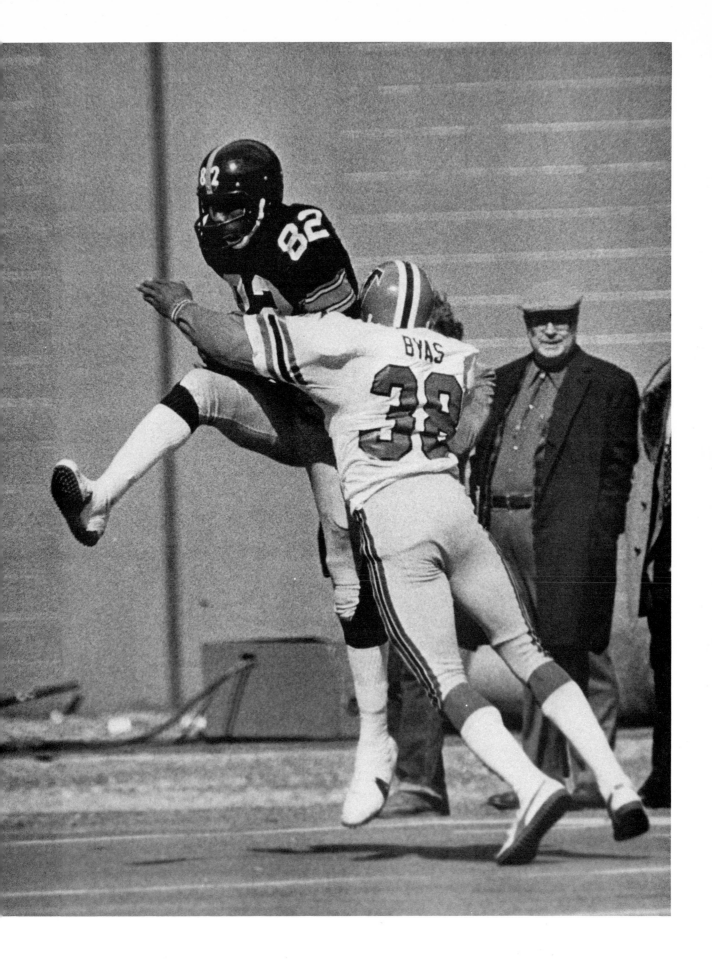

Bennie Cunningham caught sixteen passes with an average gain of 20.1 yards before being knocked out of action in the sixth week of the season against Atlanta.

ham got injured he was heading for the best season of his three-year career. He had already caught sixteen passes for 321 yards, an average of 20.1 yards a reception. For a tight end that's a remarkable record.

But in the sixth game of the season, against the Atlanta Falcons, Cunningham hurt his leg and was finished for the year. It was a tough break, because Cunningham, at 6′ 4″ and 247

pounds, is the biggest tight end in the NFL. He is mobile and extremely difficult to bring down. That's what makes him so dangerous after he catches a ball.

After Cunningham got hurt, Randy Grossman took his place. Grossman, at 6′ 1″ and 215 pounds, is the smallest tight end in the league. He is also the only Jewish player in the NFL. His size didn't attract the pro scouts. In

Sure-handed Randy Grossman grabbed thirty-seven passes during the season.

fact, Steeler trainer Ralph Berlin signed him as a free agent in 1974.

Grossman was a more than adequate replacement. He caught thirty-seven passes for 448 yards. Although his speed is average, he has good hands and the ability to get open.

"With all those big guys out there, I'm dealing in areas below their vision," explained Grossman. "I always thought I was underrated by

people who rate people. I was confident that I could do the things that had to be done. I was never big enough to be a tight end, but everyone has a picture of themselves, of what they think they are. I guess I have a bigger picture of myself."

Much like guard Sam Davis. At thirty-five Davis is the oldest of all the Steelers. Nobody gave him much of a chance when he was signed

Mike Webster (52) established himself as an all-Pro, and possibly the best center in football, in 1978.

as a free agent in 1967. Yet he has survived twelve years in the pits and has played longer for Pittsburgh than any other players currently on the team. Despite his age Davis is considered one of the top pulling guards in the league. He lost his starting job in 1974 following a foot injury but regained it in 1976.

"I felt stronger than I've felt the last five or six years," said Davis. "I have my quickness back. Everyone looks at us as having the smallest offensive line, but no one relates to us as having the quickest and strongest.

"People just don't respect the Pittsburgh team as having an explosive offensive line. When they talk Pittsburgh everybody concerns themselves with Bradshaw, Franco Harris, Lynn Swann. People like to read about our different offensive weapons before they get involved with the offensive line.

"I'm unrecognized. Our offensive line is unrecognized. I think we do a nice little job. The reason I survived is that I was raised to take care of myself. I was not raised to look at my teammates and worry about what they were doing. I guess you'd have to say I did it by myself, and I'm glad I did, because it's the reason I'm still here."

Davis and Rocky Bleier are the only two remaining players from the pre-Noll era. But since then the Steeler offensive line has developed into one of the finest in the NFL. Tackle Jon Kolb was added first, then came guard Gerry Mullins, all-pro center Mike Webster, and tackle Larry Brown, who started his career as a tight end and was switched to tackle in 1977. Now everybody recognizes the Pittsburgh offensive line.

From top to bottom, Gerry Mullins, Larry Brown, and Jon Kolb.

Joe Greene

He heard the whispers. They were ugly. They started long before the 1978 season began. Then they grew louder, and the louder they became the angrier he became. No one likes to hear them. No player likes to hear it said that he is finished, washed up. Those are the nastiest whispers of all. And when training camp began there were a great many fans who believed it. They, too, felt that it had to end some time. After all, every player has to reach the end. Injuries the past two years had taken their toll. He was now thirty-two years old; he had played the game for nine years. It was time to say goodbye. The only thing wrong was that Joe Greene wasn't ready to call it quits.

It was no wonder Greene was filled with fury when training camp opened. The whispers were out in the open and they sounded almost believable to everyone but Greene.

"They wrote me off," exclaimed Greene. "They said I was washed up, could no longer play, things like that. My friends kept telling me how they'd read about what was wrong with my back. If there was something wrong that was my business. But there wasn't anything wrong. Did it bother me? Sure it did. I was upset, to say the least. I was angry."

Greene's anger drives him to a dangerous plateau, where his performance level is highest. Opponents know that. His teammates realize it. There is nothing more devastating during a game than an emotionally riled Greene. He overwhelms opponents, simply intimidates them. His attitude is infectious. It's what the Steel Curtain is all about.

Although Greene didn't have to prove anything to himself, he had to show everyone else that he was an even better all-around performer than before. He could no longer be the reckless, driving hunter of his earlier years with the Steelers. Now, in 1978, he assumed a new role. The Steeler defense changed with him. Instead of depending on individual brilliance the Steelers advocated team defense. Greene was still expected to perform at peak efficiency, but now his performance was welded into a team effort.

It worked, too. It didn't prevent Greene from being double-teamed in every game as he had always been. But his responsibilities were narrowed. He wasn't expected to chase the quarterback on every play, nor was he expected to play with diminished ferocity. That could never happen. Greene just wasn't expected to carry the whole defense by himself. He was now a part, a very integral part, of the whole.

Greene was comfortable with his new role. A great deal of pressure was lifted from his shoulders. He had absorbed more injuries in the last two years than in the rest of his career. There were injuries to his back, neck, shoulder, and groin, the kind that hurt, that limited his effectiveness. But 1978 was different. Greene was healthy and mean and tough, so much so that he led the Steeler linemen with seventy tackles, five fumble recoveries, and four quarterback sacks. Joe Greene was indeed alive and well.

"The realization that I could get my job done better with a conservative approach was impor-

Although double-teamed most of the time Joe Greene still manages to harass opposing quarterbacks.

tant," remarked Greene. "I think that all comes with realizing that as time goes on things must change, and you react accordingly. I'm only fooling myself if I think I can go out there and play like a sprinter when I'm not. Like rushing the passer. I never thought I had the ability to rush the passer with 100 percent confidence. Oh, I had confidence, you always do. But not the kind you need, and the reality of that is you're a disservice to your team. I was trying to play a role I couldn't perform.

"Now I try to see everything that happens. See all the defensive linemen. Try to communicate with everybody. That's the conservative approach. We do things up front that other teams don't. We play formations and we play hunches, but we do it together. We don't put a guy out of position if we're not covering for him first. What I do is communicate. I feel good things about the people I play with. I talk about what I think we're capable of doing. I talk to the players. Sometimes I step on some toes.

"When the season began I don't think any one of us knew how good this team was. We knew we were good, but we weren't sure if we could get into the playoffs. Then I started to see small things, small things like a couple of plays in our overtime win over Cleveland. In crucial situations we did exactly the right thing. We played well when we had to play well. By the time we got through Denver and Houston in the playoffs I started to see the signs. Good signs. The kind that gave me a real good feeling.

"This club had all the emotion of the first Super Bowl. That's because this time we didn't have any idea this would be as good a ball club as we are. As hungry as the other times? I think so. I thought our '76 club was worthy of being in the Super Bowl, but last year was a disappointment to all of us. The thing that made us hungry was being away for two years. I like to go to the Super Bowl every year. What else do you play for? All I have to look forward to is the postseason games.

"It's all been so good. I felt so super, like I was on an unreal but natural high. I'm so spaced out about this club, what it's done, what it can do. I think this has probably been one of my better years. Maybe not the best; I didn't have the pass rush that I would like to have had. Overall, my effectiveness and the role I played

with the ball club was probably the best ever. It was more of a team concept on the defensive line. We did a lot of things together as a group on the football field. It's not an individual thing. At the beginning it was. My style was one of individual play."

The adjustment was tough for Greene to make, yet he made it. And the bottom line was that the Steelers were better defensively. They allowed only 195 points over the sixteen-game regular season, the fewest in the NFL. L. C. Greenwood, who played next to Greene on the line, appreciated his contributions in making the team concept work.

"Joe probably played better ball this year than in his entire career," remarked Greenwood. "Before, he just ran all over the field. But now he's matured a lot and he knows more about what he's doing, so he doesn't have to take the chances he once did. He can take short cuts without a lot of guessing.

"Now that he's learned the game he's played the game the way it's supposed to be played. And I feel it was his best year, because he did a lot of things that you may not see out there. He did things that the fans might not have seen, but I saw them because I'm playing next to him. Joe is a great asset to this team, especially to the defense. Teams can't man-block him. They have to have at least two men on him each play. That frees somebody else."

It isn't strange that Greene didn't feel his play in 1978 had been his best. He's like that. The big defensive tackle is his own severest critic. Yet the good things he did didn't go unnoticed. George Perles, for one, noticed a lot of things. He is the Steelers' defensive coordinator, who put the front four together seven years ago and molded them into the Steel Curtain. Greene has always been one of his favorites.

"I'll tell you what he means to the ball club," exclaimed Perles. "Everybody knows what he is physically. But what he means to this team mentally, emotionally, I can't put into words. He's the most important person on this team. Besides being a football player, the emotions, the enthusiasm, the toughness, the meanness are the intangibles that are all there. We have a reputation for being tough, and a lot of our reputation is due to him.

"Greene's got things you can't measure with

scales and tape measures and strength machines. He's got leadership. As a defensive tackle Joe hasn't lost anything from his peak years. He had some injuries, and there were times when he wasn't as up emotionally as this year, but Joe never lost his ability.

"Physically, he's a guy who can take all the strength and quickness, collect it, and fit it together like a spring, and then explode. He has this way of coiling himself up and coming off the ball that very few people can withstand. The defense are the biggest, toughest, strongest, meanest people.

"Let's face it. This is an animalistic world and people look up to strength, especially football people. Joe Greene has all that. He radiates it. On the field he demands and gets more respect than anybody in the NFL. In all my years I don't know anybody who ever challenged him in that area. But of all the guys we have Joe is the easiest to get along with. He knows that everything we think and do is designed to help us. He's aware of everything that is going on, is very interested in the game plan, and is free to make suggestions.

"Greene has all the ingredients of greatness. He may be the fastest man I have ever seen for his size and weight. He realizes that football is a mental as well as a physical challenge. He's always studying films and scouting reports, mapping out strategies to deal with upcoming opponents.

"But there is more than that, something that sets him apart from other superstars. The guy has pure team spirit and an unbending desire to win. Good statistics, personal commendations mean nothing to Joe Greene unless he wins. Most superstars don't understand the necessity of dedicating themselves to an overall team effort. L. C. Greenwood, Dwight White, Steve Furness are good strong players, but Greene makes them better. He knocks out one player, then helps the guy beside him.

"There is something about him that I can't put my finger on, yet other people feel it, too. I remember walking into the locker room with Joe for the Pro Bowl one year. Here we had superstars from all over the league, and they all seemed humbled by his presence. This may sound incredible, but Joe commanded respect without having to utter a single word.

"He's got something. Underneath that calm exterior you have a dangerous man. It's like he has a switch in an electric fuse box somewhere in his head, and that switch is almost always on safety. But he'll let it out when pushed too far. If someone plays dirty, irritates him, the man may not necessarily be responsible for his actions. He's a man and a half when that happens. I'd like to see someone cut him or hold him or do something illegal on him right at the start of every game. That's the way to get him up. It gets him fighting mad."

Such a time occurred several years ago when the Steelers were playing the Cleveland Browns. Bob DeMarco, the Cleveland center who lined up in front of Greene, gave Joe an elbow to the throat. It hurt. Greene felt it was an illegal blow. The referee didn't signal any penalty. Incensed, Greene ran halfway across the field toward the Cleveland bench. He caught up with DeMarco and belted him in the mouth. Dazed, DeMarco went to the bench spitting out blood and a couple of teeth. Undaunted, Greene walked over toward the Browns' bench and braced himself for a challenge. There were no takers.

There was another time in Philadelphia when Greene stopped the game. The Eagles were beating the Steelers and frustration was welling inside Greene. Losing and being held on practically every play was too much for Greene to take. Since the referees weren't calling the penalties, Greene decided to take matters into his own hands.

Before the Eagle center could snap the ball, Greene reached down and took the football out of his hands. He then threw the ball high into the stands and angrily stalked off the gridiron.

"Everybody looked at him," recalled former Steeler linebacker Andy Russell. " 'He can't be doing this,' we thought. We watched the ball spiral into the seats. It seemed like it took forever. The crowd was dead silent. And the players, there we were, we didn't have a ball, we didn't have a left tackle. It was like he was saying, 'Okay, if you won't play right, we won't play at all.' Nobody else would do such a thing. Anybody else would get in trouble with the league, with the coaches. But Joe did it. In a moment the crowd exploded. They loved it."

There was a moment, however, when the

crowd didn't love him. In fact, Greene came ever so close to igniting a massive free-for-all on the field and bringing extra excitement to millions of television viewers. The incident attracted special attention because it occurred during a playoff game against the Denver Broncos in 1977.

In the closing minutes of the first half Greene delivered a punch to the ribs of Denver guard Paul Howard. Everyone in Mile High Stadium and those watching on television saw it. Everyone except the referees. No penalty was indicated. It infuriated the fans, who began to yell, "Get Joe Greene," as Howard was being helped off the field.

On the very next play Greene found himself in the center of another altercation. This time Greene punched Mike Montler, the Denver center. Montler swung back but missed. The officials stepped in, threw their flags, and slapped Greene

with a 15-yard unsportsmanlike conduct penalty. They also had to cool tempers, which by now were flaring on both sides. After the next play, Greene walked off the field satisfied. He had recovered a Bronco fumble.

When the first half ended a minute later, the air was still hostile. As the two teams were trotting off the field, Denver coach Red Miller ran after the officials and began protesting vigorously about Greene's violent style of play. Miller was hot. Once underneath the stands he vehemently protested to Chuck Noll. At that point Perles stepped into the middle and told Miller to go back to his locker room. Miller exploded. He challenged the burly Perles to a fight. Cooler heads prevailed, however, and the two were separated before any blows were thrown.

"Look, I'm really a nice guy," said Greene. "At least I try to be. Most of the time. When I'm

Greene tied for the team lead in opponents' fumbles recovered in 1978.

not being hassled. I don't like it when people call me mean. I've always been big and strong ever since I was a kid. Strength and quickness are my primary assets, but that doesn't mean that I go around beating on people.

"Nobody wants to be known as mean. It kills me when little kids are afraid of me because of my size. Fathers pushing them saying, 'It's all right. Ask for his autograph. He won't hurt you.' That sort of thing bothers me. I'll sign them for kids, they're all right. Sometimes adults will come up and stick a piece of paper in your face when you're eating, the fork halfway up to your mouth. I don't sign them then. People don't understand how that feels. They'll come up and shove a piece of paper at you like you're not even human, just some kind of machine that plays football and writes its name. We're human. We bleed like them, cry like them, eat like them.

"That's what's wrong with professional football. People think we're supermen. We're not. None of us is particularly unique. Football is repetition, repetition, repetition. Everyone connected with it tries to attach too much charisma to it, but it's repetition. And what is football, really? Just a game. There's very little in football that's creative. It's a great game, but when people try to dress it up, make it more than it is, that's garbage, like most of the stuff about the game in the newspapers.

"I'm not saying there haven't been any changes, but what are people going to see one year that they haven't seen before? Repetition. When I go out there now I'm doing the same things I've been doing since I was thirteen years old. You don't play for money or for success, I don't care what anyone says. You play because football is something that you can do well and it is fun. Underneath, that's what the game is, winning and fun."

Yet, it wasn't always that way. Born in Temple, Texas, Greene was raised by his mother, to whom he is devoted. He didn't exactly have what is considered a normal childhood. While other kids his age were out playing, Joe was working in the cotton fields. Greene never forgot those years.

"Maybe it would have made me stronger in some ways in which I'm weak if I had a father around," recalled Greene. "Given me some stability. I often wonder, but I always knew my mother loved me. No matter how hard it was, she always took care of us. I chopped cotton some, picked cotton. When I was twelve I told myself I would never go back into the fields. I had a burning desire to be a success at something.

"Not necessarily football. I often sit around and reminisce. Times were—I guess they were tough. I miss 'em. It's been a long time—since high school, early college days—since I've felt at ease. I feel anxieties, pressures, feel that people are going to ask me for an autograph even when they don't. Sometimes I feel good about giving autographs, when people are really nice and it means something to them.

"I never got into trouble when I was a kid, but it's strange that I got the reputation of being a bully. I didn't deserve it. Before I started playing football I got my butt kicked constantly. It was always some old, little guy. At one point I was more round than tall. I was a bit timid, shy. I still am, a bit. Then I started playing football, and I guess that all kind of went away. I started taking my aggressions out on other people.

"In the eighth grade I weighed 158 pounds, but they didn't even give me a uniform. I quit. The next year I weighed 203 and started getting what you might call confidence. My sophomore year I weighed 235. By my senior year I weighed 250. From my sophomore year on I was a middle linebacker. I loved that position. If there was a tackle being made somewhere I was on it. We didn't win, though. I got a reputation for being the dirtiest ballplayer that ever came out of that area. When we were losing I'd act the fool. I didn't do that in college because we won. I've never acted crazy in the pros unless we were losing.

"I'll tell you how crazy I used to be. A team came to Temple and beat us. We had this little diner in town. I came in there, and the other team was eating. Their quarterback had an ice cream cone. I took it away from him and smeared it all over his face. He didn't do anything. He went back to the team bus. Then I heard somebody call my name. I turned around and a soda bottle hit my chest, and the guy I'd done that way ducked back into the bus. Like a damn fool, I went at the bus—in the front door. They all went out the back door."

Later Greene went to North Texas State. Coincidentally, the school's nickname was the Mean Green. He carried the "mean" with him into the pros.

Yet, the Steelers had certain misgivings about Greene before making him their number one draft pick in 1969. Their scouting report on him wasn't very encouraging. In fact, none of the Steeler scouts recommended taking him at all. What the scouts wrote raised more than a few eyebrows: "Puts on weight, tendency to loaf. . . . Physically, this boy has it all. Mentally, he's disappointing in that he only uses his abilities in spurts. Will need a heavy hand but can play. . . . I would question taking a boy like this in the first round as he could turn out to be a big dog."

Although some other pro scouts rated Greene highly, his reputation did not exactly overwhelm Pittsburgh. One Pittsburgh newspaper carried a headline that read, "Steelers Draft Joe Who?"

For a while the Steelers wondered about Greene. He was late in reporting to training camp because of a contract squabble. When he finally arrived he was a bit heavy. He didn't seem to appreciate going to a team with a record of 2–11–1 the year before. Greene was used to a winning atmosphere at North Texas State.

The Steeler veterans looked upon Greene with a skeptical eye. He quickly had them talking to themselves, however. He was genuine, all right. He learned to react quickly to some new moves he had never seen in college. At the same time he proved that he was too strong to be overpowered by sheer force. The big 6' 4", 275-pound rookie made his presence felt around the league once the season began. He had an outstanding season and was named rookie of the year. It was the only award that the Steelers won that year, finishing with a dismal 1–13 season. But in Greene they had the cornerstone on which to build their defense.

"I had accomplished a lot very quickly," recalled Greene, "but when I looked in the mirror after my first pro season with all my awards and trophies I was still in last place.

"Yet, when you are a rookie, it's beautiful. A lot of things happen out there that you aren't even aware of. I wish I could go back to the way it was my rookie year, just hit somebody or get hit and not worry about the consequences. The Man has a way of taking care of rookies and fools. My rookie year I had a good time.

Chuck Noll's first draft choice in 1969, Greene was selected as
the NFL's defensive rookie of the year and played in the Pro Bowl that year.

Sunday was a fun day. I got kicked out of games twice. I wish I could get that involved again. Now, I've got so many things in my head that when I get on the field I'm a robot. I have paralyzed myself with analysis."

Greene immediately took charge as the leader of the defense his rookie season. That he was thrown out of two games showed how much he wanted to win. The "Mean Joe" nickname became even more appropriate; it was one he wouldn't lose.

In the fourth game of the season the Steelers

were playing the New York Giants in New York. Fran Tarkenton was the Giants' quarterback. Greene, knowing Tarkenton's reputation as a scrambler, was intent on nailing him behind the line of scrimmage. On one attempt in the third quarter he just missed tackling Tarkenton.

"Before I walked back to the line I told Tarkenton I wasn't going to miss him the next time," Greene recalled.

On the next play Greene came charging again, determined to tackle Tarkenton. As he grabbed him and knocked him down the crowd groaned.

Tarkenton had already thrown the ball, but Greene didn't know it. The referee immediately threw Greene out of the game and Greene didn't understand why. Later he saw the films of the game which revealed his late hit. With Greene out of the game the Giants went on to win, 10–7.

After the game Greene was quoted as saying he was "sorry he didn't do a complete job." The way it came out, everyone thought that Greene wished Tarkenton had been carried off the field on a stretcher. But according to Greene that wasn't the case at all.

"The writer misinterpreted what I had said," he explained. "I said I didn't like being thrown out of the game and I was sorry we didn't win. I take pride in my personality, in my attitude toward people, and this really hurt me. I was going to write Tarkenton a letter and tell him that I didn't mean it the way it came out, but I never got around to it."

A month later Greene got thrown out again, this time against the Minnesota Vikings. "Clint Jones was running with the ball, and he had a bunch of tacklers hitting him," remarked Greene. "He was still on his feet when I came over and hit him, too. Then Jim Vellone of the Vikings came up and hit me on the back. I yelled to the referee to throw his flag and he did.

I started clapping my hands, but then I saw him walk the wrong way. The penalty was on me!

"On the next play I rushed the passer, and I was trying to get past Vellone. I didn't appreciate his hitting me in the back. It was a pretty good shot and it could have ended my career. So we began swinging at each other. I was thrown out and he wasn't.

"Going after the quarterback is like playing king of the mountain. When you get the quarterback you're on top of the mountain. That's the name of the game: Get the Quarterback. He's the brains of the team. I learned a long time ago that if you kill the head the body will die. And the quarterback is the brains of the team.

"Look, I believe if a guy runs through me and he gets a few yards, and if I catch up with him then or later, he's going to pay the price. You don't get anything free. You've got to pay. Just like if I get to the quarterback I'm going to pay for it. They're going to give me all sorts of knocks.

"I don't take cheap shots, though. If a guy is going down I might hit him. But I don't hit a guy when he's on the ground. I try to be where the ball is, and when I get there I don't want to be standing around twiddling my thumbs."

Ironically, Greene met up with Tarkenton again in Super Bowl IX. This time Tarkenton was playing for the Minnesota Vikings. It was a game in which the Vikings were slight favorites to win. After all, it was the Steelers' first Super Bowl and the first time Pittsburgh had ever won a conference championship in forty-two years.

The Steelers did a thorough job in producing a 16–6 victory for their first world championship. They limited the Vikings to only seventeen yards on the ground and applied enough pressure on Tarkenton to take away his passing game. One big reason was Greene, who recovered a fumble and knocked down a pass in furious pursuit of Tarkenton. He never stopped coming at Tarkenton the entire game.

"Joe Greene was fantastic," proclaimed Perles. "No one ever played a game like that."

It was the biggest win in the history of the Steelers. Greene knew what it meant.

"Even in my wildest dreams I didn't think I'd get as big a charge out of winning the Super Bowl as I did," exclaimed Greene after the game. "Winning is a lot bigger than I thought it would be. I love it, man, I really do. I feel so good I'm almost weak.

"It's more than wearing the ring and being number one. This is our first time. We've never been here before, but we never considered losing. It's not all fun and games. We knew we had a job to do. The Vikings were a worthy opponent. I feel compassion for them."

It's just like Greene. There is a certain softness to him. He has sensitivity. He understands pain. The two years after Super Bowl X were painful for Greene. He carried around his injuries quietly, never once using them as an excuse. That was why Super Bowl XIII meant so much more to him. He came back in victory after two frustrating years.

"This was a great win for us," Greene sighed. "It was great to be back in this game after three years. Dallas was the defending champions. One of us was going to be the first ever to win three Super Bowls. That meant something.

"Our best football is still in front of us. Our best games were in the playoffs. We were just starting to get into the groove. Our offense scored something like 100 points, and that's a tremendous effort against the caliber of teams you face in the playoffs.

"Overall, this is probably the best Steeler team of all, because of the maturity of some of the other players, like Bradshaw, Swann, Stallworth, and Lambert, and the consistency we had during the regular season, and the way we came on in the playoffs. Collectively, the Pittsburgh Steelers will probably be the best team of all time. We got three Super Bowls."

And one Joe Greene.

The Defense

Dwight White (78), Loren Toews (51), Joe Greene (75), and L. C. Greenwood (68) combine to stop a Kansas City rush at the line of scrimmage.

The defense had always been there, or so it seemed. It was the one group with personality that had surfaced in the early years of the Noll era. Whenever anyone began discussing the Steelers the topic was defense. In 1969, when Noll began reconstructing the ruins in Pittsburgh, the Steelers had one topnotch player on defense, linebacker Andy Russell, a bonafide all-Pro. When the Steelers made defensive tackle Joe Greene their number one choice they had two.

"Defense is the ultimate in team function," explained Noll. "You must play it as a team. You may hear about great linebackers or defensive backs, but unlike offense, no one or two individuals make a defense. Great running backs can change the entire complexion of any game in an instant. Not so on defense. It takes a special kind of man to be a defensive player. He has to get his satisfaction from a job well done. If he does his job nobody notices. If he gets burned everybody notices."

What few people realized in 1969 was that besides Greene the Steelers had drafted another excellent player in L. C. Greenwood on the tenth round. Perhaps no one noticed him because of all the hoopla about Greene or because Greenwood was so far down on the list. Tenth round draft choices are not generally considered good prospects to make a pro team.

But one thing nobody could miss about Greenwood was his size. The rookie from Arkansas AM & N was a towering 6′ 6½″ tall. Strangely enough he had gone to college on an academic scholarship. Perhaps it was his intelligence that made him attractive to the Steelers.

"I had a good childhood in Canton, Mississippi, but I worked hard," said Greenwood. "I was the oldest. My father went to work in a factory every morning at six, came home at four, then worked in the garden and around the house until midnight. Every day but Sunday. He figured that I should work like that, too.

"He worked me hard enough that I'm glad I made enough money in football so I never have to work that hard again. When I was about fourteen he said, 'Hey, you're a big boy now. You've got to deal with life.' From then on, any money I got I earned. I went to work in a factory and started scheming on what I could do in life to keep me from working hard the rest of my life."

It wasn't that Greenwood found playing with the Steelers easy. It took him two years to become a starter. But when he did he was ready. In 1971 he led the Steelers in sacks with eleven and the NFL in fumble recoveries with five (which also tied a Pittsburgh record).

What Greenwood gave the Steelers was quickness. His quickness and height, exaggerated by long, outstretched arms, was a definite obstacle for opposing quarterbacks. His quickness also provided him with tremendous range for someone his size on running plays.

Yet it took several more years for Greenwood to be recognized. He tried to achieve recognition earlier. So others would recognize him more easily, Greenwood wore high-topped yellow shoes. They alone made him conspicuous on the football field.

After Super Bowl IX Greenwood began to win the recognition he deserved as one of the NFL's top defensive ends. He was irrepressible against the Vikings, continually charging after Fran Tarkenton. He penetrated the backfield so quickly and so often that Tarkenton was off balance the entire game and never could get his passing attack going. Greenwood slapped three of his passes away.

A week before the game Greenwood studied films of Minnesota at home. He observed how other defensive ends tried to contain Tarkenton. Some would play him on the outside and concede the inside passing lanes; others would play him inside and let Tarkenton work the outside. Nothing was effective.

So, Greenwood thought, why not play Tarkenton the same way he played other quarterbacks? He felt he would be more effective if he could merely apply pressure to Tarkenton's passing pocket.

"L. C.'s plan was right, of course," remarked George Perles, who was the defensive line coach at the time. "By playing his position with its normal route to the passes, he could take away that passing lane we were set to concede to Tarkenton. It was his idea and he made it work.

"Greenwood is a thinking man's player. It's not intimidation as it is with some linemen. He likes to set guys up, then get past them. I've seen quarterbacks get off the deck after being sacked by him, and you can tell by the expression on their faces they have no idea where he came from or how he got there so fast. It's after times like this that the intimidation process begins, but only because Greenwood has won the battle of wits."

"I like to play those big guys, the ones with the reputations," confessed Greenwood. "I guess they like to play me, too, because both of us are considered to be among the best. But I like the big, bulky tackles who may not be as agile as the smaller ones. They know you can't fight your way through them with all that heft, so they figure they got you beat at the start.

"But I like to set them up. I'll go outside for a couple of plays, watch them move with me, then I'll take off inside. They come back to take away the inside and I'll spin around them. Pretty soon you've got them fighting for their lives, and that reputation doesn't mean too much right then.

"Our defensive team did a hell of a job. My job was to contain Tarkenton on the sprintouts, protect the outside, and then pursue him from behind. We concentrated on stopping the run, then the pass. I thought the Vikings looked a little tight."

So was Greenwood the first time he reported to training camp. He didn't know how good his chances were of making the team and was even thinking about returning home. That's how insecure he felt about pro football.

"The Steelers drafted me tenth and Clarence Washington, who I'd been in college with, eleventh," he remembered. "Nobody paid much attention to us for a couple of weeks. One night Clarence said, 'C'mon, let's go home.' I said, 'Dig this, Clarence. They gave us a little money to sign. If we go home now we'll have to give it back. I don't know about you, but I don't have anything left to give them. If we stay they'll cut us and pay our way home.' "

Greenwood stayed. Two years later he was joined on the other end by Dwight White. The Steel Curtain was coming together. White was drafted on the fourth round out of East Texas State. He wasn't as big as Greenwood, but then who was? White was still plenty big at 6' 4" and 255 pounds. White was strong and loved contact, so much so that he made the starting team as a rookie.

The 1971 draft was an excellent one for Pittsburgh. It also produced defensive tackle Ernie Holmes, who completed the front four, linebacker Jack Ham, safety Mike Wagner, and Gerry Mullins and Larry Brown on offense.

When White joined the Steelers he had already acquired the nickname, "Mad Dog," because he played with such intensity. He was surprised that the name had preceded him to Pittsburgh, especially since he had acquired it as a high school player in Dallas.

"I had transferred from Lincoln High School to Madison High, and we wound up playing Lincoln for the city championship," recalled White. "They really whipped us. Sticks Anderson, who I had played with at Lincoln, was their quarterback, and he was running out the clock, lying on the ball, letting us think about getting beaten so badly. When he did it one more time, I really bashed him, and he looked at me and said, 'Hey, man, that's cold-blooded.' But I couldn't stand to think about being beaten, and I had to do something. After that the players started calling me 'Mad Dog.'

"When I went to college I tore up my knee playing linebacker. I came back the next year and they made a defensive end out of me. I didn't know the basics of the position, so when the ball was snapped I'd just go crashing in there. Sometimes I'd make a great play; sometimes I'd get killed. One day the coach said, 'White, you play football just like some crazy, mad dog.' The name I had acquired in high school stuck.

"When I came to Pittsburgh I thought it was all over, but pretty soon it was 'Hey, Dog, what's happening?' "

White, too, gained prominence in the 1975 Super Bowl game against the Vikings. Super Bowl games have a way of leaving lasting impressions on people. Yet until the game began, White didn't know whether he would be able to play. He spent the week before the game in a hospital with a serious case of flu. He wasn't even listed in the starting lineup the day of the game. The night before the game he reported from the hospital, weak and with a distinct loss of weight, and naturally, he hadn't worked out at all.

"I had pleurisy, and I was in the hospital all week before the game, and the doctor told me I couldn't play," revealed White. "But the good pro does what he's not supposed to.

L. C. Greenwood led the Steelers in sacks with nine and now has a career total of 54½.

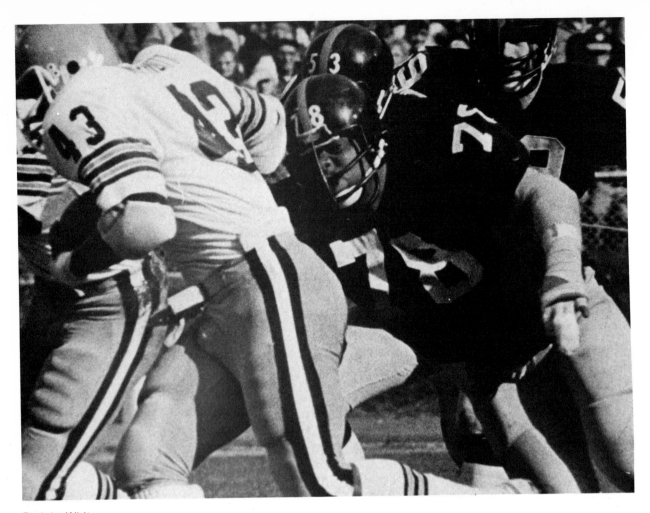

Dwight White

"You do what you have to do. It's like that in life. On the football field I can be as nasty as anyone who ever played. I can be wild, but it takes patience for me to concentrate, and the more control I have of myself, the better I play."

It was White's intensity that took him from a hospital bed to the football field, not once but twice. On Thursday morning he left the hospital and attended team meetings. Early the next morning, however, he suffered severe chest pains, and the doctors ordered him back to the hospital. Still he was determined to play. He didn't want to miss Pittsburgh's first Super Bowl. So he walked up and down the hospital corridors to avoid becoming weak from being bedridden.

On Saturday he left the hospital a second time. He had lost nineteen pounds. On Sunday he got off the team bus and quietly walked into the dressing room in Tulane Stadium, still not knowing whether he could play. Steve Furness had worked in White's spot all week and was ready. The doctor and Noll would decide whether White would play or not. Then the Steelers went out on the field.

"When we were working on our drills," recalled Joe Greene, "White told me, 'Give me a hit.' I whacked into him and he said, 'Do it again.' So I did. Noll heard the cracks as our pads hit and he spun around to look. I think it was then, when he saw Dwight going through the regular routines without thinking too much about what was happening, that he decided he could play."

Noll approached White. He had made his decision. "He came up," said White, "put his hand on my forehead, and told me, 'The doctor thinks you'll be okay. So do I.' That was all there was to it. In the locker room before we went out for the kickoff all he told me was not to pace

John Banaszak

myself, go as hard as I could for as long as I could, and then come out when I got tired. I just never got tired until we had it locked up."

White started all right, and when the game was over he had left his mark. A few minutes after the game began he slammed Minnesota's Dave Osborn into the ground. He kept on playing and never stopped. After it was all over, White was near exhaustion. He couldn't even find the strength to take off his uniform.

"I kept reading in the papers that I wasn't going to play, but no way I wasn't going to be there. No way. I had pleurisy, lots of pain around my ribs. Every day I'd spend a couple of hours inhaling this medication from a plastic breathing device. It must have worked.

"I'm going back to the hotel and die," he moaned after the game.

Later he went to a diner, ate a cheeseburger, then went to his room and slept for sixteen hours. The next day, when the team arrived in Pittsburgh after the biggest win in its history, the team doctor took a look at White and put him in a hospital for ten days.

"That's what our football team is all about," exclaimed Noll. "Dwight White getting out of a hospital bed and then playing the kind of football game he did. You think our guys didn't know what he was going through out there and that it didn't help us win?"

Nobody realized it more than Perles. He was the architect of the now highly acclaimed Steel Curtain. He had a feeling of satisfaction.

"Dwight is the most emotional of the group," remarked Perles. "That is hard to imagine sometimes, but he builds his game around emotion. He works through the week to become angry so that when he goes on the field he will be driven by pure emotion. That he demanded to play is what sets him apart. He is the most high strung of the linemen, and when he gets it into his mind that he must play or must tackle or must get to the quarterback then there isn't anything that you can do or say that will keep him from doing just that.

"He knows he has the ability to play, but he knows, too, how to reach back and get the extra factors that sometimes are more important than pure ability. He plays with more emotion than anyone on our team. And that is saying something, considering that we dwell on the emotional aspects of the game during all our preparation periods.

"White always asks, 'How did I do?' If he is criticized, it hurts his pride. Dwight gets his licks in on every play. A back who comes out to fake him may find himself clotheslined if he wanders too close. The next time he comes out he'll be looking for Dwight and forget what he's supposed to be doing. That's called 'getting the message across.' He could be a defensive tackle with no problems. And he'd be a great one, because of his physical and mental attributes."

Just playing means a great deal to White. He played in seventy-nine consecutive games before an injury sidelined him in 1976. He bounced back in 1977 and had six and a half sacks. In 1978 he played in twelve straight games before an injury stopped him in the twelfth game of the season.

Fortunately, John Banaszak was able to help out. He is a valuable backup player who is considered one of the team's best pass rushers. He can also play defensive tackle.

Steve Furness can play both positions too.

Furness became a regular in 1977 and led the team in quarterback sacks. He has exceptional strength and his versatility enables the Steel Curtain to operate effectively.

Certainly no linebackers in the NFL function better than Pittsburgh's. In the vintage 1971 draft the Steelers picked Jack Ham of Penn State on the second round. That pick was without question one of the best the Steelers ever made. Ham started as a rookie and has been a strong side starter ever since. In fact, he has missed only one game, in 1973.

Ham's forte is pass coverage. He is agile enough to cover the short pass and speedy enough to protect against the long pass. His pass drops are amazing. In a playoff game against the Oakland Raiders several years ago Ham dropped forty yards downfield to break up a pass.

The 6' 1" 225-pound Ham has a knack for being where the ball is. In his rookie year he led the league's linebackers in pass interceptions with seven and recovered four fumbles to tie for the team high. He is a very intelligent performer who rarely makes a mistake and shows an innate ability to diagnose plays quickly. Ham has the knack for making the big play, but his trademark is consistency.

It is difficult to grade Ham from one game to another. There just isn't any variation in his play. His consistency is taken so much for granted that there is very little talk about him. It caused one coach to remark one night, "When was the last time Ham played a bad game?" Nobody could answer.

Noll was so high on Ham that he wanted to draft him on the first round. "The first round?" snapped a friend. "Don't waste that choice. You'll get Ham on the second round."

"Don't be too sure of that," answered Noll. Luckily, Pittsburgh did secure Ham on the second round, after making Frank Lewis their first round selection.

Why was Noll so excited about Ham? "Because of his brains, his intelligence," remarked Noll. "It stamped him as a number one choice. He's a winner. He makes the big play. He's a defensive player who makes things happen—interceptions, recoveries, forcing fumbles, blocking kicks. Even though he's on defense, he's an offensive threat. He gets you the ball."

Steve Furness

When Ham joined the Steelers they were making progress. In Noll's first two years they were 1–13 and then 5–9. The improvement was most noticeable on defense. In a preseason game against the New York Giants Ham intercepted three passes. He became an instant starter.

"Fortunately, there wasn't a lot of difference in playing defense at Penn State and with the Steelers," disclosed Ham. "Chuck Noll and Joe Paterno had similar ideas how defense should be played, and pro ball didn't turn out to be a completely new learning experience for me.

"But there was confusion, though. God, the week before our first preseason game against Green Bay I was really confused. But something happened that I never expected to see in the pros. The guys helped me. Andy Russell and Chuck Allen were real pros. Here I was, battling them for their jobs, and they went out of their way to make things easy for me."

Jack Ham (59)

Ham's exceptional mobility, quickness, and speed have made him one of the best linebackers of all time.

(Far right) Jack Lambert led the team in tackles and assists in 1978.

Yet Ham never expected to play with the Steelers. They never made contact with him in his final year at Penn State. He really wasn't looking forward to joining them, either.

"I didn't want to get drafted by Pittsburgh," admitted Ham. "I thought I'd get drafted by the Giants or San Diego. Even though I'm from near Pittsburgh, I wasn't particularly interested in playing for the Steelers. I would have preferred to play on a team farther away, out west maybe. I'd lived all my life in Johnstown or Penn State and going to Pittsburgh, well, it wasn't exactly my idea of being a well-traveled athlete."

But the Steeler fans made him feel right at home his second year. The 11–3 season excited the fans and a number of player fan clubs sprang up. There was one for Ham, although he didn't know it at first.

"I didn't know anything about it until Andy Russell pointed the sign out to me one day. 'Dobre Shonka,' it said," smiled Ham. "I'm Polish, but it was so long since I had heard any Polish spoken I didn't even know what it meant. I had to ask my mother. She told me it meant 'Good Ham.'

"That was really something. The fans have been great. They've made it a lot of fun playing football in this town."

That's about as excited as Jack Ham gets. He's very quiet, unlike Jack Lambert. Lambert is a pent-up fury who explodes on a football field. The 6′ 4″, 220-pound middle linebacker may not have bulk, but his upper body strength and his range more than make up for it.

In some ways Lambert was a surprising number two pick by the Steelers in 1974. He had a fine career at Kent State University and the

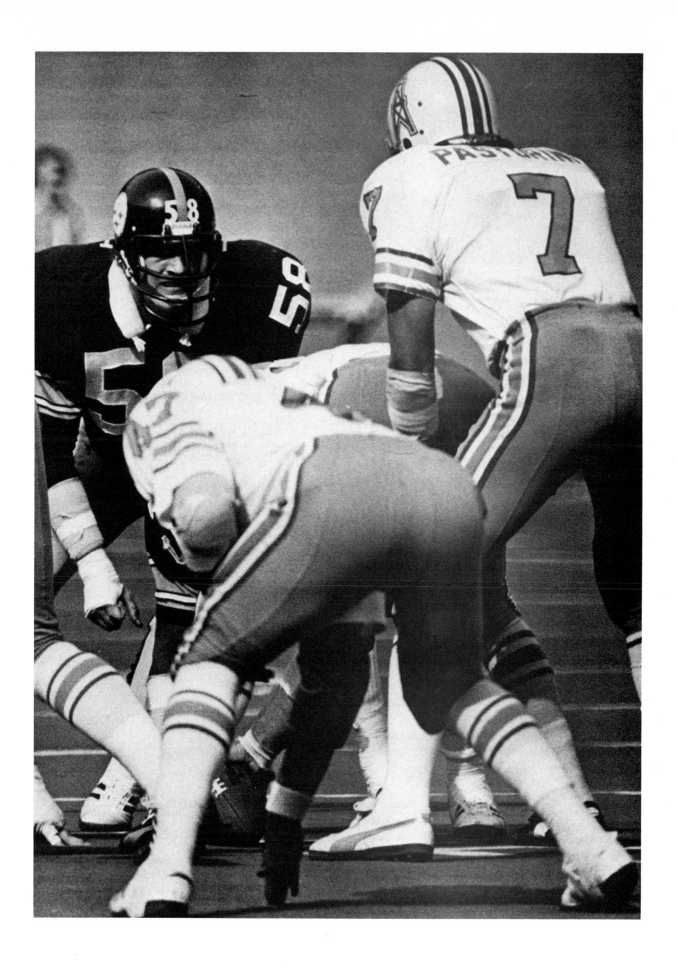

Steelers liked his aggressiveness, yet they weren't sure how high to draft him. Finally, when there were only five seconds left of the allotted fifteen minutes they had to make a decision, the Steelers picked Lambert.

What they didn't fully realize at the time was that they had found their middle linebacker for at least the next dozen years. Lambert immediately became a starter and played in the Steelers' first Super Bowl in 1975.

It didn't come easily, though. Lambert worked hard to succeed. He didn't allow his second round selection to make him overcon-fident. Instead he drove between Kent State and Pittsburgh every week from April until July, when training camp began, to look at films.

"I felt I needed every edge I could get," he revealed. "The Steelers originally told me they wanted me as an outside linebacker, even though they already had Jack Ham and Andy Russell. I figured I'd learn all the keys and coverages for both outside and middle linebacker, so I'd be ready if they decided to switch me.

"The thing was, I never played against the so-called national powers at Kent State. I went to a couple of the postseason all-star games and

One of the lightest middle linebackers in pro football, Lambert compensates for his lack of bulk with exceptional upper body strength, great speed, and quickness.

found out I could play against them. But Pittsburgh was tough to break into. And my rookie year was the year of the players' strike. I didn't get a chance to hit any veterans until the third week of the preseason. That's when I knew I would make it. When the veterans went down the same way the people I hit in college did, then I felt better about everything."

Even the Steelers thought they had seen everything Lambert could do after his first two years. He had been the enforcer, but in Super Bowl X against the Dallas Cowboys he showed all the world he could take charge. And he did

so on a play in which he wasn't directly involved.

With twenty-six seconds remaining in the first half the Cowboys were ahead, 10–7. Roy Gerela trotted on to the field to try a 36-yard field goal that would tie the score. He missed. Dallas safety Cliff Harris patted Gerela on the helmet, saying, "Thanks, Roy. You're our best player."

Lambert reacted. In an instant he reached Harris, picked him up in his massive arms, and threw him to the ground. As Harris sat embarrassed on the ground Lambert pointed a finger at him. Millions of television viewers saw and so did the officials, but they didn't penalize Lambert a yard. Lambert carried his rage to the dressing room. He was riled.

"Normally, I don't say much on the field," explained Lambert. "I prefer to show my emotions physically instead of verbally. I believe in playing football as hard as I can on every play. Yes, I'm very aggressive and very physical. On the field I guess I'm just plain mean.

"I love contact. I believed the game is designed to reward the ones who hit the hardest. If you can't take it you shouldn't play. I don't believe in cheap shots or arrogant gestures and I'm definitely opposed to doing much talking on the field, especially if it's the kind where you're just gloating or poking fun at the other guy. There's no place for that in football.

"So when Harris did what he did to Gerela I responded the only way I know how. There was nothing uncontrolled about it. I'm always under control on the field, but I play hard and I hit hard. What the Steelers are all about to me is hard hitting and intimidation, physical intimidation gained only by outhitting the next guy on every play.

"I never want to see us intimidated. Never! And until Harris overreacted that's exactly what Dallas was doing, intimidating us. It had never happened before while I'd been with the club and I never want it to happen again. After the Harris incident we went back to being the Steelers I love and respect. Once we took physical command I knew we'd win."

Lambert had accounted for seven tackles and assisted in seven others when the game was over, but what he did to Harris was not reflected in the statistics. Yet it had a direct bearing in the Steelers' 21–17 triumph. Dwight White, for one, realized it.

"He got us going," White disclosed. "He got hollering at everybody and we just got caught up in it. His spirit was contagious. We weren't the same team in the second half. He was the catalyst we needed to get us back to playing the way the Steelers are supposed to play. Once he got shook up, we all got shook up, and if I were on the other side I wouldn't want to see that happen."

Even Joe Greene appreciated Lambert's emotional display. Greene had to remain on the sidelines the second half with an injury.

"The first day I knew Lambert," said Greene, "I realized he was the kind of man I wanted behind me if I ever had to go into the streets to fight. The dude is mean, real mean. You don't mess around with Lambert."

In Super Bowl XIII the Cowboys didn't. The game was certainly hard-hitting, but it was devoid of any incidents. Before the game Harris had tried to bait Lambert, but Lambert kept his cool.

"Harris said that you're bananas most of the time," someone told Lambert. "Then he changed that to all the time, on and off the field."

"He's a fine one to talk," snapped Lambert. "If they think we're getting too rough for them maybe they ought to stay in the NFC where they belong. They started it all with the Gerela business. If somebody sticks a finger in your face, you're going to be rolling around in the dirt some.

"I always wanted to get at the ball. An outside linebacker has to have more discipline to guard against the sweeps and outside plays. In the middle I can go to the ball right away, which suits my personality. At outside linebacker I'd find myself moving toward the ball, and if the play went outside, I wouldn't be there."

Lambert was there during the 1978 season. He easily led the Steelers in tackles with 125 and was involved in fifty-nine others. The total of 184 was an all-time Steeler record. That's the kind of football the Steelers like.

Yet Lambert's style is not without controversy. His overly aggressive play attracts it. He was thrown out of a 1978 game against Cleveland on a call he didn't feel was justified.

"I supposedly hit quarterback Brian Sipe late," fumed Lambert. "The films showed I did not. Officials are overreacting. I agree the quarterback should be the most protected player, but not when he runs with the ball.

"'I think all quarterbacks should wear dresses,' I remarked after the game. I couldn't believe all the hate mail I got after I said that. People thought I was a male chauvinist. They said my mother should be ashamed of me."

Lambert's style will never win him any popularity contests. In Pittsburgh they love the way he plays, but everywhere else he is hated. His image is that of a wild man. He doesn't like it.

Roy Gerela sets up one of his twelve field goals.

"Image, I'm sick of it," he declared. "You know, the Steelers' image always has been that of this dirty, rough team. That's bull. We don't take cheap shots and we don't go outside the rules unless provoked. But while we were looking at the Cleveland film we saw something on the extra point try. One of the Browns came up to the line and went right at our guy's knees. There was no reason for it other than to injure.

"That's dirty football, and the Steelers have too much pride to play like that. We don't look for trouble, but I guess I got to admit trouble has a habit of finding me. It's beginning to get out of hand. All the stuff upsets me because I am not a dirty football player. I don't sit in front of my locker before a game thinking about getting into fights or hurting somebody. All I want to do is to be able to play football hard and aggressively, the way it's meant to be played. But when somebody deliberately clips me or comes off the bench to bait me—well, I'm not going to stand for it."

Loren Toews

Robin Cole

The one who has to stand him the most is Bleier. They room together in training camp, yet their personalities are completely opposite. Somehow they survive.

"Yeah," quipped Bleier, "I'm short and good-looking, and he's tall and ugly. He's so mean no one else will room with him. They probably felt that I was the only guy who could keep him off the streets and away from wild women."

"That's not it," explained Lambert. "He's married and I'm single. That's the worst thing, and he makes a lot of strange noises. He snores at night. I hit him with a pillow 200 times, roll him over, then put a sheet over his head.

"Rocky was in Vietnam, you know, and in the middle of the night he'll say, 'He's behind a bush.'"

It's no wonder Lambert's so mean; he never gets any sleep.

A year before the Steelers drafted Lambert they selected linebacker Loren Toews. He was designated to replace Andy Russell. After Russell finally retired after the 1976 season Toews took over. Toews faced a strong challenge, however, from Robin Cole, Pittsburgh's first round choice in 1977. They will both see considerable action, since Toews is judged better against the pass and Cole against the run.

As the 1978 season began the defensive secondary was the one area of doubt. Could safety Mike Wagner bounce back from a serious neck injury? How good was Donnie Shell? Who would fill the remaining cornerback spot?

Mike Wagner had cracked a vertebra in the third game of the 1977 season. He had also undergone surgery for a hamstring problem that had bothered him since high school. Wagner did a lot of skiing and leg conditioning exercises during the off-season. When he reported to training camp for the 1978 campaign, however, he was given a new assignment. Wagner was switched from strong safety, the position he had played in two Pro Bowls, to weak safety, where, it was felt, he would get less contact.

"They told me that there would be less contact at weak safety," said Wagner. "But you know what? I was playing at weak safety when I broke my neck. That season of watching as a fan taught me what football really means to me."

Wagner showed just how much it meant. He led the secondary in tackles, ranking right behind team leader Jack Lambert.

Donnie Shell, Wagner's partner at strong safety, was another valuable find, who was signed as a free agent in 1974. He was a standout on the special teams his first three years. It wasn't until 1977 that he started in the secondary. Despite missing two games he still led the secondary in tackles.

Shell began the 1977 season as a strong safety but switched to the weak side after Wagner was hurt. His main problem there was lack of experience, but he made up for it with hard work. Shell is acknowledged to be one of the hardest tacklers in pro football because of his aggressiveness and physical style of play.

(Right) Mike Wagner blitzes in on Roger Staubach during Super Bowl XIII.
Donnie Shell

Mel Blount
(Right) Ron Johnson
(Far right) Craig Colquitt led the NFL in average net yards punting in his rookie season.

The one secure spot in the Steeler secondary was at cornerback. In eight years Mel Blount had missed only one game. There was no concern about his dependability, especially since he led the Steelers in interceptions for the third straight year in 1977 and appeared in three Pro Bowls.

At 6′ 3″ Blount is the ideal size for a cornerback. He may well be the best cornerback in the NFL for man-to-man coverage. In 1975 he enjoyed one of the greatest years any cornerback has ever had in the NFL. He led the league with eleven interceptions to set a new Pittsburgh record. Blount was the first Steeler defensive back to hold an NFL record since Bill Dudley led the league in interceptions in 1946.

In 1978 Blount picked off four more passes to run his career total to thirty-nine. He ranks second behind Jack Butler, who has fifty-two.

Ron Johnson was the rookie who filled the remaining cornerback position. That doesn't happen too often in the NFL. Noll scouted Johnson personally in the Senior Bowl. His 4.5 speed and excellent quickness and strength make up for his 5′ 10″ height.

"As a rookie I knew other teams would try to test me," admitted Johnson. "At the start of the year they were throwing at me. I figured a quarterback is only as good as the time he has to throw, and our front line didn't give passers much time. With my strength and speed, I can jam a receiver and still run with him."

Used as the fifth defensive back, Tom Dungy contributed immensely. He led the Steelers in interceptions with six and also played on the special teams. Signed in 1977, he was the first free agent to make the Steelers since 1975. He spent a great amount of time studying films to help make the transition from a college quarterback to a defensive back.

Besides the secondary, the other area of noticeable improvement was the performance of the special teams. Their play was the best the Steelers had enjoyed in many years. Larry Anderson was among the AFC's kickoff return leaders. Randy Reutershan handled punt returns, and Jack Deloplaine and rookie Rick Moser also contributed.

Field goal kicker Roy Gerela improved somewhat over his 1977 performance, when he was hampered by a groin injury. He hit on forty-four of forty-five extra point attempts but only twelve of twenty-six field goal attempts. He ranked seventh among the league's kickers with eighty points.

The one kicking surprise was rookie punter Craig Colquitt. He was the first kicker the Steelers drafted since 1971. He might be the last for a long time. Colquitt finished sixth in the AFC with a 40.0 average, but he led the entire NFL in net punting average with 35.2. Colquitt kicked only four balls in the end zone the entire season, quite a feat.

The Steelers had it all.

The 1978 Season

Bottom Row: Field Manager Jack Hart, Craig Colquitt, Roy Gerela, Terry Bradshaw, Mike Kruczek, Cliff Stoudt, Rocky Bleier, Tony Dungy, Mike Wagner, Alvin Maxson, Equipment Manager Tony Parisi. **Second Row:** Head Coach Chuck Noll, Ron Johnson, Larry Anderson, Donnie Shell, Franco Harris, Laverne Smith, Sidney Thornton, Rick Moser, Randy Reutershan, Nat Terry, Mel Blount, Defensive Coordinator George Perles. **Third Row:** Offensive Backfield Coach Dick Hoak, Loren Toews, Mike Webster, Dennis Winston, Jon Kolb, Robin Cole, Sam Davis, Jack Lambert, Jack Ham, Willie Fry, Tom Dornbrook, Linebacker and Secondary Coach Woody Widenhofer. **Fourth Row:** Offensive Line Coach Rollie Dotsch, Steve Furness, Tom Beasley, Ted Petersen, Gary Dunn, L. C. Greenwood, Fred Anderson, Gerry Mullins, Ray Pinney, Joe Greene, John Banaszak, Defensive Assistant Dick Walker, Strength Coach Lou Riecke. **Top Row:** Trainer Ralph Berlin, Assistant Trainer Bob Milie, Steve Courson, Dwight White, Larry Brown, John Stallworth, Theo Bell, Randy Grossman, Andre Keys, Jim Smith, Lynn Swann, Bennie Cunningham, Receiver Coach Tom Moore.

Something was different. The players could feel it. When they reported to their training compound at Latrobe, Pennsylvania, they sensed a new awakening. It was as if everybody had been saying to himself that this year was going to be special. The last two years had not been very good ones. Oh, yes, the Steelers had managed to win the Central Division title both years, but when the time had come to compete in the playoffs for the Super Bowl gold they had been eliminated. That wasn't like the Pittsburgh teams of 1974 and 1975, which had won consecutive Super Bowls. Only the 1966–67 Green Bay Packers and the 1972–73 Miami Dolphins had equaled that accomplishment.

But in 1976 the Steelers were victimized by a series of crippling injuries. To the surprise of most experts, who had picked them to repeat, Pittsburgh lost four of its first five games. That hadn't happened since 1969, Noll's first year as coach. But the Steelers overcame their unexpected adversity and finished the season with nine consecutive victories. In the opening-round playoff game they overwhelmed the Baltimore Colts, 40–14, and appeared to have a date with destiny to become the first team ever to win three straight Super Bowls. But the triumph over the Colts was extremely costly. Franco Harris and Rocky Bleier were injured badly enough that neither played in the AFC Championship game against the Oakland Raiders. Their absence was too much of a handicap to overcome; the Steelers lost to Oakland, 27–7.

In 1977 the club was beset with problems off the field, even before the season began. Noll was a party to a football law suit brought in California by Oakland defensive back George Atkinson. The emotion of the trial provoked some unkind statements about the "criminal" element in professional football. Some of Noll's own players took it personally. Mel Blount and Jack Lambert were extended holdouts.

The Steelers' equilibrium was disrupted. Pittsburgh's once strong defense surrendered 243 points, the most since 1971. By the time the season ended the Steelers had set club records for penalties and turnovers, ranking second in the NFL in these areas during 1977. Even so, they won their division with a 9–5 record. But when the Steelers were upended by the Denver Broncos, 34–21, in the opening playoff game, many felt that they were on the decline.

There was too much pride in Pittsburgh to permit a collapse, however. When the players checked into their dormitory at St. Vincent College on a hot July day they already had a positive attitude about the 1978 campaign. It was strictly their doing. Management had not made any major personnel changes. The squad was basically the same one that had won the previous two years. The only difference was that for the first time the players were embarking on a 16-game regular season schedule. The dedication to winning had to run deeper. The players knew it. They were ready mentally.

Noll realized this. Mental preparation was one side of the change. The other was execution. Noll reasoned that his squad could no longer rely on sheer brute force, so he decided to make use of the team's finesse and experience. Instead of relying predominantly on the running of Franco Harris he designed a much more balanced offense. He wasn't too concerned with his defense, despite the 243 points they yielded in 1977. Noll was certain that cohesiveness would return with Blount and Lambert in training camp from the start. He also knew that Lambert, L. C. Greenwood, and Mike Wagner, all-pros in 1976, had missed a total of nineteen games with injuries in 1977.

Noll concentrated his changes in the offense to achieve balance. He did so for two important reasons. The offense had depended too much on Harris to make the big play. Opposing teams were stacking their defenses to foil the Pittsburgh running game by playing their safeties up close and exposing their cornerbacks to single coverage on the Steeler wide receivers.

Bradshaw would have to play an even more important role than before. The often maligned quarterback had demonstrated his leadership the previous year. Despite suffering a broken left wrist in the fourth game of the season Bradshaw had played in every game and even with his handicap had turned in one of his finest efforts. For the first time the players had voted him the team's most valuable player.

"I knew something was different when training camp began," recalled Bradshaw. "I could smell it. Last year there were so many problems, and they affected us all. They carried right through the season. It would affect my concentration during the week. All the players said, 'Well, it's not going to affect me, I'm going to play my own game,' but it's not that easy. I couldn't put it out of my mind. I'd go home every night and think about it, about the way our team was being torn apart. It just wasn't the family we'd had in the past, the team that had taken years to build. I tried to play good football and avoid controversy and hide my feelings, but it's tough when you're upset every day and you try to hide it."

Mike Webster felt it. He knew there had been a disruptive force in the 1977 Steelers that wouldn't be present this time around. In fact, the players were prepared not•to let anything affect their performance.

"Something bad happened to us in 1977," remarked Webster. "We did terribly. There was a festering situation on the club. We weren't close, weren't together. We had so many problems. Contracts were one of them. People walking out on us was another. General unhappiness. It was a mess. Some people can take that sort of thing and play. Some can't.

"But when we gathered at training camp this year we decided we'd handle it like professionals. We'd forget all about the hassling and do our own jobs. It's surprising how neatly everything fell into place, how the guys on the team drew closer and closer. We became a very unselfish bunch.

"The talent was there, no doubt about it. We were better from top to bottom, and there was more of it. We had terrific depth and balance. Another thing: The coaching staff opened us up more on offense. We weren't going to run the ball eighty-five times a game and throw only three passes.

"We were a very hungry team, more so than we've ever been before. It's a strange phenomenon, but after you've had a lot of success—and don't forget we won back-to-back Super Bowls in '74 and '75—you lose that hunger."

Still, the skeptics weren't quite convinced. Though they considered the Steelers one of many contenders on their past success alone, no one gave them a clearcut edge over the rest of the American Football Conference. But they came on like nobody expected.

"For the most part, this team was written off at the beginning of the year," Bleier said. "A lot of people didn't think we would be able to come back with eight, nine, and ten-year veterans like Joe Greene, L. C. Greenwood, and Dwight White. A lot of people just never thought we had that much of a chance."

The Steelers weren't exactly overpowering during the shortened preseason action. They split the four games they played, winning their first two, against the Baltimore Colts and the Atlanta Falcons. But what caused a little concern was that they then lost their next two to the New York Giants and the Dallas Cowboys.

Game One: Buffalo

In the regular season opener the Steelers faced the Buffalo Bills in Buffalo. The Bills were undergoing a rebuilding program that saw them trade their long-standing star, O. J. Simpson, and hire a new coach, Chuck Knox, who had been successful with the Los Angeles Rams for a number of years.

The Steelers began slowly. They played a scoreless first quarter in which, as expected, their offense had trouble moving. They gained only twenty-three yards in all and produced only two first downs.

In the second period, however, Bradshaw got them going. He began a drive on his own 35-yard line with a 20-yard completion to Stallworth. He climaxed the march seven plays later with a 14-yard touchdown pass to Stallworth for the Steelers' first touchdown of the new season.

The next time Pittsburgh got the ball Bradshaw drove them seventy-two yards. Again he started with Stallworth, this time on a 34-yard strike. On third down he set up the touchdown with a 12-yard completion to Swann on the 1-yard line. Harris took it over the goal to give the Steelers a 14–0 lead before the half ended.

Taking the second half kickoff, the Steelers stayed on the ground. Bradshaw called nine straight running plays, alternating between Harris and Bleier. After two passes failed Gerela was short with a 49-yard field goal attempt. It was the only serious scoring attempt by either team in the third quarter and the score remained unchanged. It was evident that the Steelers were in control. They had 245 total yards, whereas Buffalo had only fifty-nine, showing minus seven yards passing.

In the opening minutes of the final quarter the Steelers scored for the third time. Bradshaw moved them into position with a 25-yard com-

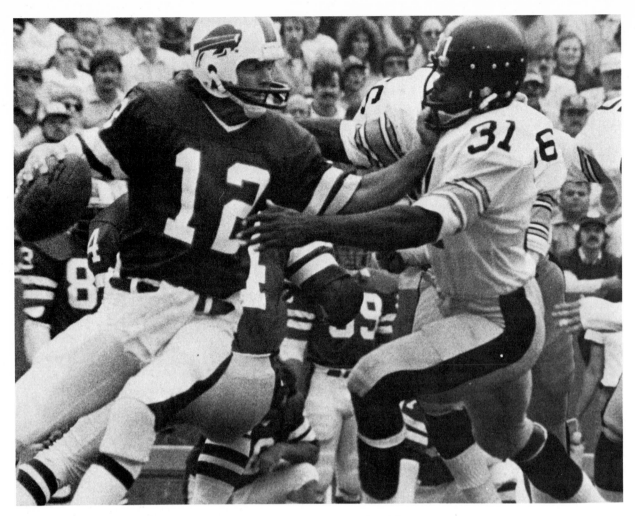

Donnie Shell catches Bills' quarterback Joe Ferguson with a safety blitz.

pletion to Cunningham. Thornton went in from the 2-yard line and Pittsburgh bolted to a 21–0 lead.

Buffalo tried to get back into the game with a new quarterback. Veteran Bill Munson replaced Joe Ferguson and threw a 22-yard touchdown pass to former Steeler Frank Lewis. Then, midway through the quarter, the Bills narrowed the Steeler lead to 21–10 when Tom Dempsey kicked a 32-yard field goal.

Bradshaw clinched the game on the next offensive series. He led Pittsburgh seventy-three yards, connecting on all four passes he threw. The final strike was a 15-yard touchdown to Bell that gave the Steelers a 28–10 lead. The Bills' Munson hit Reuben Gant with a meaningless three-yard touchdown pass with less than a minute to play.

The Steelers won the opening game of the season, 28–17, and gained an impressive 359 total yards on offense. Most of it came from the arm of Bradshaw, who was fourteen for nineteen for 217 yards.

1ST WEEK, 1978 SEASON

PITTSBURGH	0	14	0	14	28
BUFFALO	0	0	0	17	17

Pittsburgh: 5:55, second period—Stallworth, 28-yard pass from Bradshaw (Gerela, kick).
Pittsburgh: 11:10, second period—Harris, 1-yard run (Gerela, kick).
Pittsburgh: :48, fourth period—Thornton, 2-yard run (Gerela, kick).
Buffalo: 4:20, fourth period—Lewis, 22-yard pass from Munson (Dempsey, kick).
Buffalo: 8:08, fourth period—Dempsey, 32-yard field goal.
Pittsburgh: 13:04, fourth period—Bell, 15-yard pass from Bradshaw (Gerela, kick).
Buffalo: 14:24, fourth period—Gant, 3-yard pass from Munson (Dempsey, kick).

Game Two: Seattle

Pittsburgh fans got a chance to see their team for the first time in the second week of the season. If nothing else Three Rivers Stadium was the place to be on a warm, cloudy day with the temperature at seventy-eight degrees. It was perhaps too warm a day for football, yet 48,277 fans decided to drink their beer outside.

The Steelers were facing the Seattle Seahawks.

The exciting three-year old expansion team had lost a thrilling opener to the San Diego Chargers, 24–20. In Jim Zorn the Seahawks had a dangerous young quarterback who was headed for stardom. Against the Chargers he completed twenty-one of thirty-nine passes for 329 yards and two touchdowns.

The teams played a scoreless first period. Neither club penetrated far enough even to attempt a field goal, but near the end of the

Lynn Swann hauls in a pass from Bradshaw and moves downfield.

quarter the Steelers got a drive going. Lambert recovered a fumble at midfield and Bradshaw had guided the Steelers to the Seattle 15-yard line when time expired.

It didn't take long for Bradshaw to score from there. On the first play of the second quarter he reached the 4-yard line with an 11-yard pass to Grossman. On the next play he found Swann in the end zone and the Steelers jumped to a 7–0 lead.

Pittsburgh scored again the very next time they got the ball. They began on their 24-yard line, and in just seven plays Bradshaw took them the rest of the way. The payoff was a 20-yard touchdown pass to Thornton. The Steelers moved into a 14–0 lead. The next time the Seahawks got the ball they scored. Zorn led them eighty yards in only eight plays, the biggest one being a 42-yard pass to tight end Ron Howard that brought the score to 14–7.

Feeling gutsy, the Seahawks tried an onside kick and recovered it on the Pittsburgh 46. They reached the 24-yard line before being stopped. Efren Herrera's 41-yard field goal try was short and wide. With only nine seconds left Gerela tried a 52-yarder which also fell short, and the score remained 14–7 as the half concluded.

The Steelers failed to score after receiving the second half kickoff. The Seahawks did, however, as soon as they got their hands on the ball. They threatened to tie the game after earning a first down on the Steeler 5-yard line. At that point the Pittsburgh defense tightened, and Seattle had to settle for a 20-yard field goal from Herrera that trimmed the Steeler margin to 14–10.

Beginning on their own 25 the Steelers reached the Seattle 3-yard line by the end of the third period, as Bradshaw completed six of the eight passes he attempted. In the opening minute of the fourth quarter tension mounted. The Steelers had a fourth and one on the 1-yard line. They decided to go for it and Harris plunged over for the touchdown that put the Steelers on top, 21–10. The Steelers had one more scoring opportunity, but Gerela was wide with a 31-yard field goal try. The Steelers were now 2–0.

"It's too hot to play football," snarled Lambert after the game. "I can't wait until it gets to be about ten degrees so we can start running again."

Lambert did all right. He accounted for five solo tackles, seven assists, one interception, and a fumble recovery. It couldn't have been all that hot.

2ND WEEK, 1978 SEASON

SEATTLE	0	7	3	0	10
PITTSBURGH	0	14	0	7	21

Pittsburgh: :50, second period—Swann, 5-yard pass from Bradshaw (Gerela, kick).
Pittsburgh: 6:19, second period—Thornton, 20-yard pass from Bradshaw (Gerela, kick).
Seattle: 10:28, second period—Sims, 1-yard run (Herrera, kick).
Seattle: 8:12, third period—Herrera, 20-yard field goal.
Pittsburgh: :41, fourth period—Harris, 1-yard run (Gerela, kick).

Game Three: Cincinnati

The Steelers were now presented with their first important game of the young season. In meeting the Cincinnati Bengals they were also facing their first Central Division opponent.

Cincinnati had always played tough against the Steelers, especially in Riverfront Stadium. The Bengals were hurting too. They had lost their first two games by a margin of four points, and their quarterback, Ken Anderson, was sidelined with a broken hand.

It was another warm day. Although there was a threat of rain, the temperature was still seventy-eight degrees, high enough to make Lambert growl.

On the first play of the game Harris growled. He ripped through the Bengals' defense for thirty-seven yards before he was brought down on the Cincinnati 26-yard line. After three more running plays Bradshaw completed an eight-yard pass to Bleier on the 5-yard line. From there Bleier swept around right end for a touchdown and a 7–0 Pittsburgh edge.

An interception gave Pittsburgh the ball right back. Bradshaw threw two straight passes to Swann, one for thirty yards and another for seventeen. The Steelers were suddenly on the Cincinnati 7. A three-yard loss and a five-yard penalty pushed the Steelers back to the 15, but Harris got it all back on one run as he broke

Gerela booms home an extra point over the outstretched arms of Bengal defenders.

through the middle for the touchdown, putting Pittsburgh in front, 14–0.

In the opening minute of the second period the Bengals got on the scoreboard. Culminating a drive that they had begun near the end of the first period, they reached the Steeler 16-yard line before stalling. Chris Bahr then delivered a 33-yard field goal to cut Pittsburgh's margin to 14–3.

With less than two minutes remaining in the half, however, Bradshaw struck. He took the Steelers eighty yards in just five plays. One was a 48-yard completion to Cunningham and another was a 28-yard touchdown strike to the big tight end. It provided Pittsburgh with a comfortable 21–3 halftime advantage.

The first time the Steelers got the ball in the third period they scored. Once again Bradshaw was the instrument. Starting on his own 11-yard line, he directed the Steelers eighty-nine yards in just eight plays. The three passes he threw were all successful, the last one being a 12-yard touchdown aerial to Swann. Pittsburgh's lead swelled to 28–3.

In the final period the Steelers controlled the game with the run. Since the defense was turning back the Bengals, Bradshaw threw only one pass. He was replaced by Mike Kruczek, who kept the ball on the ground the rest of the way to preserve the Steelers' 28–3 triumph. Pittsburgh's record was now 3–0, which kept them tied for first place with the Cleveland Browns.

Bradshaw had a fine afternoon. He was fourteen for nineteen for 242 yards and two touchdowns. In all, the Pittsburgh offense produced 447 yards.

Heat or no heat, Lambert had another big game. He led the Steelers in tackles with eleven.

3RD WEEK, 1978 SEASON

PITTSBURGH	14	7	7	0	28
CINCINNATI	0	3	0	0	3

Pittsburgh: 3:20, first period—Bleier, 5-yard run (Gerela, kick).

Pittsburgh: 5:45, first period—Harris, 15-yard run (Gerela, kick).

Cincinnati: :40, second period—Bahr, 33-yard field goal.

Pittsburgh: 13:44, second period—Cunningham, 28-yard pass from Bradshaw (Gerela, kick).

Pittsburgh: 7:03, third period—Swann, 12-yard pass from Bradshaw (Gerela, kick).

Game Four: Cleveland

Although the season was still young, the Steelers were confronted with a mini-crucial game when they returned home to Three Rivers Stadium the fourth week of the campaign. Facing them were the dangerous Cleveland Browns. Like the Steelers, they were undefeated and shared the lead in the Central Division.

Down through the years the Browns-Steelers series had been one of the heated rivalries in pro football. Pittsburgh had won only twenty of the fifty-six games played. With a new coach, Sam Rutigliano, the Browns had high hopes of replacing the Steelers as Central Division champions.

The game was billed as the Blue Collar Bowl. On a pleasant day with comfortable 61-degree weather 49,513 fans turned out to see the battle for first place.

On the first play of the game Shell brought the crowd to its feet by intercepting Brian Sipe's pass on the Cleveland 36-yard line. Bradshaw's key 24-yard completion to Swann apparently had the Steelers moving for a touchdown. They could only get down to the 2-yard line, however, and had to settle for a 19-yard field goal by Gerela to take a 3–0 lead. The first period ended that way as Cleveland's Don Cockroft missed a 48-yard attempt near the end.

The Browns tied the game in the second quarter. After they reached the Pittsburgh 26-yard line, Cockroft delivered a 43-yard field goal to even matters at 3–3. Minutes later Cockroft came through again. The Browns recovered a fumble on the kickoff and Cockroft booted a 30-yarder to lift the Browns into a 6–3 lead.

Cleveland's fired-up defense had held the Steelers to just three first downs and only seventy-nine total yards in the first half. The game loomed as a fierce defensive struggle.

Gerela tried to tie the game on the Steelers' first offensive series in the third period, but his 46-yard effort was wide. Seven minutes later, Cockroft was called upon to kick his third straight field. He did, from forty-one yards out, to push the Browns into a 9–3 lead. The period ended with the Steelers on the Cleveland 15-yard line but facing a fourth down.

Now it was Gerela's turn. On the first play of the final period has was accurate with a 33-

Center Mike Webster opens up a large hole in the Cleveland defense.

Unable to find his primary receiver downfield, Jets' quarterback Matt Robinson moves out of the pocket to avoid Joe Greene's rush.

yard field goal attempt that cut Cleveland's edge to 9–6. It was a battle of field goals.

Gerela got the next shot. With just 2:35 left he tied the game at 9–9 with a 36-yard field goal. Regulation time ran out with the score still tied.

Going into overtime, Pittsburgh won the coin toss and chose to receive the ball. Beginning on the Steeler 21, Bradshaw carefully guided his squad to the Cleveland 37, where he faced a second and nine. He called a "Fake 84 Reverse Gadget Pass."

Bradshaw took the ball and handed to Bleier, who gave the ball to Swann on an apparent reverse. But then Swann lateraled the ball back to Bradshaw, who threw a long, looping pass to Cunningham for a touchdown and a dramatic 15–9 win. The stands exploded.

"They couldn't beat us man to man," snapped Cleveland safety Thom Darden, who chased

Cunningham on the winning catch. "They just lucked out. We'll see them when they come to Cleveland."

What everyone *could* see was that Pittsburgh was 4–0.

4TH WEEK, 1978 SEASON

CLEVELAND	0	6	3	0	0	9
PITTSBURGH	3	0	0	6	6	15

Pittsburgh: 3:17, first period—Gerela, 19-yard field goal.
Cleveland: 8:33, second period—Cockroft, 43-yard field goal.
Cleveland: 9:16, second period—Cockroft, 30-yard field goal.
Cleveland: 10:28, third period—Cockroft, 41-yard field goal.
Pittsburgh: 3:07, fourth period—Gerela, 33-yard field goal.
Pittsburgh: 12:25, fourth period—Gerela, 36-yard field goal.
Pittsburgh: 3:43, overtime—Cunningham, 37-yard pass from Bradshaw (no kick).

Game Five: New York

The triumph over the Browns was significant. It demonstrated that the Steelers had the character to prevail in a tough situation. Such character is a vital ingredient in champions. Joe Greene sensed it.

"I started to see things, small things like a couple of plays in the Cleveland game," revealed Greene. "In crucial situations we did exactly the right thing. We played well when we had to play well."

Now the Steelers had to play the New York Jets in New York. The Jets couldn't be taken lightly. They were going through a major rebuilding program under second-year coach Walt Michaels and had split their first four games.

The first time the Steelers went on offense they scored. A weak punt gave them possession at midfield. Bradshaw took it from there. In nine plays he got them a touchdown on a 10-yard pass to Swann in the left corner of the end zone. The quarter ended with Pittsburgh ahead, 7–0.

The Jets drove sixty-four yards in seven plays to tie the game in the early minutes of the second period, when Bruce Harper ran eleven yards for a touchdown.

Bradshaw got the Steelers in front again with 6:48 remaining in the first half. He took the

Steelers sixty-six yards in eight plays, hitting Stallworth with a 14-yard touchdown pass. Pat Leahy boomed a 47-yard field goal with just one second left, however, to whittle Pittsburgh's halftime margin to 14–10 and give Jet fans hope. New York had actually outgained the Steelers in total yardage, 188 to 135.

Pittsburgh came out fired up after intermission and took control of the game. The Steelers took the second-half kickoff and traveled sixty-three yards in just six plays. Bradshaw connected on three of four passes, the last a 26-yard strike to Swann in the left side of the end zone that gave the Steelers a 21–10 lead.

The next time the Steelers got the ball they scored again. The Jets were bogged down deep in their own territory, largely because of a 10-yard sack by Greene on third down. With the ball on the 6-yard line, the Jets were forced to punt from their end zone. Pittsburgh wound up with excellent field position on the New York 29.

Bradshaw threw five passes in the seven-play series and connected on three of them. With a first down on the 3-yard line, he twice gave the ball to Thornton, who punched it across on his second attempt. Pittsburgh jumped its lead to 28–10 with eight minutes left.

The last time the Jets had the ball they scored. Kevin Long ran in for a touchdown from the 2-yard line to make the final score 28–17. Bradshaw finished the game with seventeen completions in twenty-five attempts for 189 yards and three touchdowns. Swann caught seven passes for 100 yards. The Pittsburgh air attack was growing explosive.

5TH WEEK, 1978 SEASON

PITTSBURGH	7	7	14	0	28
NEW YORK	0	10	7	0	17

Pittsburgh: 6:10, first period—Swann, 10-yard pass from Bradshaw (Gerela, kick).
New York: 1:03, second period—Harper, 11-yard run (Leahy, kick).
Pittsburgh: 8:12, second period—Stallworth, 14-yard pass from Bradshaw (Gerela, kick).
New York: 14:59, second period—Leahy, 47-yard field goal.
Pittsburgh: 2:22, third period—Swann, 26-yard pass from Bradshaw (Gerela, kick).
Pittsburgh: 7:02, third period—Thornton, 1-yard run (Gerela, kick).
New York: 13:55, third period—Long, 2-yard run (Leahy, kick).

Game Six: Atlanta

Pittsburgh was one of three unbeaten teams in the NFL and the only undefeated team in the AFC. The other two clubs with unblemished records were the Los Angeles Rams and the Washington Redskins of the NFC.

In meeting the Atlanta Falcons in Three Rivers Stadium, the Steelers were facing their first NFC opponent of the season. Although the Falcons had a weak offense, they were considered one of the stronger defensive teams in the NFC.

The Steelers didn't wait to test the Atlanta defense. They took the opening kickoff and marched eighty-five yards before being repelled on the Falcon 3-yard line. As a result, Gerela was asked to salvage something out of the long drive and did, with a 21-yard field goal. The sustained attack consumed an almost unbelievable 9:58.

The first time the Steelers went on the attack in the second quarter they scored again. This time Bradshaw took them all the way, negotiating eighty yards in nine plays. Bleier scored the touchdown when he broke loose from the 8-yard line to give Pittsburgh a 10–0 lead.

With just 2:39 left in the half the Steelers got the ball again. This time Pittsburgh went sixty-one yards in six plays, Bradshaw himself scoring the touchdown on a six-yard rollout. When the first half ended Pittsburgh had an easy 17–0 lead. The Steeler offense had already accumulated 212 yards, while the defense had limited the Atlanta offense to sixty-one yards.

The Falcons had the ball for over five minutes in the beginning of the third quarter and still couldn't score. On their next effort, however, they managed to reach the Pittsburgh 11-yard line, only to see Fred Steinfort miss a 31-yard field goal try, his second miss of the day.

Bradshaw struck quickly. On a third and two from the Pittsburgh 28-yard line he fired over the middle to Stallworth. The rangy receiver caught the ball, broke several tackles, and began a clear run upfield. He was finally caught on the 2-yard line and stopped after a 70-yard gain. Two plays later, Bleier ran it in to put the Steelers on top, 24–0.

When the Steelers took control of the ball for the first time in the final period they scored again. Bradshaw led them seventy yards in eight plays, hitting on four of five passes. His last pass was an 11-yard touchdown to Stallworth. Pittsburgh's bulge was now 31–0. With eight minutes left Noll sent in his reserves.

Just 2:03 remained when the Falcons finally scored. Steve Bartkowski threw an 11-yard touchdown pass to Wallace Francis as the Falcons averted a shutout, 31–7.

Bradshaw enjoyed another fine game, completing thirteen of eighteen passes for 231 yards and a touchdown. Harris recorded his first 100-yard game of the season, gaining 104 yards, as Pittsburgh produced 387 yards in all against Atlanta's heralded defense.

6TH WEEK, 1978 SEASON

ATLANTA	0	0	0	7	7
PITTSBURGH	3	14	7	7	31

Pittsburgh: 9:58, first period—Gerela, 21-yard field goal.
Pittsburgh: 7:09, second period—Bleier, 8-yard run (Gerela, kick).
Pittsburgh: 14:01, second period—Bradshaw, 6-yard run (Gerela, kick).
Pittsburgh: 13:42, third period—Bleier, 2-yard run (Gerela, kick).
Pittsburgh: 3:08, fourth period—Stallworth, 11-yard pass from Bradshaw (Gerela, kick).
Atlanta: 12:57, fourth period—Francis, 11-yard pass from Bartkowski (Steinfort, kick).

Game Seven: Cleveland

It was time for the Steelers to go to Cleveland in a return meeting of the Blue Collar Bowl. Thom Darden said that the Browns would be ready for them. So were 81,302 fans, the largest crowd of the season to watch the Browns. (Actually, the game was a complete sellout, with 82,400 tickets distributed.)

Pittsburgh entered the game with a shiny 6–0 record. Cleveland trailed the Steelers by two games with a 4–2 mark. This game was crucial for the Browns. A loss would drop them three games behind. They couldn't afford that. They couldn't allow the Steelers to run away and hide from the rest of the Central Division.

Cleveland had an opportunity to score first after the kickoff, but Mel Blount intercepted Brian Sipe's pass at midfield and ran it back thirty-five yards to the Brown 15-yard line. Pittsburgh got to the 6-yard line, but failed to con-

Greenwood (68) and Greene (75) close in on Falcons' quarterback Steve Bartkowski.

Jack Ham pulls down Cleveland's star running back Greg Pruitt.

vert on a third and one play. Gerela contributed a 23-yard field goal, however, to put Pittsburgh in front, 3–0.

Donnie Shell then recovered a Cleveland fumble on the Brown 48-yard line. But, Bradshaw could only complete an 18-yard pass to Swann before stalling. Gerela then hit a 43-yard field goal to give the Steelers a 6–0 edge with six minutes left in the quarter. The game was following the pattern of the first meeting between the two teams.

With just 1:44 left in a hardfought second

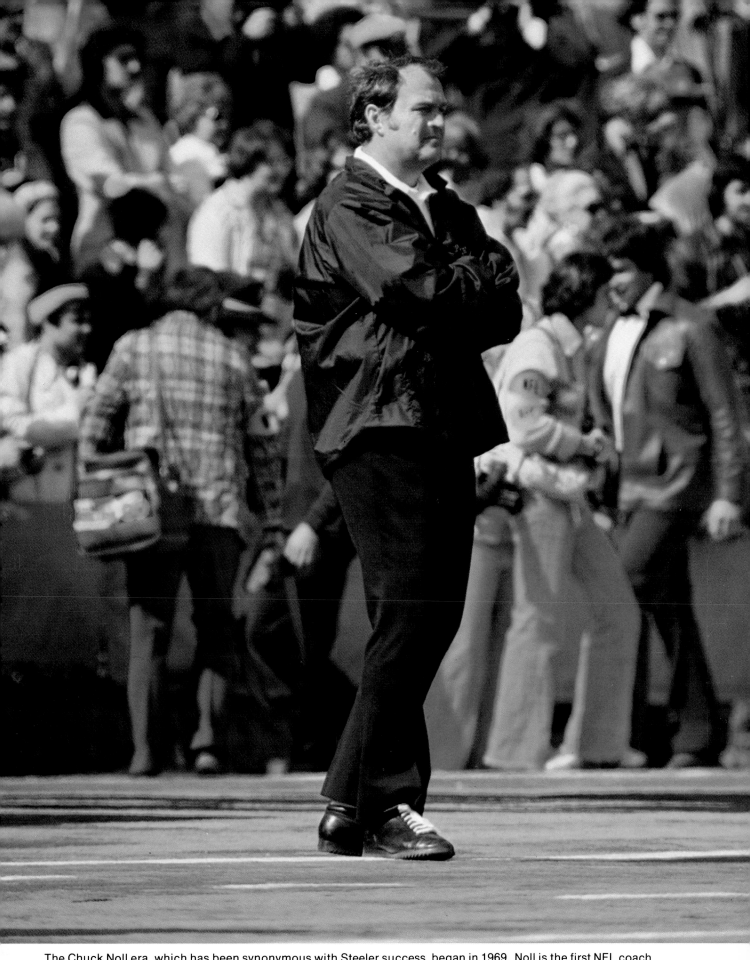

The Chuck Noll era, which has been synonymous with Steeler success, began in 1969. Noll is the first NFL coach to win three Super Bowl championships.

Precision-jumping Lynn Swann leaps behind Cincinnati defensive back in bid to catch ball.

(Left) Pittsburgh fans won't forget the year Terry Bradshaw had in 1978. The strong-armed quarterback had his best season ever by hitting on 56.3 percent of his passes for 2,915 yards and twenty-eight touchdowns to rank second in the NFL.

A determined Franco Harris starts his move outside to avoid the arms of Dallas' defensive end Ed "Too Tall" Jones in Super Bowl XIII.

(Right) Rangy wide receiver John Stallworth looks the ball into his hands in 28−17 victory over the New York Jets.

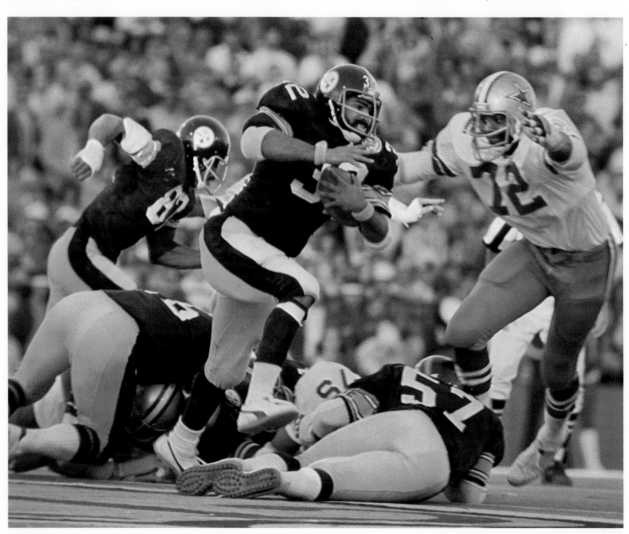

A snarling Jack Lambert, a bloody bandage in his hand, looks menacingly at action on the field.

(Right) Defensive tackle Joe Greene stretches his 6′ 4′′ frame in attempt to defend against a pass.

The defenders. From left, Joe Greene (75), Jack Lambert (58) and L.C. Greenwood (68).

Tall as cornerbacks go at 6′ 3′′, nine-year veteran Mel Blount intercepted four passes in 1978 giving him a career total of thirty-nine, second highest in Steeler history.

(Left) Four Denver Broncos combine their efforts to hold back L.C. Greenwood in AFC championship playoff game.

John Stallworth and Lynn Swann are the most prolific wide receivers in pro football. Between them in 1978, they caught 102 passes for 1,678 yards and twenty touchdowns.

Demonstrating his magic, wide receiver Lynn Swann catches a pass all alone in the end zone.

Leaning forward, Rocky Bleier carefully cradles the ball as he runs to daylight.

Biting his lip, a taut Steve Furness watches play from the sidelines.

Reliable Jack Ham, the most versatile outside linebacker in the NFL, reaches out to stop Dallas running back Robert Newhouse.

period, Cleveland scored. Sipe hit Dave Logan with a 17-yard touchdown pass to send the Browns into a 7–6 lead.

It was short-lived. Larry Anderson settled under the kickoff on the 5-yard line and started to run. He broke into the open and sped ninety-five yards for a touchdown. The Steelers walked off the field at halftime leading, 13–7, on a play that stunned the Browns. Cleveland had outgained Pittsburgh 185 to 67 and made ten first downs to the Steelers' five.

In the early minutes of the third period Mike Wagner stopped a Cleveland drive with an interception on the Steeler 11-yard line, bringing it back to the 31 before being downed. Bradshaw took it from there. He connected with Swann on a 28-yard touchdown pass to culminate an eleven-play, 69-yard drive. Pittsburgh moved into a 20–7 lead.

With 2:12 remaining the Steelers increased their margin to 27–7. Bleier put the finishing touch to a ten-play, 71-yard drive by scoring from the 1.

The Browns tried to come back. They scored in the opening minutes of the fourth period when Sipe hit Reggie Rucker with an 18-yard touchdown aerial to make the score 27–14. Midway through the quarter, however, Bradshaw put the game out of reach. He fired a 32-yard touchdown pass to Stallworth to seal a 34–14 victory.

Pittsburgh remained undefeated with a 7–0 record. Only the Rams could match it, as Washington suffered its first defeat. More importantly, the Steelers jumped into a three-game lead in the Central Division race. Darden would have to wait until next year.

7TH WEEK, 1978 SEASON

PITTSBURGH	6	7	14	7	34
CLEVELAND	0	7	0	7	14

Pittsburgh: 3:33, first period—Gerela, 23-yard field goal.
Pittsburgh: 8:33, first period—Gerela, 44-yard field goal.
Cleveland: 13:16, second period—Logan, 17-yard pass from Sipe (Cockroft, kick).
Pittsburgh: 13:30, second period—Anderson, 95-yard kick return (Gerela, kick).
Pittsburgh: 5:22, third period—Swann, 28-yard pass from Bradshaw (Gerela, kick).
Pittsburgh: 12:48, third period—Bleier, 1-yard run (Gerela, kick).
Cleveland: 3:35, fourth period—Rucker, 18-yard pass from Sipe (Cockroft, kick).
Pittsburgh: 7:30, fourth period—Stallworth, 32-yard pass from Bradshaw (Gerela, kick).

Game Eight: Houston

A large Monday night television audience would get its first look at the unbeaten Steelers. So would the Houston Oilers. With a 4–3 record they had moved into Three Rivers Stadium to challenge the Steelers. Somebody had to. Pittsburgh was on the verge of a runaway.

Like the Steelers, the Oilers were a very hard-hitting team. They were tied with Cleveland for second place and now posed the main threat to the Steelers in the Central Division. Rookie running back Earl Campbell, who was on his way to a 1,000-yard season, gave the Oiler attack a new dimension it had never had before. No longer could opposing teams be concerned only with defending against quarterback Dan Pastorini's passing.

Nobody scored in a closely played first quarter. The Steelers came closer, but the only time they had the ball, Gerela's 31-yard field goal attempt was wide.

Two minutes into the second period, Houston scored. On an 80-yard drive that began late in the first period and consumed a total of thirteen plays, Campbell scored from the 1-yard line. Houston led, 7–0.

Pittsburgh deadlocked the game on the ensuing series of downs. Starting on their 32-yard line, the Steelers moved sixty-eight yards in eight plays. The touchdown was a 25-yard aerial from Bradshaw to Swann, a well executed play.

Minutes later Pittsburgh got the ball back. Shell recovered a fumble on the Houston 24-yard line, but after moving for one first down the Steelers bogged down. Nevertheless, Gerela put the Steelers ahead, 10–7, when he hit one from thirty yards out. But with only one second left in the half, Toni Fritsch responded for Houston with a 39-yard field goal that tied the contest at 10–10.

The Steelers took the second half kickoff but couldn't move. When the Oilers got the ball, they did, marching seventy yards in eleven plays, with Campbell scoring from the 3-yard line to give the Oilers the lead, 17–10. That's how the third quarter ended.

Houston came right back in the fourth period the first time they went on offense. This time they drove seventy-eight yards in nine plays with Campbell going over for the third time, from

"Dirt" Winston's shoestring tackle prevents this Houston kickoff return from moving farther upfield.

the 1-yard line. Houston increased its lead to 24–10.

Bradshaw quickly tried to rally the Steelers. He moved them fifty yards in ten plays, the payoff being a six-yard touchdown pass to Swann to slice Houston's lead to 24–17.

Bradshaw wasn't through yet. With 1:45 left in the battle, he steered the Steelers to Houston's 14-yard line, but his fourth down pass to Swann in the end zone fell incomplete. Houston prevailed, 24–17.

It was a major victory for the Oilers. They pulled to within two games of the Steelers. There was still a race in the AFC Central Division.

Pittsburgh suffered its first loss of the year, despite outstanding defensive play by Mike Wagner, who had eleven tackles, and Jack Ham,

who had ten. The Steelers were human, after all.

8TH WEEK, 1978 SEASON

HOUSTON	0	10	7	7	24
PITTSBURGH	0	10	0	7	17

Houston: 2:05, second period—Campbell, 1-yard run (Fritsch, kick).
Pittsburgh: 6:31, second period—Swann, 25-yard pass from Bradshaw (Gerela, kick).
Pittsburgh: 9:17, second period—Gerela, 30-yard field goal.
Houston: 14:59, second period—Fritsch, 39-yard field goal.
Houston: 9:54, third period—Campbell, 3-yard run (Fritsch, kick).
Houston: 4:37, fourth period—Campbell, 1-yard run (Fritsch, kick).
Pittsburgh: 9:40, fourth period—Swann, 6-yard pass from Bradshaw (Gerela, kick).

Game Nine: Kansas City

There was no panic in Pittsburgh. Chances are remote that any team could ever go through a season undefeated in an expanded sixteen-game schedule. Besides, the Steelers were still the team to catch in the Central Division. A two-game lead at the halfway point of the season was certainly commendable. Not many experts had felt that they would get that far.

Unquestionably the Kansas City Chiefs weren't going very far. They arrived in Pittsburgh in last place in the Western Division with a 2–6 record. It presented the Steelers with a good opportunity to rebound after a physically tough Monday night game.

Kansas City attempts to pick up Shell's safety blitz.

The Chiefs managed to score first. They picked off a Bradshaw pass and got the ball on the Pittsburgh 11-yard line. They couldn't get a touchdown but got a 25-yard field goal instead from Jan Stenerud for a quick 3–0 lead.

Pittsburgh took the kickoff and drove straight down field with it. They put together a seventy-three-yard march that required thirteen plays. Harris scored from the 1-yard line to give the Steelers a 7–3 lead.

When the second quarter began Pittsburgh was working on a drive that had started on their 17-yard line late in the first period. They kept the attack going and completed the 83-yard distance in thirteen plays. Harris dazzled the crowd with an eleven-yard draw play for his second touchdown as the Steelers pushed ahead, 14–3.

The next time the Steeler offense appeared on the field they scored again. On a third down play Bradshaw and Stallworth teamed up on a perfectly timed pass in the middle of the field for a 23-yard touchdown. Pittsburgh's advantage swelled to 20–3, but Gerela missed the extra point attempt.

In the third period the Chiefs gave the Steelers a scare. They scored the first two times they touched the ball. Ted McKnight shook loose around left end for a 14-yard touchdown run that made the score 20–10. On the next series, Bradshaw fumbled and the Chiefs recovered on the Pittsburgh 25-yard line. Three plays later Tony Reed cut back around left end and ran for a 16-yard touchdown that narrowed Pittsburgh's lead to 20–17.

Near the close of the third period the Steelers got an unexpected touchdown. Andy Belton had moved for five yards before he was stripped of the ball by Robin Cole. Donnie Shell picked up the loose ball on the Kansas City 17-yard line and ran all the way for a touchdown to provide the Steelers with breathing room, 27–17, as the quarter came near its end.

With only two minutes remaining in the game, the Chiefs managed to score again as Arnold Morgado ran for a two-yard touchdown. The game ended 27–24.

Kansas City had outgained the Steelers, 327 yards to 215. It wasn't exactly an artistic success, but it was a win nevertheless. Pittsburgh now led the division by three games as the Oilers were upset by Cincinnati.

Game Ten: New Orleans

If the Steelers had taken Kansas City too lightly they couldn't afford any complacency against their next opponent, the New Orleans Saints. It is understandable that no team in the NFL can maintain a high level of efficiency week after week after week. Letdowns are common, and they are something that coaches are wary of with each approaching game.

The Saints were a pesky team that was having unexpected success. They had a 5–4 record, certainly no match against Pittsburgh's 8–1 performance. But New Orleans quarterback Archie Manning was enjoying his finest season after three pain-wracked years of injuries. He ranked among the top quarterbacks in the NFC, and the Saints' defense enabled them to play close games throughout most of the season.

Midway through the first period the Steelers opened the scoring. Actually it was the first time they performed on offense. A Pittsburgh drive that began on the 20-yard line expired on the New Orleans 10-yard line. Gerela kicked a 27-yard field goal that gave the Steelers a 3–0 lead.

The second quarter was half over when the Saints retaliated. Manning completed a 70-yard drive in eleven plays by tossing a five-yard touchdown pass to Rich Mauti to send the Saints in front, 7–3.

New Orleans almost scored again as the first half was ending. On third down at the Pittsburgh 5-yard line Manning was hit by Loren Toews. He fumbled, and Greene captured the

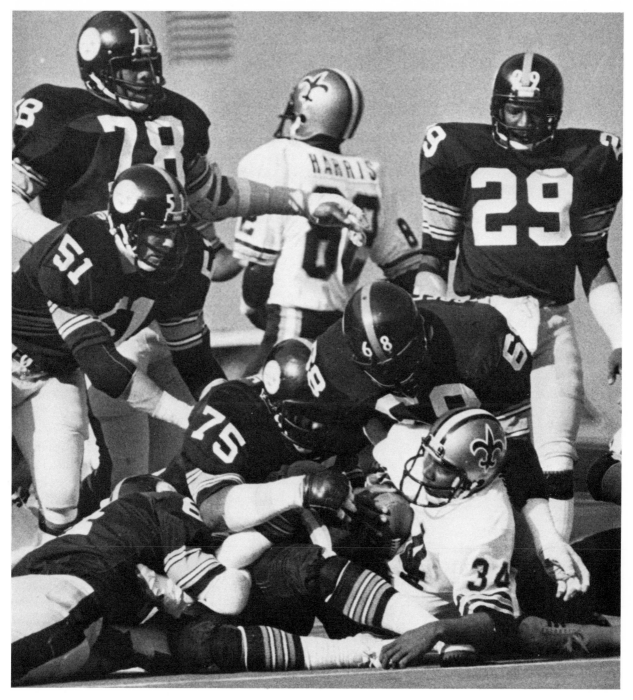

Furness (64), Greene (75), and Greenwood (68) combine to stop this Saints' rush for no gain.

ball for the Steelers on the 9-yard line, four seconds away from the conclusion of the first half.

Bradshaw ignited the Steelers after they took the second half kickoff. He started on the 23 and moved the ball to the New Orleans 28. On fourth down Pittsburgh needed four yards and went for it. Bradshaw passed to Swann, who made a leaping catch on the 6-yard line. Bradshaw went

right back to him for a touchdown pass and a 10–7 Steeler lead.

With less than two minutes left in the third period the Steelers added to their margin. Gerela booted a 21-yard field goal to stretch Pittsburgh's lead to 13–7.

Just after the final period began the Saints went ahead. Tony Galbreath culminated an 80-yard drive, which started in the third period and took just eight plays, with a five-yard touchdown run. It sent the Saints in front, 14–13.

Anderson's fine 54-yard return on the kickoff gave the Steelers excellent field position on the Saints' 34-yard line. After getting one first down the Steelers could only get as far as the 14. Gerela was sent in to kick a 31-yard field goal. His kick hit the right upright, however, and the Saints clung to a 14–13 lead.

When the Steelers got the ball back with 5:33 remaining they had to move quickly from their 34. They did. Bradshaw directed them sixty-six yards in eight plays, collaborating with Bleier on a 24-yard touchdown pass with only two minutes left in the game.

Despite yielding 421 yards to New Orleans Pittsburgh pulled the game out, 20–14, to remain three games ahead of Houston. It was the second close win in a row.

10TH WEEK, 1978 SEASON

NEW ORLEANS	0	7	0	7	14
PITTSBURGH	3	0	10	7	20

Pittsburgh: 8:40, first period—Gerela, 27-yard field goal.
New Orleans: 8:24, second period—Mauti, 5-yard pass from Manning (Mike-Mayer, kick).
Pittsburgh: 5:50, third period—Swann, 6-yard pass from Bradshaw (Gerela, kick).
Pittsburgh: 13:38, third period—Gerela, 21-yard field goal.
New Orleans: 1:28, fourth period—Galbreath, 5-yard run (Mike-Mayer, kick).
Pittsburgh: 13:09, fourth period—Bleier, 24-yard pass from Bradshaw (Gerela, kick).

Game Eleven: Los Angeles

Perhaps Pittsburgh was looking ahead to its west coast meeting with the Los Angeles Rams. It was a rare Sunday night game, an attractive pairing for millions of fans on national television.

In winning nine out of ten games the Steelers had the best record in the NFL. Los Angeles with an 8–2 mark had the second best. It was a match-up of two teams who were heading for the playoffs in their respective conferences. Some bold forecasters remarked that perhaps this would be a preview of the two teams in Super Bowl XIII.

The Rams desperately wanted to go to the Super Bowl. They had never been there, al-

though they had repeatedly won the Western Division championship. They had an adequate offense, led by quarterback Pat Haden, wide receiver Ron Jessie, and running backs Larry McCutcheon and John Cappelletti, but the strength of their team lay in its defense.

The game attracted 63,089 fans. Actually, many more tickets were sold, but the 8,325 others who owned them didn't bother to show up. Perhaps the cool weather that lowered the temperature to forty-nine degrees dissuaded them.

Los Angeles didn't display any offense after receiving the opening kickoff. Tony Dungy recovered a Ram fumble on the Los Angeles 41-yard line, and Pittsburgh moved to a first down on the 13. Bradshaw's pass was intercepted, however. After that neither team threatened, and the first period ended in a scoreless tie.

In the second quarter both teams missed field-goal attempts, the Rams first. Pat Corral tried one from twenty-five yards away that sailed wide. Then with only fifty-three seconds left in the half, Gerela lined one up from the thirty-one yard line, but it, too, was wide. The first half produced no points and very little offense. The Steelers had six first downs and 121 total yards, while the Rams had five first downs and 100 yards.

Pittsburgh got on the board first. They grabbed the second half kickoff and moved seventy yards in eight plays to register the game's first touchdown. It came on a 14-yard pass from Bradshaw to Swann, who was playing before his hometown fans. The Steelers led, 7–0.

After the kickoff the Rams threatened to tie the game. They drove to the Pittsburgh 9-yard line, where Mike Wagner sacked Haden for an 11-yard loss on third down. Corral then kicked a 37-yard field goal to narrow Pittsburgh's edge to 7–3, which was the score at the end of the third period.

The Steelers were victimized the entire final period by poor field position. It gave the Rams an opportunity to score much more easily. With less than six minutes left to play, they did. Beginning on their 44-yard line, they moved fifty-six yards in eight plays, with Haden throwing a 10-yard touchdown pass to Willie Miller. The play enabled the Rams to beat the Steelers, 10–7.

It was as if Pittsburgh's offense hadn't existed.

It managed only fifty-nine yards in twenty-five rushes. Bradshaw was only eleven of twenty-five for 115 yards. In the final twenty-six minutes, Pittsburgh, in seven offensive series, lost thirteen yards.

11TH WEEK, 1978 SEASON

PITTSBURGH	0	0	7	0	7
LOS ANGELES	0	0	3	7	10

Pittsburgh: 3:53, third period—Swann, 14-yard pass from Bradshaw (Gerela, kick).
Los Angeles: 10:44, third period—Corral, 37-yard field goal.
Los Angeles: 9:33, fourth period—Miller, 10-yard pass from Haden (Corral, kick).

Game Twelve: Cincinnati

The loss to Los Angeles left the Steelers with a 9–2 record. Houston won again to improve its record to 7–4 and climb to within two games of Pittsburgh. The Oilers began to think in terms of overtaking the Steelers in the remaining five weeks of the season. That they would face Pittsburgh in two weeks gave them hope.

But in this twelfth week of the season the Steelers faced the Cincinnati Bengals. The Bengals were having a horrible season. Normally a strong divisional contender, Cincinnati was 1–10 and had a new coach, Homer Rice, who had

Rams and Steelers hunt for a fumble.

Lambert breaks through to stop Bengal running back Boobie Clark behind the line.

replaced Bill Johnson a month before. Surprisingly, Cincinnati's only victory of the season had been over the Oilers.

In fairness to the Bengals, they were beset with injuries all season long. The major blow had been to their quarterback Ken Anderson. Anderson, his left wrist still weak from a break, was ready to face the Steelers for the first time, however.

The game began slowly before 47,578 in Three Rivers Stadium. It wasn't until 12:24 that Cincinnati scored the first points, when Chris Bahr booted a 29-yard field goal.

In the next 2:04, the Steelers began to move. They had driven from their own 36-yard line to the Cincinnati 21 when time ran out in the first period. The Bengals, playing the run scrappily, surrendered only eight yards on the ground, four each by Harris and Bleier.

Pittsburgh kept its drive going when the second period began. Finally, on second and goal at the 1-yard line, Bleier broke through for a touchdown that sent the Steelers on top, 7–3. The 64-yard drive took twelve plays.

Near the end of the half Anderson ignited the Bengals. He connected on four consecutive passes to set up a 48-yard field goal attempt by Bahr. With only fourteen seconds on the clock Bahr came through. The Steelers' lead at halftime was only 7–6.

Offensive football was conspicuously lacking in the third period. The closest either team came to adding to its point total occurred near the period's end. Greene recovered a Bengal fumble on the Cincinnati 18. In the next three downs, however, the Steelers could manage only one yard. Gerela was sent in to try a 24-yard field goal, but missed as his kick hooked wide to the left.

On the fourth play of the final quarter Bahr tried to put the Bengals ahead. He attempted a 48-yard field goal that veered wide to the left. As it turned out, that was the closest Cincinnati came to scoring the rest of the game. The Steelers never came close enough to attempt another field goal. They managed to win the defensive struggle by the narrowest of margins, 7–6.

Another weak Steeler offensive performance created some concern. Pittsburgh gained only seventy yards on the ground and eighty-four

through the air for a total of 154, 20 yards fewer than they had made the week before.

12TH WEEK, 1978 SEASON

CINCINNATI	3	3	0	0	6
PITTSBURGH	0	7	0	0	7

Cincinnati: 12:24, first period—Bahr, 29-yard field goal.
Pittsburgh: 2:43, second period—Bleier, 1-yard run (Gerela, kick).
Cincinnati: 14:46, second period—Bahr, 48-yard field goal.

Game Thirteen: San Francisco

Pittsburgh returned to the west coast for their thirteenth game of the season. This time they were meeting another NFC opponent, the San Francisco 49ers, in a Monday night game. They still had a two game lead over the Oilers; the Steelers were 10–2 and the Oilers, whom Pittsburgh was to play the following week in Houston, were 8–4.

Like Cincinnati, the 49ers were experiencing a woeful season. They had achieved only one victory; their 1–11 record, the same as the Bengals', was the worst in the NFL. They had already begun to look toward next season. There was nothing else to do.

The preseason acquisition of O. J. Simpson had done little for San Francisco except sell more tickets. The 49ers' collapse wasn't Simpson's fault, however. He was injured early in the campaign and was through for the year. So was his running mate Wilbur Jackson. Their quarterback Jim Plunkett was traded to the Oakland Raiders, and his replacement, Steve DeBerg, was out with an injury that left third-string Scott Bull in control.

The Steelers scored first. After reaching the 11-yard line they had to settle for a 42-yard field goal to take a 3–0 lead.

In the closing minute and a half of the first quarter, the Steelers began to put a drive together. Bradshaw opened the second quarter throwing, hitting his first two passes and leading the Steelers to the 49ers' 22-yard line. He tried to hit Swann in the end zone, but missed. Bradshaw came right back to him, however, and Swann was all alone as he caught a 22-yard

Ron Johnson snares one of his four interceptions for the year against San Francisco.

touchdown pass to send Pittsburgh into a 10–0 lead. The 80-yard drive took eleven plays.

The next time the Steelers took possession they scored again. This time they started upfield from their own 34. Bradshaw took them sixty-six yards in thirteen plays, the touchdown resulting from a 25-yard pass to Swann who was again free in the end zone. At the half the Steelers were in control, 17–0. They had scored more points than in their two previous games combined.

Pittsburgh was a bit sloppy in the third period and didn't come close to scoring any more

points, while the 49ers started to make a game of it. They recovered Bleier's fumble on the Steelers' 5-yard line and scored with a minute remaining when Paul Hofer drove across from the 2-yard line to make the score 17–7.

Bradshaw provided a dramatic touchdown with just over two minutes remaining in the contest. He returned to the field after watching two plays from the sidelines. On second and ten from the 49ers' 11-yard line, he drilled a touchdown pass to Stallworth to account for the Steelers' final points in a 24–7 triumph.

The Steeler offense had awakened. They finished the game with twenty-two first downs and 380 total yards. Bradshaw hit thirteen of twenty-one passes for 195 yards and three touchdowns, as Swann caught eight passes for 134 yards. The Oilers were next, in Houston.

13TH WEEK, 1978 SEASON

PITTSBURGH	3	14	0	7	24
SAN FRANCISCO	0	0	7	0	7

Pittsburgh: 3:17, first period—Gerela, 42-yard field goal.
Pittsburgh: 1:24, second period—Swann, 22-yard pass from Bradshaw (Gerela, kick).
Pittsburgh: 10:19, second period—Swann, 25-yard pass from Bradshaw (Gerela, kick).
San Francisco: 13:55, third period—Hofer, 2-yard run (Warsching, kick).
Pittsburgh: 12:50, fourth period—Stallworth, 11-yard pass from Bradshaw (Gerela, kick).

Game Fourteen: Houston

The victory over San Francisco enabled Pittsburgh to become the first team in the NFL to win eleven games. It also kept the Steelers two games in front of the Oilers in the race for the Central Division championship.

Houston still entertained high hopes of overtaking Pittsburgh. So did the 54,261 fans who showed up at the Astrodome. If the Oilers could beat the Steelers they would be only one game behind them. In the final two weeks of the season they could hope to tie Pittsburgh and possibly be awarded the division title by having beaten the Steelers twice. This was the biggest game of the year to the Oilers.

Behind Jon Kolb's blocking, Bradshaw lets fly one of his two touchdown passes against Houston.

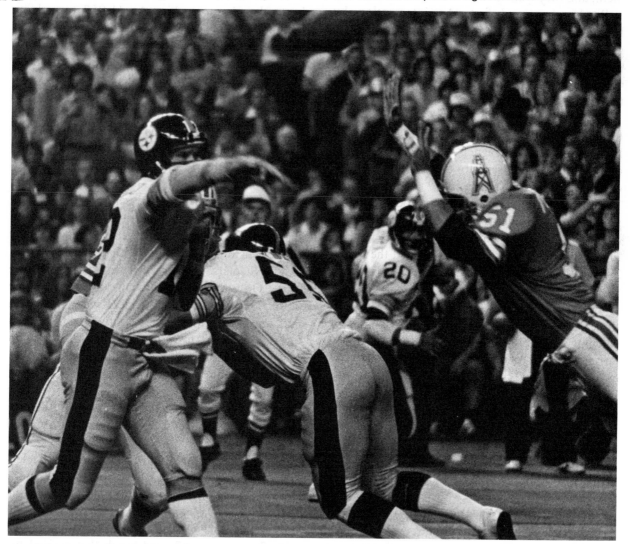

The last time the two teams had met, six weeks ago, the Oiler defense had done an excellent job of stopping Harris. They had limited him to just fifty-six yards and forced Bradshaw to put the ball up more than he had wanted. It was expected that the defenses of both teams would again dominate play.

The Steeler defense had a specific mission. They had to stop Earl Campbell, who had already run for 1,000 yards. By shutting down the rookie star they would make Dan Pastorini throw more, and the Oilers would not be in a position to control the game with Campbell's running.

The first quarter showed that the game would be a physical one. Each team wanted to assume control with hard-hitting tackles. They were going all out, especially the Steelers. A victory would clinch the division championship for them, and they wanted it.

Pittsburgh scored first. An interception by Lambert on the Pittsburgh 49 gave the Steelers good field position. Bradshaw carefully guided them to the 23-yard line before being stopped. Gerela then connected on a 41-yard field goal to give the Steelers the first points, 3–0.

As the quarter ended, the Steelers found a way to stop Campbell. On his last carry he was hit hard by Shell and Wagner, so hard that he not only fumbled but went to the sidelines with a cracked rib, never to return.

Midway through the second period the Oilers got a break. Bradshaw fumbled the snap, and Houston recovered on the Pittsburgh 15-yard line. Four plays later Tony Fritsch tied the game, 3–3, with a 37-yard field goal. The half ended without further scoring.

The score remained 3–3 until there were just three minutes left in the third quarter. After catching a Pastorini pass, Mike Barber was jarred by Mel Blount and fumbled. Shell recovered the ball on the Steeler 48-yard line. Pittsburgh moved to a first down on the Houston 4. Thornton got to the 1, but Houston stopped the Steelers cold on the next two downs. After a delay of game penalty set the Steelers back to the 6, Gerela kicked a 23-yard field goal to give Pittsburgh a 6–3 lead as the quarter drew toward its conclusion.

Not until 11:18 of the fourth quarter did Bradshaw seal the victory. He directed the Steelers eighty yards in eleven plays, throwing a

five-yard touchdown pass to Stallworth for a 13–3 victory. The Steelers clinched the Central Division championship in a bruising physical battle in which at least seven Oilers and four Steelers left the game with injuries.

14TH WEEK, 1978 SEASON

PITTSBURGH	3	0	3	7	13
HOUSTON	0	3	0	0	3

Pittsburgh: 11:31, first period—Gerela, 41-yard field goal.
Houston: 11:26, second period—Fritsch, 37-yard field goal.
Pittsburgh: 12:18, third period—Gerela, 23-yard field goal.
Pittsburgh: 11:18, fourth period—Stallworth, 5-yard pass from Bradshaw (Gerela, kick).

Game Fifteen: Baltimore

It was almost too cold for Steeler fans to celebrate the championship. As 41,957 turned out in Three Rivers Stadium to cheer their heroes snow was falling heavily. Since it was a Saturday game the contest was being televised nationally as part of an NFL doubleheader.

Pittsburgh's opponents were the Baltimore Colts, who were having a frustrating season. Picked by many to win the Eastern Division title, the Colts' record was 5–9. Their woes were to a great extent the result of a shoulder injury to quarterback Bert Jones. Though Jones had been sidelined most of the season, there was a chance that he might return to action against the Steelers, but his tender shoulder and the slippery field prevented his doing so.

The Steelers' 12–2 record was the best in the NFL. Only the Rams with an 11–3 mark came close. Nevertheless the Steelers wanted to win and finish with the best credentials in their conference in order to gain the home field advantage in the championship playoffs.

Despite the weather Bradshaw came out throwing. On the second series of downs, he looped a 31-yard touchdown pass to Stallworth that gave the Steelers a 7–0 lead midway through the first period.

When the second quarter began the Steelers scored again. Though they began with poor field position on their own 13-yard line, as the first period was ending, Bradshaw got them out of the hole with one play. He collaborated with Swann on a 62-yard bomb that carried the

Bradshaw prepares to hand to Harris (32) as Bleier (20) and Davis (57) pull to take out the Colts' defense.

Steelers into Baltimore territory. Then he hit Thornton with a 24-yarder to the 3. On the first play of the second quarter Harris went over for a 14–0 Pittsburgh edge.

Greenwood set up another touchdown for the Steelers. He recovered a fumble on the Colt 2-yard line. On the first play from scrimmage, Harris went over to build Pittsburgh's margin to 21-0 with nine minutes remaining in the half.

Two minutes before halftime the Colts scored. Quarterback Bill Troup found Roger Carr in the end zone for a five-yard touchdown pass that léft Pittsburgh in front, 21–7, when the first half ended.

Baltimore got back into the game early in the

third period. Bradshaw was hit hard and fumbled, and Colt linebacker Derrel Luce picked up the ball and ran forty-four yards for a touchdown. Toni Linhart missed the conversion, however, leaving the score 21–13.

Larry Anderson gave the Steelers excellent field position on the kickoff. He raced fifty-seven yards before he was downed on the Baltimore 18-yard line. Three plays later Bradshaw passed to Grossman for a 12-yard touchdown and a 28–13 Pittsburgh lead.

In the early moments of the final period Bradshaw closed out the scoring, again with the pass. He capped a twelve-play, 64-yard drive with a 29-yard touchdown pass to Jim Smith. The

Steelers won, 35–13, as Bradshaw had a big day. He completed eleven of eighteen passes for 240 yards and three touchdowns. More importantly, the Steelers were assured of the home field advantage in the playoffs.

15TH WEEK, 1978 SEASON

BALTIMORE	0	7	6	0	13
PITTSBURGH	7	14	7	7	35

Pittsburgh: 7:48, first period—Stallworth, 31-yard pass from Bradshaw (Gerela, kick).
Pittsburgh: :04, second period—Harris, 3-yard run (Gerela, kick).
Pittsburgh: 6:00, second period—Harris, 2-yard run (Gerela, kick).
Baltimore: 13:06, second period—Carr, 5-yard pass from Troup (Linhart, kick).
Baltimore: 4:07, third period—Luce, 44-yard run on fumble recovery (kick failed).
Pittsburgh: 5:55, third period—Grossman, 12-yard pass from Bradshaw (Gerela, kick).
Pittsburgh: 2:10, fourth period—J. Smith, 29-yard pass from Bradshaw (Gerela, kick).

Game Sixteen: Denver

For the second straight week the Steelers were on national television. They met the Broncos in Denver on Saturday, in the second half of another NFL doubleheader.

The Broncos were a troublesome club for the Steelers. In 1977 Pittsburgh had lost twice to the Broncos, both times in Denver. They had lost 21–7 during the regular season and then in the opening game of the AFC playoffs, 34–21.

Denver had already won the Western Division crown for the second straight season. It was tougher for them this time around, however. In 1977, the Broncos had finished with a 12–2 record. This year, facing the Steelers, Denver had only a 10–5 slate. Still, they were a rough team and tough to beat at home, where 74,104 Broncomaniacs came out to Mile High Stadium.

Sidney Thornton is taken down after picking up several yards against Denver in the second half.

Just before the first period came to a close Pittsburgh scored. The Steelers marched fifty-two yards in ten plays, Harris scoring a touchdown on fourth down from the 1-yard line to give Pittsburgh a 7–0 lead.

The score remained unchanged until 11:37 of the second quarter. In just two plays Bradshaw got the Steelers a touchdown. It was set up by Tony Dungy, who recovered Riley Odoms' fumble on the Denver 42-yard line. Bradshaw didn't wait to go to the air. He drilled a 17-yard pass to Stallworth on the 25-yard line. Then he came right back to Stallworth in the end zone to give the Steelers a 14–0 lead.

Pittsburgh got the ball again with just 2:05 left. Bradshaw took advantage of it. Looking sharp, he directed the Steelers fifty-eight yards in eight plays. There were only twenty-three seconds left when Bradshaw called a time out. He wanted to talk over a third and nine situation on the Denver 10-yard line. When play resumed he threw a touchdown pass to Jim Smith and the Steelers jumped into a 21–0 lead, completely dominating the Broncos. The defense held Denver to only three first downs and forty-six total yards.

The Broncos started the second half with a new quarterback, Norris Weese, who replaced Craig Morton. On his second series of downs Weese got the Broncos a touchdown, hitting Haven Moses with a 25-yard pass. When the quarter ended Denver still trailed, 21–7.

In the early minutes of the fourth period Mike Kruczek, who had started the second half for Pittsburgh, threw an interception. Denver took over on its own 48. Five plays later Jim Turner kicked a 45-yard field goal to cut Pittsburgh's margin to 21–10.

Weese kept trying. With only 1:13 showing on the clock he completed a nine-play, 76-yard drive with a 30-yard touchdown pass to Odoms. The final score remained 21–17, but not before the Steelers had had a scare. A 49-yard face penalty in the end zone gave the Broncos the ball on the Steelers' 1-yard line with seven seconds left, but Greene and Lambert stopped Lonnie Perrin's plunge for the winning touchdown.

Pittsburgh finished with an impressive 14–2 record, and looked forward to their second season, the championship playoffs.

16TH WEEK, 1978 SEASON

PITTSBURGH	7	14	0	0	21
DENVER	0	0	7	10	17

Pittsburgh: 14:22, first period—Harris, 1-yard run (Gerela, kick).
Pittsburgh: 11:37, second period—Stallworth, 25-yard pass from Bradshaw (Gerela, kick).
Pittsburgh: 14:45, second period—J. Smith, 10-yard pass from Bradshaw (Gerela, kick).
Denver: 9:13, third period—Moses, 25-yard pass from Weese (Turner, kick).
Denver: 5:56, fourth period—Turner, 45-yard field goal.
Denver: 13:47, fourth period—Odoms, 30-yard pass from Weese (Turner, kick).

The AFC Playoff

Super Bowl fever gripped Pittsburgh. One could feel it in the air. The Steelers had offered no suspense in winning the Central Division. Their 14–2 regular season record was the best in the team's forty-five-year history. Nobody had come close to catching them once they had opened the campaign with seven consecutive victories. But this was a new season. What remained ahead on the road to Miami were the playoffs.

One thing was certain: The Steelers would have the advantage of playing in Three Rivers Stadium. Their brilliant record guaranteed that. In the opening round of the championship playoffs they would face the Western Division champions, the Denver Broncos. Should they emerge victorious, then they would meet the winner of the Houston-New England game the following week in Three Rivers.

The Steelers entered the playoffs with a psychological edge. Steeler fans are a rabid lot, and their feelings for the team, running at fever pitch, recalled the euphoria of 1974 and 1975, when the Steelers won back-to-back Super Bowls.

The intensity started to build at the Press Box Bar on Market Street. The clientele at the downtown spa wanted to hang it all out for John Banaszak, the big defensive end who had stepped in and done the job when Dwight White was hurt. They had in mind an even larger banner than the one they had already hung at Three Rivers. That piece of embroidery measured sixty feet long and twelve feet high, which was certainly large enough to spell "Banaszak." The trouble was that the present banner hindered

the view of Steeler ticket holders who were not necessarily active members of the Banaszak Fan Club.

"We just thought it was too large," explained Joe Gordon, the Steelers' publicity director.

"So, what's the next step, order them to take it down?" someone wanted to know.

"No," exclaimed Gordon, "I was just trying to reason with them. I wasn't trying to commit suicide."

That was the start of it. In a small Pittsburgh suburb called Port Vue, another Steeler aficionado, Bob Bubonic, was getting ready for the game. Night after night he would comb the head of a furry animal. Bubonic has a special place in Steeler fan lore. He is the person in the gorilla costume who parades in the stadium at the head of Gerela's Gorillas. The gorilla has been a fixture at Steeler games since 1971, when kicker Roy Gerela first joined the team. Every week the members of the fan club would drive up to Esser's Costume Store and rent a gorilla suit at $100 a pop. After years of appropriating such an expenditure from the club's treasury, the membership decided to invest and bought a suit for Bubonic.

Members of Franco Harris' Italian-American Army were starting to muster. They had banded together back in 1972, when Harris was a rookie. At the time Myron Cope, a 5' 7" effervescent Pittsburgh radio and television announcer, began heralding the Army's exploits. The biggest victory the Army ever achieved occurred its first year, when Tony Stagno, a local baker and president of the club, made Frank Sinatra a member,

Stallworth was Bradshaw's favorite target all day against the Broncos.

Joe Greene and the front four kept Morton constantly under fire.

complete with a bread, cheese, and wine ceremony in Palm Springs. Nothing could possibly top that.

Except perhaps beer sales. Through the years Pittsburgh has had the reputation of being a shot and beer town. A week before the Denver game the beer was beginning to flow. Joe Litman, head of S & S Beer Distributors, noticed it. His orders were much higher than they had been the previous week. A football buff himself and a close friend of Len Dawson, who once played for the Steelers, and of Hank Stram, Litman followed the fortunes of the Kansas City Chiefs closely. In the last few years, however, his allegiance had swung to the Steelers.

"The Steelers are a cinch," snapped Litman. "They'll go all the way. I don't care who they'll meet in the Super Bowl, they'll win that one, too. I've already ordered my Super Bowl tickets. The Steelers are the best team in the NFL. Pittsburgh fans will be celebrating for a month."

Even Joe Gordon got that feeling. He had been with the Steelers for a number of years and he could gauge the excitement that was generating.

"They are all stirring about these days," he remarked. "You can sense it around town. There is a kind of happy feeling. They are ready to participate."

One in particular was Dan Farish, a twenty-four-year-old bartender. Gordon saw him every morning for three days as he entered the Steeler offices. Farish and two others, John Butler and Barry Smith, had been waiting in line for fifty-four hours to buy tickets not only to the Denver game but to the AFC championship contest the following week.

The three had arrived at 4 A.M. Sunday morning, well in advance of the ticket windows' opening at 10 A.M. Tuesday. All were from nearby Turtle Creek, and they came well prepared for the cold. They were equipped with sleeping bags, a heater, radio, food, lounge chairs, and, equally important to a bartender, five cases of beer and two fifths of liquor.

"All I want for Christmas is my two front seats," Farish sang gleefully to passersby. "We think we are going to set a National Football League record for the longest wait for Steeler tickets."

He might well have. And if Gordon didn't keep any records of such happenings in the past, Farish and his two friends may very well have started a new log among Steeler statistics. Even Denver fans with their Broncomania would have marveled at the trio.

The feeling that something wonderful was about to happen permeated the Steeler dressing room, too. Lynn Swann, the marvelous wide receiver, expounded on it. He was so happy that he was thinking "Super Bowl," even though there were two more games to win first. He drew a parallel to the Steeler teams that had won Super Bowls IX and X.

"I'd say this team has much more maturity and professional experience it is capable of using all the time," said Swann. "It's one thing to have experience and know what you can do and can't do, and another thing to use this experience during a game. On this team each individual is taking more responsibility for what we have to do. We're making sure we're more mentally prepared so that we don't have to rely so much on one person.

"The first few years, when Joe Greene and the front four came in, the defense was doing a great job and waiting for the offense to do something. And maybe the defensive backs are waiting for the defensive line to make a great play and the linebackers are waiting for the secondary. And everyone's waiting for Franco to run 1,000 yards or make an Immaculate Reception or for Terry Bradshaw to play up to his potential or Terry Hanratty to do it. Every year we were waiting for the next first round draft choice to make the team go.

"All of a sudden we were there in 1974. The next year everyone just flowed. We had a large number of rookies, fourteen, the first championship year, and those two teams just felt this is where we were supposed to be. The guys were unaccustomed to anything else.

"After two years of having the disappointment of coming close and not making it, you get more analytical: 'I'm not going to wait for Franco to get his 1,000 yards. I'm going to make the catch to win the game.' Franco is not going to wait for the line to open up the perfect hole. He's going to bust through and pick up three or four yards by himself. The offensive line is saying, 'I'm not going to let Franco set up all the blocks. I'm going to blow my man out of there.' Terry

Bradshaw says, 'I'm going to study more and read defenses better.'

"It's not a question of hunger. We've always had that. It's taking on responsibility. It's the idea of responsibility, the burden of responsibility on each individual, as opposed to the individual putting it on the rest of the team. That's the maturity of the ball club. Our mood right now is very good. It's healthy. It's very up. We're confident, but it is a hard-working confidence. We realize we have the talent and the ability to go all the way. We're not about to blow it by thinking we have an overwhelming amount of ability.

"Defensively, these are two of the better teams in the NFL. I expect a hard-hitting game. Everything is on the table. There's no tomorrow, no second chance. They [the Broncos] play the 5-3 well. They get good pressure from their three down linemen and their linebackers react very well to the ball. Their strongest asset is their reaction to the ball. That was one of the reasons they lost to Dallas in last year's Super Bowl.

"What Dallas does is that they come out in one formation, shift to a second and possibly a third, fake the pass, look downfield, and throw a screen. When Roger Staubach gets rid of the ball, instead of having five, six, seven guys or more reacting to one ball carrier, the defense is split up, and that's when a little panic sets in. We have a very basic offensive scheme. We don't come out in multiple formations. We don't do a lot of shifting. We just come after you.

"Myself, I think I can play better. A lot of things I did I wasn't happy with. I should have had well over 1,000 yards. My number of catches should have been higher. I felt I should have made a catch in the first Houston game that could have tied the score and maybe made us 8–0 instead of 7–1. I pride myself on doing the tough things that get me above being an average receiver. I can take being imperfect. I can handle my life as it is now. Sure, nobody's perfect; but why can't you try to be perfect? If you think you've reached perfection, where else can you go?"

Most certainly to the Super Bowl. That's what Swann and the rest of the Steelers were thinking, but the Broncos offered the first obstacle. Two weeks earlier Pittsburgh had defeated the Broncos in Denver in the final game of the regular season, 21–17. It was a game in which the Steelers had jumped into a 21–0 first half lead, only to have the Broncos close strongly, so strongly that they almost pulled the game out at the finish.

The Broncos had a strong regard for Swann. In the last game he had been doubled all day by the Denver zone and caught only one pass for five yards. They had also employed this strategy in the opening-round playoff contest of the 1977 season. Denver had defeated Pittsburgh then, 34–21, and blanketed Swann, allowing him only one catch for six yards.

Denver was hoping to return to the Super Bowl for a second straight year. The strength of its team was the defense. Though the Steelers led the NFL in fewest points allowed with 195, the Broncos were right behind with 198. In eight of the games they had played during their 10–6 season, the Broncos had held their opponents to a touchdown or less. They were indeed tough on defense.

The Broncos were also riled. They were upset at some remarks attributed to Steeler players after their season-ending game. They felt that the Steelers had regarded the last win as meaningless and saw this game the same way, since they had already defeated Denver. The remark was misinterpreted. What the Steelers had tried to say was that they had already won their division and that whether they won or lost on that final day wouldn't matter. What did matter was their performance in the playoffs.

A light rain on Saturday was responsible for the few empty seats in Three Rivers Stadium. A vocal crowd of 48,921 nevertheless turned out. Most of them brandished large yellow towels, which had been the fashion throughout most of the season. So what if they got a little wet? Their owners could still wave them to exhort their heroes to greater heights.

They would get the opportunity to wave them at the defense first. Denver won the coin toss before the game began and elected to receive the ball. They clearly wanted the opportunity to score first and then let their solid defense take charge. That had been the pattern of many of their victories the past two years. After all, the Denver offense wasn't exactly explosive. Opportunistic was a better description.

Rick Upchurch, a dangerous kick return spe-

With Sidney Thornton (38) leading the way Franco Harris cuts upfield.

cialist, settled under Gerela's kickoff on the goal line. The speedy wide receiver started to run for daylight. He almost found some, too, before being tripped up on the 23-yard line. As the Steeler defense came on the field the yellow towels began to flap throughout the stadium.

Denver quarterback Craig Morton began conservatively enough. He handed the ball to Jon Keyworth twice. The first time he got two yards over right tackle. Then he busted up the middle for five yards. Morton was faced with a third and three on the 30-yard line. Suddenly Morton went up top. He threw a 19-yard pass to wide receiver Haven Moses, and the Broncos had a first down on their 49-yard line.

The Broncos, moving ever so cautiously, advanced to the Pittsburgh 42-yard line. They were helped along by a five-yard penalty. On third and one, however, Rob Lytle was denied a first down by the middle of the Steeler defense. Denver had to punt.

Bucky Dilts placed the Steelers in poor field position. Although his punt traveled only thirty-one yards, it forced Jim Smith to signal for a fair catch on the 11-yard line. Harris tested the Bronco defense first and didn't gain anything.

Randy Grossman starts off the line against Tom Jackson.

It was Bleier's turn next and he made three yards. Bradshaw signaled for a quick pass to Harris. He guessed that the Denver defense would be swarming. He was right. They bore in fast and almost sacked him. His pass fell short and now Pittsburgh had to punt.

Craig Colquitt's kick didn't travel much farther than Dilts', only thirty-four yards. What was worse, Upchurch made a big runback of twenty-two yards before he was brought down on the Pittsburgh 26-yard line. The Broncos had outstanding field position.

Lytle tried to run but was dropped for a yard loss by Ham. Surprisingly, Morton didn't hesitate to pass. He was successful, too. He fired a 16-yard pass to wide receiver Jack Dolbin. The Broncos had a first down on the Steeler 11-yard line. They appeared ready to move in for a touchdown, just the way they had hoped to before the game began.

But they suffered a setback. Denver right tackle Tom Neville was caught holding, an infraction that pushed the Broncos back to the 20-yard line. After Lytle gained four yards Morton decided to pass again. Mel Blount reacted quickly to a flare pass to Lytle and dropped him for a yard loss at the 17. Settling for a field goal, Morton stayed on the ground. He gave the ball to Keyworth, who was driven down for a three-yard loss by the onrushing Greene. Still the Broncos were within field goal range, and Jim Turner successfully booted a 37-yarder. The Broncos were in front first, 3–0.

There was 5:50 remaining in the first quarter when the Steeler offense returned. Larry Anderson's 27-yard runback placed the ball on the Pittsburgh 34. Bleier could manage only a yard. On second down Bradshaw threw to Stallworth but missed. On a third and nine Bradshaw called a pass. He knew the Broncos would be playing it, and he also thought that they would double on Swann, so he came right back to Stallworth and this time completed his first pass of the game, a 19-yard advance to the Denver 46.

Pittsburgh then brought the crowd to its feet with a rare play. Bradshaw handed the ball to Harris, who faked a run and lateraled the ball back to Bradshaw. Looking for Stallworth deep downfield, Bradshaw threw, but the pass fell incomplete. Bernard Jackson had interfered with Stallworth, however, and the Steelers were awarded a first down on the Denver 12-yard line. Now it was the Steelers who were threatening for the first time as the clock wound down.

Bleier swung around right end for three yards, but on the very next down he was caught holding on a pass play. The ball was brought back to the 19-yard line. Undaunted, Bradshaw went to his passing game. His second down pass to Harris was incomplete. On third down he looked for Stallworth again. They teamed up for a 16-yard completion and a big first down on the 3.

Now Bradshaw turned to Harris. He made it to the 1-yard line. On second down he broke through left guard for a touchdown. Bradshaw had led the Steelers sixty-six yards in eight plays. A few seconds later Gerela's Gorillas moaned; Gerela failed to kick the extra point and the Steelers' lead remained at 6–3, with 2:33 left in the opening period.

The Broncos couldn't do anything with the ball after the kickoff. Donnie Shell and Robin Cole collaborated on a third down sack of Morton, dropping him for a seven-yard loss to the 15. Denver's troubles were aggravated when Dilts could manage only a 28-yard punt. Theo Bell made a fair catch on the Denver 43. Harris' three-yard run brought the period to an end.

As the second quarter began the Steelers were in excellent field position. They had a second down on the Bronco 40-yard line. Bradshaw wanted to pass. He threw a flare to Stallworth that didn't gain anything. He came back to his rangy receiver a second time with success, zipping a 22-yard pass to Stallworth that gave the Steelers a first down on the 18. Pittsburgh was moving in for the second consecutive time.

Harris didn't give Steeler fans much time to dream about scoring. He shook loose around right end and went in for his second touchdown as the yellow towels heralded the 18-yard run. This time Gerela contributed, and Pittsburgh moved into a 13–3 lead.

After the kickoff the Broncos were in more trouble. On second down Larry Canada fumbled, and Shell recovered the ball on the Denver 26. The Steelers were primed for another score. Harris cut around the right side and picked up six yards to the 20-yard line. Then Bradshaw hit Stallworth for the fifth time, this

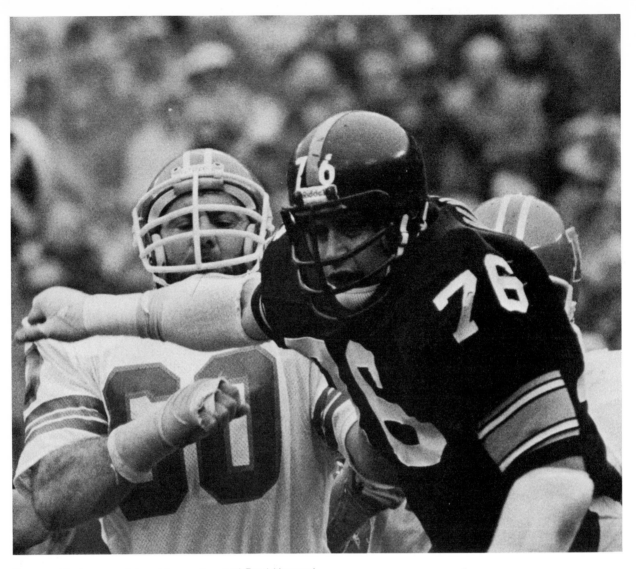

Banaszak's forearm takes him past guard Paul Howard.

time for eleven yards and a first down on the nine. Pittsburgh was driving again.

Harris was denied the right side and lost a yard when cornerback Louie Wright came up fast to stop him. Bradshaw's second-down pass to Stallworth fell incomplete. Following the pattern, he came back to Stallworth on the next play and completed a nine-yard pass to the 1. Pittsburgh had a fourth down on the 1-yard line. Bradshaw and Noll faced the biggest decision of the game. Should they go for it or take the field goal? They elected to go for it, much to the delight of the towel swingers.

Bradshaw decided to give Harris the ball. Instead of swinging right, however, Harris tried the left side and was turned back. The Broncos

had held on fourth and one. The joy was evident on their faces.

It was short-lived. The Broncos couldn't make a first down and Dilts had to punt from his end zone. Pittsburgh, putting the ball in play on the Denver 45-yard line, found itself with another opportunity to score. Bradshaw tried to go to Swann, but safety Bernard Jackson knocked the ball away. Bleier then broke over left guard for eight yards. When Harris picked up eight more around left end the Steelers had a first down on the 29.

Harris went the same way and gained seven yards. Carrying for the third straight time, he went over right guard for six yards and another first down on the 16. Harris again—this time he could find only two yards. Bradshaw passed to tight end Randy Grossman for the first time and gained seven yards. Pittsburgh had a third and one on the 7. Bradshaw asked Harris to try again but he was stopped short. Gerela was sent in and kicked a 24-yard field goal that provided Pittsburgh with a 16–3 margin.

Following the kickoff, Denver coach Red Miller decided to shake up the offense. He sent in Norris Weese, an agile but less experienced quarterback, to replace the veteran Morton. In his first series of downs Weese couldn't get the Broncos going, and Dilts had to punt again. It was another short punt, twenty-eight yards. Pittsburgh had possession on the Denver 39.

But the Steelers misfired. Bradshaw fumbled on an abortive play and linebacker Tom Jackson recovered the loose ball on the Pittsburgh 49. Denver had 3:56 in which to score and get back into the game.

Weese didn't wait. On first down he rifled a 28-yard pass to Dolbin on the Pittsburgh 21. After a 10-yard holding penalty on Denver guard Tom Glassic Weese went back to the air. He threw to Dolbin again, this time for twenty yards and a first down on the 11-yard line. Lonnie Perrin moved for eight yards around right end and the Broncos were on the 3. There were just two minutes left when Dave Preston went around right end for the Broncos' first touchdown. Turner's conversion narrowed Pittsburgh's lead to 16–10.

Anderson provided the Steelers' attack with a good start when he returned the kickoff thirty yards to the Pittsburgh 46. Bradshaw wanted to get more points on the scoreboard before the half was over. There was 1:49 left. His first pass to Bleier was no good. On second down, however, he hit Swann for the first time with a 14-yard strike on the Denver 40.

Again Bradshaw missed with a pass to Bleier. He then switched to the run, and Harris gained five yards. The Steelers signaled for a time out with 1:08 left. Realizing that Swann would be double-teamed, Bradshaw looked to Stallworth. He found him open on the 25, but a 15-yard penalty on Mike Webster brought the ball back to the Denver 40.

Time was expiring. This time Bradshaw went to Grossman for a 22-yard completion to the 18 and a first down. A tripping penalty against

Denver carried the ball to the 9. Bradshaw had one more shot at a touchdown. He tried Stallworth, but overthrew him. Still Gerela had enough time to boot a 27-yard field goal that gave Pittsburgh a 19–10 lead as the first half reached its conclusion.

Although the Steelers appeared in control, they hadn't completely dominated the first half action. A nine-point lead was certainly not insurmountable. They appeared to be more effective through the air. Bradshaw threw eighteen times, a rather high number, and completed ten for 130 yards. Seven of the receptions were made by Stallworth. The outcome was still in doubt; the Broncos had a reputation of being a strong second-half team.

The Steelers received the second-half kickoff. If they could add to their lead they would be in a strong position to take full command of the game. That was what Bradshaw had in mind when he set his offense on the Pittsburgh 33-yard line. He had to be wary of any adjustments in the Broncos' pass coverage.

After earning two first downs the Steeler drive stalled on the Denver 46. On third and fifteen Bradshaw tried a bomb to Swann. He wanted a quick touchdown, but his pass was knocked down in the end zone. After Colquitt's punt the Broncos went on the attack deep in their own territory, on the 16-yard line.

Miller stayed with Weese at quarterback. Weese didn't wait to make things happen. He knew the Broncos needed a lift. On first down he passed twenty-four yards to tight end Riley Odoms. The Broncos were now on the 40. Two penalties gave the Broncos another first down. Weese then scrambled for ten yards and another first down on the Steeler 45, but Lambert was flagged for unnecessary roughness and the 15-yard penalty placed the ball on the Pittsburgh 30-yard line.

The Steelers had been slapped with three consecutive penalties. Weese sensed that they were upset, that the momentum might be turning in Denver's favor. He wanted to strike quickly through the passing lanes while the Steelers were in disarray. His first two passes failed, but he tried again. He hit on a 14-yarder to Moses and a first down on the 16.

Preston tried to run and was stopped after a two-yard advance. Weese returned to the pass but failed to connect with Moses. On third down he decided against the pass and went with a draw play to Otis Armstrong. The Steelers were waiting however, and dropped him after a three-yard gain.

That brought up fourth and five on the 11-yard line. A field goal would certainly give the Broncos a lift. Turner lined up a 29-yard try. He carefully marked the spot for his holder. The ball was snapped. Greene made a great charge at the line and penetrated deep into the Denver backfield. Then he reached up with his huge hand and blocked Turner's kick. The biggest defensive play of the game had a far-reaching magnitude. It stopped Denver's momentum and sent the Broncos off the field with their heads down. Neither team threatened for the rest of the quarter, and when it ended, Pittsburgh maintained a 19–10 lead.

The Steelers needed a spark, something to give them emotion for the final fifteen minutes. Early in the fourth quarter Bradshaw gave it to them. It came without warning, on one play. It was enough to put the game out of Denver's reach and insure Pittsburgh's position in the AFC championship game the following week.

Pittsburgh was in control of the ball on the Denver 45-yard line. There were some twelve minutes left when Bradshaw thought over a second and eight play. He looked at Stallworth in the huddle and called the bomb. As Stallworth streaked toward the Denver goal line, Bradshaw dropped back and cocked his strong right arm. The pass was unerring. Stallworth, running a deep post, leaped high into the end zone. He stretched his arms over cornerback Steve Foley, caught the spiral, and tumbled over the end line. It was an unbelievable catch. In his excitement Swann couldn't wait to clutch his partner Stallworth, who couldn't hold back his joy. It was the game-breaking touchdown. Gerela's conversion stretched the lead to 26–10.

But the Steelers weren't finished. Dennis Winston recovered Upchurch's fumble of the kickoff on the Denver 29-yard line. Bradshaw wanted to put the game away on first down. He tried Stallworth again in the end zone but missed. On second down a holding penalty on rookie running back Rick Moser brought the ball back to the Denver 38-yard line. Bradshaw

remained unruffled. He called another bomb in the huddle, this time for Swann.

The graceful Swann had been watched closely all afternoon. He had only one reception for fourteen yards, far below his norm. Swann took off. He needed all his speed and his moves to beat the coverage. He did. Bradshaw delivered the ball into his arms for a 38-yard touchdown. In less than a minute Bradshaw had produced two bombs to his two favorite receivers. The final one clinched it. Gerela's extra point merely made it 33–10. With just over ten minutes left to play there wasn't enough time for the Broncos to come back, not the way the Pittsburgh defense had been playing.

Noll was satisfied. In the waning minutes of the contest he began substituting. One by one he took out his stars so that they could be acknowledged by the happy throng. It wasn't raining anymore and the towels were waved furiously as each player left the field. It was indeed a complete victory, offensively and defensively, the kind that Swann had talked about earlier in the week. Everyone did what he was supposed to do. Like Bradshaw.

"We figured that they would rotate their pass defense to Swann and double-cover him," Bradshaw disclosed. "I couldn't see any sense getting Lynn killed by throwing into double coverage. I went to the weak side of the zone. I had a lot of room inside with Stallworth and I kept firing away at him. I also knew that Foley would be backing off John so he wouldn't get beat for a touchdown like he did in Denver. He was giving John a big cushion."

Almost lost in the excitement of Bradshaw's dramatic bombs was the fact that Harris ran for 105 yards in twenty-four carries. That gave him a total of 1,155 in twelve post-season games —against the best teams, too. It was the equivalent of producing a 1,000-yard season under the NFL's old twelve-game schedule.

"I didn't realize that," said Harris, who also set a postseason touchdown record of twelve with the two he had scored. "I guess I just feel it's a thing where everything goes. It's not a sixteen-game schedule, where you have to pace yourself sometimes. In the playoffs there's no second chance if you lose. Today we played a team that we had some tough situations with

Sam Davis leads the way off the line.

before, and I think a lot of people didn't think we could beat them. It was an emotional thing. I guess it's changed from Oakland to Denver."

The excitement of victory carried over to Greene. His block on the third period field goal attempt had turned the momentum. It was a money play.

"Steve Furness and I double-teamed their center," explained Greene. "We usually hit the gaps on the side of the center, but we noticed in the films that Maples has a hitch in his snap so we decided to double-team him. While he was hitching we got a good start, and we penetrated about three or four yards.

"We never put Denver down. I think all that kind of talk earlier in the week was coming from Denver maybe to put some psychology on them. I think we're a better football team, but you have to go out and show it, and today I think we did that."

They certainly did. The AFC championship was next.

THE AFC PLAYOFF

DENVER	3	7	0	0	10
PITTSBURGH	6	13	0	14	33

Denver: 9:10, first period—Turner, 37-yard field goal.

Pittsburgh: 12:27, first period—Harris, 1-yard run (kick failed).

Pittsburgh: 1:36, second period—Harris, 18-yard run (Gerela, kick).

Pittsburgh: 8:54, second period—Gerela, 24-yard field goal.

Denver: 13:04, second period—Preston, 3-yard run (Turner, kick).

Pittsburgh: 14:53, second period—Gerela, 27-yard field goal.

Pittsburgh: 3:29, fourth period—Stallworth, 45-yard pass from Bradshaw (Gerela, kick).

Pittsburgh: 4:03, fourth period—Swann, 38-yard pass from Bradshaw (Gerela, kick).

Jon Kolb (55) and Ray Pinney (74) stand up linebacker Randy Gradishar as Bleier (20) moves through the hole.

The AFC Championship

Bradshaw was sick. On Thursday before the biggest game of the year he came down with all the symptoms of the flu. He felt weak, he had a fever, he didn't want to eat, and he felt nauseous all the time. Still he showed up for the Steelers' practice on Friday morning. He worked a little with the offense but had to quit. It became too much for him. After the defense took over the practice session in the cold and damp of Three Rivers Stadium, Terry Bradshaw went into the locker room and vomited.

Bradshaw certainly had had better days, yet he didn't seem too concerned about his ailment. He dressed, got some medication from the trainer, and quietly went home to rest.

"It won't bother me for the game," assured Bradshaw. "I only missed a little work out there today when I went inside to throw up."

Bradshaw's health created some concern. Not enough to cause any alarm; Chuck Noll didn't seem upset by his star quarterback's condition. He played down its seriousness and insisted that Bradshaw would be ready to face Houston on Sunday in the AFC championship. Noll is never one to overreact in such situations.

Yet Bradshaw's illness brought back memories. Earlier in the week, reserve wide receivers Theo Bell and Jim Smith had been stricken with a virus but managed to recover quickly. It seemed like a familiar scene. In 1972, when the Steelers were playing the Miami Dolphins in the AFC title game, Bradshaw and about fourteen of his teammates had been bedridden with the flu. It was the Steelers' first appearance in a postseason game under Noll and the clever

coach had chided the out of town writers for bringing their unfamiliar germs to Pittsburgh without allowing his players enough time to develop immunity.

Perhaps even more important than Bradshaw's condition this year was the weather. The most promising outlook was bleak. Ice warnings were issued for Sunday. Pittsburgh was battered by a cold siege. It snowed on Friday and Saturday and temperatures were in the twenties. The snow was expected to continue the next day or give way to freezing rain. Whatever happened, the day would be far from dry.

Bradshaw had already accepted that fact. He had been experimenting with a pair of fingerless gloves designed to keep his fingers free while protecting the rest of his hands from the biting cold. Bradshaw seems unperturbed by inclement weather. Rather, he performs admirably under adverse conditions. In the snowbound next-to-last game of the season he had been brilliant against the Baltimore Colts. "It's not easy, but I don't mind," Bradshaw had said with a smile.

Bad weather or not, one thing was certain—the Houston game wouldn't be easy. Like Pittsburgh the Oilers were a very physical team. The clubs had played each other twice during the season. In the first game the Oilers had come from behind to defeat the Steelers, 24–17. More significantly, Houston had been the only team to defeat Pittsburgh in Three Rivers Stadium in 1978 and the first to win against the Steelers there in four years.

The second meeting had been just as memorable, and not only because the Steelers had de-

The Steelers shut down Earl Campbell and the Oilers' running game.

feated the Oilers in the Astrodome, 13–3. In the most aggressive game played in the NFL in a number of years thirteen Oilers and three Steelers had left the game with injuries. That's how hard these two chief Central Division rivals play against each other.

Houston was a hot club. It finished strongly in the second half of the season and reached the playoffs for the first time since 1967, as a wild card team. Besides a hard-hitting defense, the Oilers had an explosive offense fueled by quarterback Dan Pastorini, who like Bradshaw was having his finest year, and rookie running back sensation Earl Campbell, who led the entire NFL in rushing with 1,450 yards.

The Oilers had been steady and sure in their two playoff victories. In the heat of Miami they had stifled the Dolphins, 17–9. Earl Campbell's running threat had opened up numerous opportunities for Pastorini's play-action passes. The eight-year veteran had thrown for an eye-popping 306 yards despite playing with a plastic vest to protect the three broken ribs he had suffered against the Steelers in the twelfth game of the season.

A week later, in the cold of Foxboro, Massachusetts, the Oilers had rolled over the New England Patriots, 31–14, a team many thought would win the AFC title. In a game the Oilers controlled completely, Campbell had run for 118 yards and Pastorini completed twelve of fifteen passes as he threw for three touchdowns. Houston was for real, a most serious contender. They were looked upon as the league's Cinderella team.

Like Bradshaw, Pastorini had overcome years of criticism. And like the Pittsburgh quarterback he had excellent receivers to aim at, namely, wide receivers Ken Burrough and Rich Caster and tight end Mike Barber. Because Campbell was such a game-influencing force his first year, he enabled Pastorini to throw more effectively.

In many ways Campbell did for Houston what Franco Harris had done for the Steelers when he first came up. He removed a great amount of pressure from the quarterback. His consistent, big-yardage games enabled the Houston offense to control a game much more than it ever had in the past. Campbell was that good.

Steeler linebacker Jack Ham didn't lose sight of that fact. "What you do with Campbell is try to gang-tackle him," declared Ham. "I mean, Campbell is just a great running back, just awesome. You've got to get some help if you want to stop him. You've got to get people to the football when he's carrying it.

"You can't arm-tackle Campbell. No one man can bring him down, not with his great leg strength and that speed. You have to put a good hit on him and hope some of your other guys are going to be there, too. You saw what he did to New England. He ripped them. That's the problem against Houston. You know Campbell is going to get his yardage, no question about it. But you can't let him run free all day."

As the strong side linebacker, Ham was expecting to challenge most of Campbell's runs. But he also had to be wary of the pass and react quickly to his drops, something that no other linebacker in the NFL does better.

Pastorini presented still another challenge. "I came into the league seven years ago with Pastorini, and I always said he was smart and had a great arm," revealed Ham. "You have to respect his arm and his brain and his guts. The last two or three weeks he's been very impressive. He's put the ball on the money, called the smart game, and been in complete control. He's the key to their attack.

"Pastorini reads defense well and he sure knows how to handle the blitz. He was always a great quarterback, but now with Campbell there he's got a real running game and he's able to do more things. I guess the real new dimension Houston has is Campbell, and he's turned that team around. He's having a great year. Pastorini is having a great year. They've got ball control now, and their defense isn't on the field as much."

Bradshaw had seen enough of Houston over the years to realize why they had become so successful in 1978. He was aware of Campbell's value and could analyze their plan of attack.

"They'll come out and run Campbell down our throats," he reasoned. "Pastorini is going to run him on first down and on second down and come back with play-action to get our support people coming in. Then Pastorini will hit somebody behind our coverage. I think they'll try to keep us off balance.

Franco scored the Steelers' first touchdown less than five minutes into the first period.

(Left) Although he was battling the flu, Bradshaw thrived in the adverse weather conditions.

"The idea is to use Campbell to control the game. The best way to counter that is to tackle him, of course. I don't know who, but somebody's got to do it. I don't know what we are going to do, just play as hard as we can, I guess, and hope that he gets a charley horse or something."

Noll, too, analyzed the effectiveness of Houston's offense. His strategy was to force Pastorini to throw the ball more. He didn't want the Oilers to control the game on the ground, with Campbell. If his defense could neutralize Campbell then it could dictate what Houston could do.

"What we want to do is make them throw the football," Noll disclosed. "What we're talking about is a basic defensive philosophy, stopping

the run first. But when you make a team throw you have to avoid giving up the big play, like New England did last week.

"In a lot of their sets Campbell is the only one in the backfield, so you know he is going to carry the ball. And even when there are two guys back there you also know that he is probably going to carry the ball. Campbell is an added threat."

There was no discounting Campbell's value. The Steelers had to contain his running. That was the defensive game plan: Stop Campbell first and then play for the pass. Nothing fancy, just good execution.

"I never thought it was possible, but here's a case where one man has turned a team

Bradshaw looks for Randy Grossman as he gets by Oilers' defenders.

around," Jack Lambert offered. "It's almost impossible for one person to tackle Campbell alone. He has tremendous balance for a big man and he runs low to the ground. If you try to tackle him high he'll run right over you. The secret is to gang-tackle him.

"He's a lot like Franco. He's a big man who hurts you when he hits you, but he also has the agility to break a long one."

There was no question that it would be an aggressive game, no matter what the weather conditions. Power had to be met with power. As far as Campbell was concerned, the bad weather wouldn't affect him. He was planning to run

against the Steelers in snow, ice, rain, or whatever.

"I played in the rain quite a bit in college," mentioned Campbell. "I played one game in the ice and snow in high school. I don't think it'll play too much of a factor. I worked all week on learning the plays and learning which ones we're going to be running Sunday. I'm just going to go out and not change nothing. Just play the same type of game. I feel as though we can run on them. We have before.

"You enjoy playing against them. They are real clean and physical. I got to tip my hat to them. In the NFL, I think they are the most physical team. I think this game will be more physical than the last. You can expect anything in a game between Houston and Pittsburgh."

Bum Phillips, the Houston coach with the intriguing name, knows only too well about playing against the Steelers. In the six years he's been in Houston, the rivalry against Pittsburgh has been his greatest, largely because both teams are so alike.

"You've got to be crazy to want to play Pittsburgh three times," drawled Phillips. "But we wouldn't want it any other way right now. Do we expect another war? It usually is war when we play them. At least it always has been in the past. I don't see any reason why it should change."

Neither did Pastorini. After all, he was a target just as much as Campbell. Besides his broken ribs he also had a sore elbow and a tender knee. Against Miami two weeks before, he had resembled a mummy with all his wrappings. Yet he's a fierce competitor, much like Bradshaw. Campbell's presence in the lineup soothed his ailments.

"As Bum Phillips says, he gave the Oilers a sword to fight with," exclaimed Pastorini. "Earl gave us an added dimension we never had before, a running back who could go outside or up the middle and take three or four defenders with him.

"He's a back the defense has to adjust to. And so I can go to play-action instead of dropping back each time. People used to say that I was bomb-crazy, but that was when Ken Burrough and I were the only weapons we had.

"But now they have to respect the run, and that's the reason our line has given up the fewest sacks of any team in the NFL. Earl is one of the best running backs who ever carried a ball. So when I start getting punished I give the ball to him and let him take the punishment. He can handle it better than I can.

"Sunday's game is between the two best teams in the NFL. It will be the Super Bowl game. It will probably be the most physical game we'll ever play. Good old-fashioned football. But as far as I'm concerned, I can't get hit any harder than I did against the Patriots. That flak jacket saves me. I'm going to wear it the rest of my life."

Bradshaw, too, was looking for a hard-hitting game. Like Pastorini, he was a prime target, but he'd been in that position before. It just intensifies in a game the magnitude of an AFC championship. Over the years he had played in four of them, so he knew what to expect. That this year's rival was Houston merely made him more aware of the game's physical nature.

"Getting hit is part of the game," Bradshaw rationalized. "You don't like it, but you accept it. You just don't think about getting hit or being hurt, only of the job you're trying to do. You've got a game where people are running into each other all the time, so there is bound to be injuries.

"Houston is a good defensive team. They are a good challenge, aggressive, a hard-hitting team. I enjoy playing against them and that's the truth. They pass rush pretty well, but we have an outstanding offensive line and they have never really got to me more than once or twice so far.

"Running the ball is probably the most important thing in playing them. The last game we ran the ball fairly well and didn't throw well at all, but we won. The first game we threw well but didn't run that well, and we lost.

"If I'm convinced that I can throw the ball against them then I'll do just that. If I'm convinced that we can run it then that's what'll be. I went into our last Houston game and I know I didn't play a good game. I wanted to win so badly I didn't risk doing anything that would hurt us.

"I wound up getting myself tight as a drum. We won despite me. So I want to go into this game relaxed, win, lose, or draw. I want to walk off the field at the end and be able to say, 'Hey, I played my best.' "

For Bradshaw to feel that way the Steelers had to neutralize a strong Oiler defense. Just as Campbell and Pastorini had to be controlled offensively, Pittsburgh had to diminish the effectiveness of Curley Culp, the key to the Oilers' active 3–4 defense. Culp, a rugged 270-pound, eleven-year veteran, was the focal point of Houston's three-man line. It meant that center Mike Webster, Pittsburgh's best offensive lineman, would be occupied with Culp throughout the game. The success of Culp—and probably the rest of Houston's front seven—lay in his ability to overpower the opposing center and take command of the line play.

"Curley is a punishing player," Webster

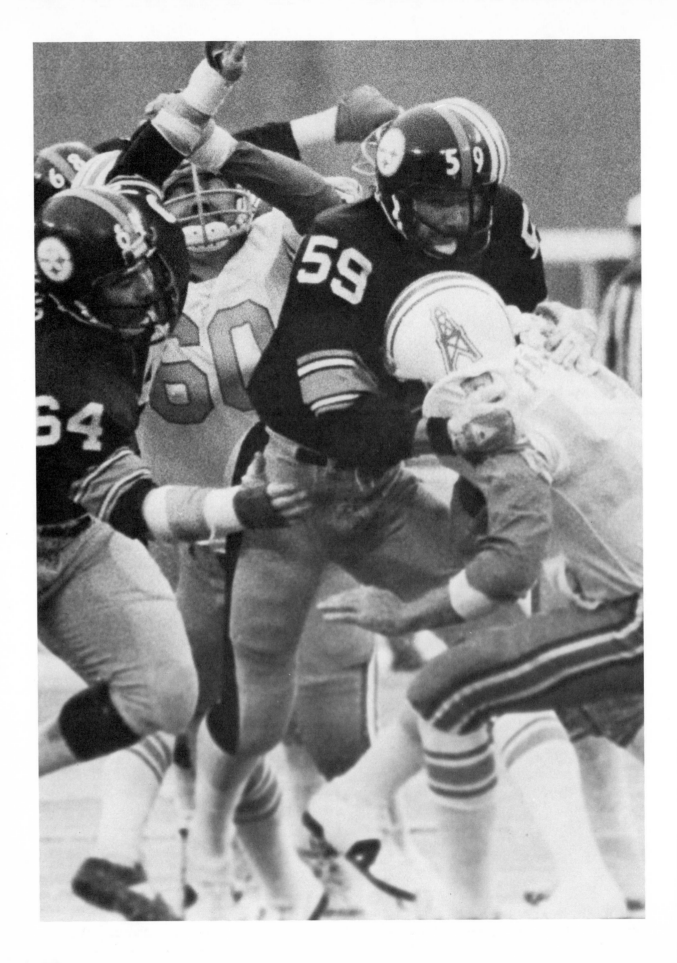

pointed out. "It's always a hard-hitting game for me against Houston, and that's the way it has to be. If I'm not physical as I can be I'm just going to be annihilated. The physical part doesn't bother me, though. I've been through it so many times, and anyway, it doesn't hurt that much. Not for long. Two, three days and I'm okay again.

"Against Curley you come out of a game all tired out, drained, because it takes such an effort to block him. There are some things I can't do to him, like taking him one on one and blowing him out. Nobody blows him out. I might get a little movement on Curley, but not the same as on other players. You just have to keep the pressure on him enough so he can't come off and make the tackle.

"Sometimes I think Curley weighs closer to a ton. There are a lot of tremendous nose guards around the league, and they all give you a beating. But Curley, he has got such massive strength he's physically my toughest opponent. He's a very quiet guy, very intense. We don't talk out there. He's got other things on his mind besides talking to me. I don't get into that, either. I have to concentrate. I can't be gabbing.

"The most I ever said to Curley was 'nice game' after it was over, but before a game, nothing. I guess maybe our matchup is really the key. The line of scrimmage is where it's going to be won or lost. We have to control it there. Our offense has to control their guys, and our defense has to contain them, Campbell, Pastorini, guys like that. We can't turn the ball over, can't make mistakes, and that's the crux of it. We not only have to score points, we have to keep their offense off the field."

What Culp and the rest of the Oiler defense wanted to do was to keep Bradshaw in the pocket. They felt he was much more effective when he scrambled out of the pocket, in much the same manner he had demonstrated against the Denver Broncos the week before. Containing Bradshaw would be a big step in shutting down the Steeler offense.

"We'll try to keep Bradshaw inside our outside containment," emphasized Houston linebacker Steve Kiner. "You can give him some

(Left) Jack Ham, with help from Steve Furness, moves in to sack quarterback Dan Pastorini.

Lynn Swann holds on as he slides toward a first down.

things. You can't eliminate their whole offense, but you don't want them to take what they want to take.

"What we have to do is also try to take Franco away from them because if Bradshaw ever establishes the running game on you he'll kill you with play-action passes. We've always been well prepared for the Steelers. A lot of ingredients go into getting ready for a team like that.

"They looked great against Denver. They always play like that when they get into the playoffs. They're really a first-class organization. To get past them is really going to be something. The way everybody's been playing, I think we can put it together.

"Pittsburgh to us has always been an obstacle. We feel like we're as good a football team as they are. We haven't had the amount of success they've had, but we've always played their butts off. We feel our quarterback is better than their quarterback. We feel our defense can play better defense than their defense, and they feel the same way about us."

That said it all. Yet all the pre-game rhetoric wouldn't influence the outcome of the game. It had to be accomplished through execution, and that's just how the bookmakers looked at it, too. They established the Steelers as favorites, offering seven points as a mark.

There was no minimizing the fact that game day was miserable. The cold snow of the night before had turned to a freezing rain, which was even worse. There was no way anyone could keep wet, cold hands warm. At least with snow the hands and the body wouldn't have been as wet. The artificial turf of Three Rivers Stadium was saturated. There were even puddles of water in various spots on the field. If anything, it was the Steelers' kind of day. They were used to playing in bad weather but the Oilers were accustomed to the covered Astrodome.

It was remarkable that 49,417 fans actually showed up, but they wanted a Super Bowl, and this was the last stop on the way to Miami. What was a little bad weather, anyway?

The referees put the game in motion with the coin flip at midfield. Houston won the toss and with it the right to carry the football first. A big roar went up as Roy Gerela kicked off. The war had begun.

John Kirden returned Gerela's kick thirty-

Jack Lambert stops Campbell for a short gain.

three yards. The Oilers began their first offensive play in good field position from their own 34-yard line. As Bradshaw had predicted earlier in the week, Pastorini ran Campbell right away. The first time Ham dropped him for a two-yard loss. The second time he gained four yards. On third and eight the Steelers played the pass effectively and dropped Caster for a yard loss. Houston had to punt.

Theo Bell brought Cliff Parsley's short punt back twelve yards to the Pittsburgh 43. It was excellent field position for Bradshaw. Harris carried first and skirted left end for four yards. Before the next play Elvin Bethea, the Oilers' end, was charged with a five-yard offside penalty. Harris then carried again and this time went up the middle for five more yards and a first down on the Houston 43.

Then Bradshaw struck. He sent Swann on a deep pattern down the sideline and delivered the ball accurately to him on the 9-yard line. The Steelers were primed to score. Harris got two yards on a play straight up the middle, designed to keep the Oilers in tight. On second down Bradshaw sent Swann and Stallworth to the right side. As they broke into the middle they took most of the Oiler defense with them. Then Bradshaw deftly handed the ball to Harris, who turned the right corner and went into the end zone untouched. Gerela added the extra point, and Pittsburgh jumped in front, 7–0, after only 4:58 had gone by.

Pastorini was determined to establish his running game after the kickoff. Five straight times he gave the ball to Campbell. Houston made only one first down, however, and Parsley punted from the Pittsburgh 48-yard line.

Beginning on his own 36, Bradshaw immediately went to the air. Since the Oilers were intently watching Stallworth and Swann, Bradshaw turned to Randy Grossman. First he hit Grossman with a 29-yard pass. Then he came right back to his tight end for another fourteen yards. In two plays Pittsburgh was threatening, on the Houston 21. Harris got two yards before Bradshaw decided to go on top again, but this time the Oilers were waiting for him. Willie Alexander picked off a pass intended for Swann on the 10-yard line.

After Campbell picked up four yards Pastorini wanted to pass. He threw to Caster, but Blount came up quickly and intercepted. He ran for sixteen yards before he was tripped up on the Oiler 26. For the third time the Steelers had the ball and for the third time they threatened.

Bleier advanced three yards to the 23. Harris didn't get anywhere and on a third-down pass Bradshaw couldn't connect with Grossman. So Gerela entered to attempt a 40-yard field goal. It fell short. Though the Steelers had the early momentum, they still had scored only once.

On first down, Pastorini, attempting to pass, was sacked for a five-yard loss by Greenwood. The Steelers then capitalized on a turnover. Campbell fumbled when he was stopped for a yard loss, and Ham propitiously landed on the ball. The Steelers were in business again.

Harris almost gave the Oilers the ball back. He, too, fumbled after gaining two yards, but Gerry Mullins alertly covered the ball on the 15. Bradshaw decided to send Bleier around the right side. He caught the Oilers by surprise, and Bleier made it to the end zone. The kick by Gerela gave the Steelers a 14–0 lead as the first quarter came to a finish.

Even though the Oilers began in excellent field position on their 47-yard line after the kickoff, they still couldn't generate any movement. Early in the second quarter they punted again. This time the Steelers had trouble holding on to the football. Bradshaw fumbled on an aborted play and lost eleven yards, and it wasn't until the ball sloshed ten yards farther back that Mullins again recovered it for Pittsburgh on the Steelers' 12-yard line. On the very next play Harris gained six yards but fumbled. Linebacker Robert Brazile claimed the ball for Houston on the Pittsburgh 19.

The Oilers had a chance to get back into the game. On a third-down play from the 16, Blount was penalized for pass interference on wide receiver Ken Burrough. Houston had a first down on the 4-yard line. Campbell got only a yard. Pastorini tried a pass to Caster that failed. On third down Campbell tried to go outside and was dropped for no gain. The Oilers had to settle for a 19-yard field goal by Toni Fritsch and now trailed, 14–3.

Following the kickoff Bradshaw had the Steelers moving and appeared ready to score another touchdown. In eight plays he drove the

Ron Johnson takes off for thirty-four yards after grabbing a Pastorini pass.

Steelers sixty-one yards to a first down on the Houston 7. After Harris fought his way for two yards, Bradshaw called Stallworth's number. But the pass was badly thrown and cornerback Greg Stemrick intercepted in the end zone.

After three plays the Steelers got the ball back. Bell's 19-yard punt return gave them the ball on the Houston 39. Harris, who was having trouble holding on to the ball, lost a yard, fumbled, but managed to recover. Bradshaw wanted to hook up with Swann and did so with a 17-yard strike to the 23. On first down Bleier got three yards, and then Harris got the ball. He fumbled once again, however, and the Steelers recovered the ball on the 30-yard line.

The weather was creating havoc on the field. The icy rain made it almost impossible to hold on to the ball securely. The outcome of the game would unquestionably be determined by which team could take advantage of the many mistakes.

Two running plays gave Houston a first down. With two minutes remaining the Oilers had the ball on their 47. Pastorini then hit running back Tim Wilson with a quick eight-yard pass to the Pittsburgh 45. The Oilers appeared headed for a score before the first half ended.

Pastorini then hit his other running back, Ronnie Coleman, for a 15-yard gain. Ham stripped him of the ball, however, and then recovered the fumble on the Steeler 31-yard line. The Oiler drive was suddenly aborted.

Bradshaw hurried onto the field. A pass interference call placed the ball at midfield. Then Bradshaw executed a 13-yard screen pass to Bleier. Using the two-minute offense, the Steelers lined up quickly, and Harris rambled around right end for eight yards to the 29. Bradshaw didn't want to waste any more time. He looped a pass to Swann in the end zone and the Steelers had their third touchdown with only fifty-two seconds left. Gerela again converted.

But there was more to come. John Dirden fumbled Gerela's kick on the 17-yard line without even being hit. Harris tried the right side and didn't get anything. Bradshaw called a pass and drilled a perfect one to Stallworth in the end zone. There were only thirty-three seconds remaining when Gerela's extra point gave Pittsburgh a 28–3 advantage.

On the first play after the kickoff Coleman fumbled and Steve Furness recovered on the

Houston 24. There were only twenty seconds showing on the clock when Bradshaw came back on the field. He immediately tried a pass to Swann in the end zone, but it was incomplete. On the next play Houston drew a five-yard offside penalty. There were only four seconds left. It was time to send Gerela in to line up a 37-yard field goal. He made it, and the Steeler margin soared to 31–3. The suspense was gone. In just fifty-four seconds the Steelers had scored seventeen points!

"Now I know how Jim Bowie must have felt at the Alamo," snapped a Houston aide in the press box.

He was right. The Steelers had gained 287 yards to Houston's fifty-four and produced sixteen first downs to the Oilers' five. In just thirty minutes of football Houston had fumbled six times and the Steelers five. The championship game was far from a Rembrandt.

There were thirty more minutes to play, yet they proved uneventful. The game was already over. Gerela kicked a 22-yard field goal in the third period that was set up by another Steeler interception. Later in the quarter Bleier was caught in the end zone for a one-yard loss and a safety. The score became 34–5, and that's the way it ended after a listless final quarter.

The Steelers had won the AFC championship convincingly in wretched weather. They had reason to celebrate long into the cold night.

"The weather was terrible, but I just threw the ball and hoped it didn't wobble," explained Bradshaw, who completed eleven of nineteen passes for 200 yards and a pair of touchdowns. "The balls were totally saturated. This was actually worse than the Baltimore game that was played in the snow. I fumbled several snaps. They were all good snaps, but my hands were cold.

"I couldn't believe what was happening just before the half. I mean, we scored a touchdown, then kick off, and they fumble it and we get it back and score again. I was looking at Chuck Noll and laughing. Here the rain is coming down, I'm chilled to the bone, the ball is miserably wet and the stickum on it is turning to grease with all that water on it, and I'm laughing. I said, 'Well, we'll go out there and see what we can do.' God, it was amazing.

"I was gonna throw early, make Houston

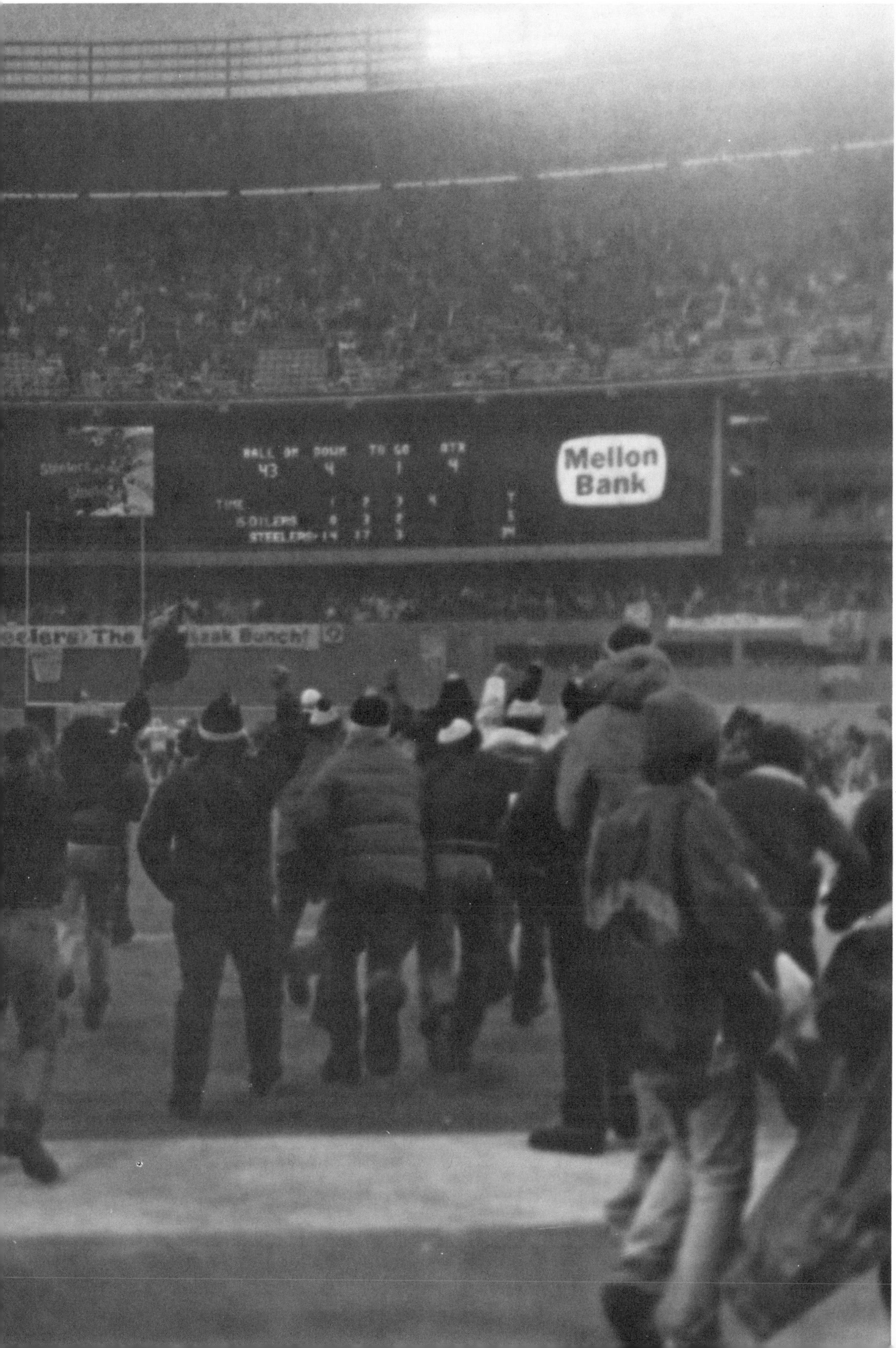
Mellon
Bank

realize it. I knew they were gonna be out to stop Franco, so my idea was to come out and throw, use a lot of play-action and back them up. Then I hit a couple and loosened them up so we could run it. We'd have been in trouble if we couldn't run the ball at all. The big thing is that I had time to read their coverages all day.

"Our big lead had to destroy them. No one's gonna score four touchdowns and a field goal in the second half of a catch-up game in that kind of weather.

"I was weak on Friday. I couldn't throw. I even messed up my play-calling today. I took tons of medication and liquids. I felt weak today before we warmed up, but then I got all pumped up and felt no effect. The virus went away automatically when I walked onto the field and the fans started going crazy. It was better than aspirin. No doctor can prescribe better medicine."

No one, player or coach, could prescribe how to hold on to the football on such an afternoon. Pittsburgh fumbled six times, as did Houston, to set new team records. The total of twelve by both teams was also a championship game record. Campbell and Harris also set ignominious records with three fumbles each.

But the bottom line was that Pittsburgh had executed when it was crucial. The offense put points on the board and the defense got them the ball. That's what football is all about.

"Our offense got 'us to the point where we didn't have to honor Houston's running game anymore," pointed out Ham, who had two fumble recoveries, a sack, and an intercepted pass. "It was tough on Pastorini. A day like this was hard to play catch-up. When you're behind like they were you can throw play action out the window."

There are some who used the rain and playing conditions as an excuse, but not Elvin Bethea. "It was raining on both sides of the field," snapped Bethea, "and in the middle."

In the end the Steelers were going to Miami. That's where the rainbow was.

THE AFC CHAMPIONSHIP

HOUSTON	0	3	2	0	5
PITTSBURGH	14	17	3	0	34

Pittsburgh: 4:58, first period—Harris, 7-yard run (Gerela, kick).
Pittsburgh: 13:51, first period—Bleier, 17-yard run (Gerela, kick).
Houston: 5:21, second period—Fritsch, 19-yard field goal.
Pittsburgh: 14:08, second period—Swann, 29-yard pass from Bradshaw (Gerela, kick).
Pittsburgh: 14:27, second period—Stallworth, 17-yard pass from Bradshaw (Gerela, kick).
Pittsburgh: 14:56, second period—Gerela, 37-yard field goal.
Pittsburgh: 7:14, third period—Gerela, 22-yard field goal.
Houston: 11:10, third period—Washington, safety (tackled Bleier in end zone).

Super Bowl XIII

The taunting had begun. As soon as Terry Bradshaw arrived in Miami he heard it. Thomas Henderson, the loquacious Dallas linebacker, fired the first verbal salvo for Super Bowl XIII by trying to offend the Pittsburgh quarterback. He remarked that Bradshaw couldn't spell "cat" if you spotted him the "c" and the "t." It was an insulting reference to Bradshaw's intelligence. Bradshaw was tired of the subject. Henderson was obviously attempting to upset Bradshaw, but Terry wouldn't have any of it. The game was too big for him to get upset over what some one else had said. Besides, he had heard it all before. He was keenly aware that responding to Henderson was just what the Dallas player wanted. Bradshaw handled it well.

"I thought it was spelled with an 'o,' " he quipped.

Dallas' free safety Cliff Harris came on even more strongly in his attempt to rattle Bradshaw. Harris remembered Bradshaw well. In Super Bowl X Harris blitzed Bradshaw in the closing minutes of the fourth quarter and knocked him out of the game with a vicious tackle. A split second earlier, however, Bradshaw had fired a beautifully timed 64-yard touchdown bomb to Lynn Swann. It was the pass that beat the Cowboys, 21–17, although Bradshaw never got to see it. He was knocked unconscious and removed from the field. It wasn't until the game was over and his teammates entered the locker room that Bradshaw found out who had won the game.

"We're going to have to knock Bradshaw out early, make him dizzy early," warned Harris.

"I'll be looking to hit him, not to hurt him, but that doesn't mean he might not get hurt."

Bradshaw saw through the Cowboys' ploy. In the five days before Super Sunday he handled the scheduled interviews with the press and the incessant questions well. If he was upset by any of the Cowboys' baiting remarks, he certainly didn't show it.

"Two things I don't do," emphasized Bradshaw. "I don't play intimidation through the press or on the field. I won't fool you. I think about it. I think about why somebody would say something like that. I think I'll send him a Bible message. If that is what Harris feels he has to do, then he'd better do it, but do it cleanly. I'm not used to this kind of attention. I would be a lot happier sitting out there by a poolside by myself, spitting tobacco."

Bradshaw didn't relish all the pregame hype, yet he couldn't escape it. Quarterbacks unquestionably attract the most attention, and with the year Bradshaw had had, it was no wonder he was in such demand by the brigade of writers who spew verbiage week-long to newspapers all across the country. It can get repetitious, but that's how big the Super Bowl is.

If Bradshaw had had a choice he would have much preferred to think quietly about the game alone. His way of relaxing would have been to pick on his guitar and warble some country and western songs. He enjoys listening to Hank Williams or Larry Gatlin. The music soothes him. A sad country song means a lot to him.

"That kind of music keeps the good things in perspective," explains Bradshaw. "It feeds part of my soul. If you go to the Super Bowl and lose, you feel inferior, you let people down. If you win, you feel dominant, important. You're either the hero or the goat, determined by what happens on the football field. There is such a big accent on winning.

"It's already been a great season. This is just the dessert. The game plan is in. I'm just here to have fun. I don't really care for all these big interviews. I'd much rather go one-on-one with a writer after a game."

The game was the thing for Bradshaw. This one was special, bigger than the rest. The long eighteen-game season had come down to one. The success of the entire 1978 campaign rested on a single game. Bradshaw thought about it in the quiet hours so much that he couldn't sleep.

"I was up at 5:30 this morning," disclosed Bradshaw. "I haven't slept since I've been here. Do you know who I thought about when I first woke up? Billy Kilmer! I don't know why, except perhaps he was on my mind before I went to bed. We had been talking about Kilmer and the racehorse he had bought. It just stayed on my mind.

"Jim Mandich and I then went to breakfast and who do you think was there? Why, Billy Kilmer! I didn't tell Billy that I had dreamt about him and telling him that he looked so young. Yet, we didn't talk football. We talked about racehorses. He didn't give me any advice about the game.

"I just enjoy the challenge of the game. I'll use whatever works out there, whatever is successful, whether it's the pass or the run. It will probably be played close to the vest starting off and open up as it goes along.

"I've known so much insecurity in my career. I can laugh about some things that happened to me and cry about some others. But now I can't build up all my hopes around one game. Of course I want to beat Dallas, but it won't destroy my whole year if I don't. Like I said, the Super Bowl is dessert, but we've already had one heck of a fine dinner.

"I like to come into a game feeling prepared and relaxed. Then we get into a tough spot and I just think, 'I'll call this little old play here, and if this guy is not open I'll turn around and hit this guy.' Take Dallas. They'll double-cover Swann and Stallworth, but soon one of them

Bradshaw moves out of the pocket early in the game.

Under intense pressure from Mike Hegman, Bradshaw fires another completion.

will slip past half that coverage. Then it's man-to-man, and we got 'em. It's not life or death. We're just playing with them."

There was no doubt that Bradshaw was loose. He didn't even show the strain of not having had enough sleep. His attitude reflected the whole season. Bradshaw was relaxed and seemed to be enjoying himself despite having to face the brigade of media people. None of his interviews grew heavy. In fact, he kept them on the light side, which eliminated any tension. He was indeed having fun.

"When he's playing like he's having fun out there, it sets the tone for the whole team," Joe Greene said with a smile. "I think that's the way he's going to play from this day until the end of his career. It's the approach he's going to go out with. It takes all that pressure off him. He used to go into every game thinking, 'I've got to perform,' and he'd be tight. This season he realized that if things don't work out one day he'd go out next Sunday and try again.

"He's not on trial any more. When you can go out there and be free, then you're going to have outstanding games. That's why I think he's going to have a good one against Dallas on Sunday."

Greene said a lot, when he expressed the Steelers' confidence in Bradshaw, who has been unjustifiably maligned practically every year he's been with the club.

"The rap Bradshaw takes is nonsense," said George Young, then pro scouting director of the Miami Dolphins. "People keep saying he's dumb, but often that's because of his style. He just plays football like it was meant to be played. He's a fine player and he's going to wind up as a Hall of Famer.

"Bradshaw is a rough, tough guy. He doesn't take anything from anybody. When he runs with the ball he looks as if he likes to run with it. When he gets hit he looks as if he likes to get hit. The Steelers have the character of the Steel City. This is an intimidating team, a blood-and-guts team. And it's best characterized by Bradshaw."

Obviously, the theme for Super Bowl XIII was intimidation. It was as if the Steelers had been cast in the role of villains. They would even look the part in their black jerseys. Everybody knows the good guys wear white. Actually,

the Steelers play hard, basic football in contrast to the Cowboys' finesse. Nor do the Steelers like to engage in the off-field banter that the Cowboys were spouting from their hotel thirty miles north, in Fort Lauderdale.

Henderson set the tone, yet none of the Steelers were affected by him. It was really the writers covering the game who were attracted to Henderson's flippant tongue. And Henderson cleverly used the press to gain as much publicity as Joe Namath had had ten years earlier in Super Bowl III. It was no wonder Henderson was called Hollywood.

"When my mouth is running my motor is running," exclaimed Henderson. "If I was mute I couldn't play this game. I put a lot of pressure on myself to see if I can play up to my mouth. I think the Steelers should be favored. The reason is because they've played the most consistent over the season. The first half of the year we didn't play as well as the last half, but I think we're peaking now.

"It's going to be like the Los Angeles game. We'll shut them out on defense, and Hollywood will have the final word again. I said the Rams didn't have any class and that's why they didn't get to the Super Bowl. The Steelers do have class, but they lack depth. That's their problem. If they lose anybody they're gonna be in trouble.

"Look at their tight end Randy Grossman. He's a substitute. With Bennie Cunningham out, that little guy's gonna have trouble over there with me. He's the smallest guy I ever played against. I've handled Russ Francis and Riley Odoms, just to name a few. Grossman's a backup tight end. How much respect can you have for a backup tight end? I mean, he's the guy that comes in when everybody else is dead. He's the last hope.

"I don't care for Jack Lambert, either. Why? 'Cause he makes more money than I do and 'cause he don't have no teeth. He's like Dracula. He should at least keep a mouthpiece in there or something. Count Lambert, that's what I call him.

"I'll tell you, they have a real intimidating defense. They're the Pittsburgh Killers. I think the best thing for our defense to do this week is pull out the acetylene equipment, welding gear, and go into the steel mill and disrupt it. I took welding. I know all about metals and steel. They got the Steel Curtain and we got the Great Wall of China. I think our defense is equal to or stronger than their defense. I think it will be a defensive struggle, but we will prevail."

Cliff Harris, who had earlier attempted to unsettle Bradshaw, now switched to his favorite topic, Lynn Swann. Unless Harris was involved in a safety blitz or Bradshaw decided to run with the ball he would not have much chance of getting a piece of the quarterback.

But Swann was another matter. The lithe wide receiver would be out in the open in no man's land. That's Harris' territory. Around the NFL he is known as a hitter. His teammates call him Captain Crash. He and strong safety Charlie Waters are perhaps the best tandem in the league.

In Super Bowl X Swann had had a fantastic game. Harris hadn't forgotten it. The amazing Swann had caught four acrobatic passes for 161 yards, including the winning touchdown near the end of the game.

As a free safety Harris goes where his instincts take him. He follows the ball rather than trying to cover a particular receiver. Swann, after his spectacular year, was certain to be around the ball. Harris was quite aware of what Swann's presence in the lineup meant.

"Sure, I'm thinking about hitting Swann if he goes for the ball," snapped Harris. "I'll hit him as clean and as hard as I can. Sure, he may get hurt from the shot. When a ball is thrown to a pass receiver there is always one moment when the receiver is in tune with the ball, one moment when he's unable to protect himself.

"If you remember those old western movies, John Wayne would always throw something at the bad guy and then punch him when he's catching it. That's my philosophy. It's all within the rules, but I want to make a receiver aware that I'm there. I want him to be looking for me or thinking about me. When his quarterback calls a pattern over the middle, I want him to be thinking, 'Oh, no.' Sometimes when a receiver comes out of the huddle he's looking at me in a different way, and then I know that it's a pass over the middle.

"Intimidation is part of the game plan for every good football team. One of the main reasons you play a physical game is because of intimidation. You see the effectiveness of it all the time. You hit receivers hard and they'll miss passes. You hit certain running backs hard and they'll stop running. Much of the belligerent talking going on for this game is a carryover from Super Bowl X. In that game thirteen Cowboys suffered injuries of some sort, and yet not a single penalty was called on the Steelers. If the officials had just one eye open they would have seen all the slugging Pittsburgh was getting away with.

"We're going to do everything we can physically, within the bounds of the rules, and try our best to intimidate them. If it works it works. And if it doesn't—oh, well."

Greene was puzzled by all the emphasis put on intimidation. In fact, he seemed a bit disturbed by it. The Steelers were made out to be the big bad bullies of the NFL. The nickname hung on him when he first joined the Steelers didn't help his image any. "Mean" Joe Greene he really isn't.

"I never can quite understand that intimidation factor," snapped Greene. "They've always called us the intimidators. We just play hard, rock 'em sock 'em football. Dallas comes out and plays the same way we do. We're similar types. That's why we have respect for them. It's competition plain and simple, not just talk about you don't like what I say or the way I dress.

"The word 'intimidate' has a bad connotation the way it's being used. Those other guys play football, too. They haven't gotten to the Super Bowl because they were a bunch of pussycats. Dallas is a physical club. They are primarily known for their finesse because they do so many things. They are capable of coming right at you, but that's not their philosophy. They like to force you into making mistakes.

"I think getting Tony Dorsett was one of the greatest steals in the NFL. It almost made them illegal, illegal in the sense that they are so good nobody can stay on the football field with them. He's that good. He fit right into their system.

"I wish I had the courage to go out and talk the way Dallas is doing. There's always a lot of talk from Texas about how good their organization is in all areas, playing, scouting, coaching. I don't doubt it. They have to be good to be in the Super Bowl year in and year out.

"Our team is in the same class, we take a

Despite this kind of defense during the whole game, Swann snagged seven Bradshaw passes.

different approach. We don't say we're the best. We just go out and do what's necessary to get the job done. It's the philosophy of this club not to talk about what we're going to do. I've been with it a long time, I'm comfortable with it, and I accept it. I'm feeling really good about this club, really. I watched a videotape of the Houston game five times, and each time there was something new that I was thrilled about."

One of the things that thrilled him was Swann's four catches for ninety-three yards and a touchdown in horrendous weather. That performance was one reason Harris was attempting to rile Swann before Sunday's game. Actually, it was not the first time that Harris tried to unnerve the swift Swann. Harris had used the same tactics in Super Bowl X.

"I read the stuff that Harris said," Swann disclosed. "He was trying to intimidate me. He said that because I had a concussion I would be afraid out there. I said to myself, 'To hell with it. I'm going out there and play 100 percent.' Sure, I thought about reinjuring myself, but it's like being thrown by a horse. You've got to get up and ride again immediately or you may be scared the rest of your life. The doctors left it up to me whether I wanted to play or not. I decided to play.

"Now he's talking again. I guess he thinks he can verbally intimidate me. The last time he made comments like that I was the most valuable player in the game. You think he would have learned."

Although it was new to him, Henderson's intimidation jive didn't concern Grossman in the least. Grossman is not one to seek the limelight, but Henderson's remarks needed some answers. Grossman didn't make a big issue of it but smiled at the sudden notoriety.

"The last time I was down here nobody knew who I was," replied Grossman, who scored Pittsburgh's first touchdown in Super Bowl X. "Anything Henderson says isn't going to inform me on what's going on. I just ignore him. Good grief, you can only reach so high a level and how much more hyped-up can you be? The only reward I want is coming back to Pittsburgh as world champions."

Henderson could bad mouth Grossman all he wanted. It didn't make any difference to Grossman, or, more importantly, to Bradshaw.

He realized that Grossman had played an important role during the season and could play an even larger role in the Super Bowl.

"People didn't show any respect for our tight end this year," Bradshaw said. "We threw more to our tight end this year and had complete success with it. The guy is underrated by NFL standards, but he did a good job. Our running game certainly didn't suffer, and he can catch the ball better than Cunningham, although he might not do as good a job running with it afterwards."

Unquestionably the best runner the Steelers had was Franco Harris. Strangely, the Cowboys didn't make any mention of him in all the pregame hysteria. Maybe they respected him too much. Quite possibly they realized that they couldn't intimidate Harris with words. Amid all the excitement Harris was nevertheless totally relaxed.

"It's a do or die situation," explained Harris. "You either win or you lose, and I don't like to be a loser. I always like to come away with something. I always feel we should win, and I go out and try to make that happen. If you don't win you go home. If we hadn't won the past two games we wouldn't be in cloudy Florida now.

"I haven't thought too much about the game. I'm just relaxing right now, but when it's time to play I'll be ready. I'll say this: It's been a good, happy year, one that I have enjoyed playing and have reached a goal we wanted to reach. There's one more big game left.

"It's hard to answer now whether this team is better than the ones of 1974 and 1975. However, I feel that we are closer as a team. I feel that we are enjoying it more, and I hope on Sunday it will get better.

"Since this has been Bradshaw's best year, maybe the pressure has been relieved from my shoulders now. I hope so. But it's going to be tough to get past Dallas' front line no matter what happens. I doubt if they'll be taking our running game lightly. It would be nice if they would, but we have so many weapons out there for them to concentrate in any one area of our offense."

Dallas linebacker D. D. Lewis, for one, was concerned about Harris' running ability. No one could tell him that Franco wasn't the key to the

Franco holds aloft the ball after his 22-yard touchdown in the fourth period.

Steelers' running attack. In Super Bowl X the Dallas defense had keyed on Harris. They had wanted to be certain that he wouldn't be effective and had succeeded in limiting Harris to an average game back then. In twenty-seven carries Harris was "held" to eighty-two yards.

"He's the running game," emphasized Lewis. "They use Rocky Bleier to keep you off balance, but their whole running game is Franco. So if you stop him you shut down their running game."

Bleier, however, had come to play. He was ready. He knew the Steeler running game was geared to Harris, but he never complained. Bleier can never be completely ignored, because he can block and catch passes as well as run. He has a sense of where it's at, both on and off the field. And to Bleier, that's important.

"Franco's record speaks for itself," declared Bleier. "He's the major carrier, then we go to the wide receivers. I get what's left over. I remember one specific play the last time we were

Jack Ham moves in on Staubach as he prepares to pass.

here. We had a fourth and eight on the Dallas 39-yard line with a minute and a half left. Noll decided to go for it. He called '36 power.' I said, 'He's got to be nuts. He needs eight and he gives me the ball.'

"This is just one in a series of games. I suppose it will go down in history to some degree. But in actuality, of what importance is it? Living through that experience in Vietnam makes you realize that whether you win or lose this game is not as important as whether you get your act together personally.

"I suppose football can be compared to conventional warfare. You have the generals with their boards out, plotting strategy, fighting over a piece of turf. The difference is that in football there is always tomorrow, always a next year.

"Football is a game, not a life or death situation. There are other experiences, more highs, more lows. It's sad that some players make it everything. In time they'll learn. In Vietnam nobody wanted to admit that it was a waste. That would be like admitting your own existence was worthless. Over time I came to agree that it was senseless, all the time and money and lives, senseless. But that doesn't answer for all the people maimed and disabled."

Bleier's roommate, Jack Lambert, plays football with savage beauty. He is not a person to taunt like Henderson. He doesn't like playing against Dallas, not because of the Cowboys' personality but because of their style of football.

"Computerized football is not my kind of football," snarled Lambert. "I'm not a very good computer. Quite possibly, playing in the old days was more fun. I used to love to play Oakland. You knew they were going to run over Art Shell and Gene Upshaw every play and run right at you. That's why I hate to play Dallas. There are so many formations you have to watch for. You have to be under control."

Lambert's sidekick, Jack Ham, was under complete control. He's not one to engage in verbal warfare. He merely shrugged his shoulders and laughed at Henderson's verbiage.

"What Henderson says doesn't affect me one way or the other," remarked Ham. "From what I see, he feels he plays better the more he puts himself on the spot. That's fine. I don't think any comments in the paper will make any differ-ence. You won't see forty-five players come out foaming at the mouth at Tom Henderson. He just makes good copy.

"I've never seen Henderson play except on television once. I don't know how good a linebacker he is. If all that talk pumps him up to play better, fine. I don't think two or three players on this team have mentioned his comments in the newspapers. That's not going to affect us one way or the other on Sunday. If you need some article to get you pumped up for a big game like the Super Bowl then you're in sad shape. This is the biggest football game of the year.

"All-Pro honors are fine. They are nice trophies to have when you're finished playing football. But I'm in this game for one thing, to come to the Super Bowl and win it. The years we weren't here, I can take all those all-Pro honors and forget about them, because you are in a team sport here. It means so much more to me to play in the Super Bowl and consider your team the best in the league. That's all my goals are. If I get all-Pro honors along the way, fine.

"I'd like to be remembered as a quality football player. I never really had any individual goals. It's too much of a team sport for me. I talked to Joe Greene after the second Super Bowl, and there is no way that you get a feeling of accomplishment like you do in winning a Super Bowl, in comparison to being all-Pro, most valuable player, or whatever. It means so much more to me than any individual goals.

"I don't take compliments well, about what's written about me in the press. We look at our game films on Tuesday and I am concerned about how well my other linebackers think I have played or how good a football player I am. I don't care if people in Texas or California know about Jack Ham. I know how I play and how my peers think about me, and that's all I care about.

"It's fine with me if people think I'm a good linebacker. If I'm a good player it's because I've got L. C. Greenwood in front of me and Joe Greene next to him. Look, I'm just a very quiet person. It's not my style to say Dallas is a bunch of bums. Sometimes people get the wrong impression and think that I'm aloof, that I don't want to be bothered with people. I enjoy my private life. I can't be Tom Henderson. It's not my style."

It was perhaps L. C. Greenwood's style. Early in his career with the Steelers, long before his gold-colored shoes, he became known as "Hollywood Bags," after quarterback Terry Hanratty dreamed up a trade that would have sent Greenwood to the Los Angeles Rams. He got hung with the nickname "Bags" and later on "Hollywood."

"He stole my nickname," snickered Greenwood. "I'm the only Hollywood around. There's no room for two Hollywoods in Miami. There's only room for one, and I'm fighting for possession of my nickname. Henderson may need that for an emotional pickup, and if that's the way he wants to get up for a game I can't complain. Me, I just work hard."

Nobody worked any harder than Joe Gordon, the Steelers efficient publicist. By the league's estimate Super Bowl XIII had more press requests than any previous one. As a result Gordon was kept busy all day and into the night. Besides the press there were the Madison Avenue types who wanted Steeler players to endorse products.

"There isn't another team that has as many players doing endorsements," remarked Gordon. "The Dallas Cowboys, for instance, have a lot of endorsements, but most are being done by one player, Roger Staubach. There's no question that we are the most marketable team in the NFL right now. We have more players who are well known than any other team in the league. After you get past the top two or three players on most teams, the rest of the guys, for the most part, are anonymous. With us it goes about ten deep."

One such advertisement appeared in a local newspaper and a magazine. It was for a hairpiece that Bradshaw was endorsing.

"It's the best endorsement deal I ever had," disclosed Bradshaw. "Why am I doing it? Because my hair's been balding for nine years and I have no inhibitions about wearing a hairpiece. When I put my wig on I feel young. This week I'm wearing my blond piece. When I wear it I get the feeling I had when I was twenty years old.

"You never know what these advertisers want. I'm a country boy. I've got a gift of gab, but that doesn't sell products. It depends on what the advertisers are looking for. If they want an intellectual look they'll take Bob Griese or somebody in golf. If they want a cowboy—well, there's a bunch of us around. Me, I can play both sides of the coin."

One advertising executive who was down from New York was Michael Severide of Uniroyal. He was there just to enjoy the game, however, and root for the Steelers. He had wisely used Greene and a number of others in a commercial in the early part of the season.

"I'm glad we got them while we did," explained Severide. "If they win on Sunday then they would be so appealing to advertisers that they could command double what they normally get."

"In one commercial I go up against a tire that's tougher than me," said Greene. "I punch the tire and make mean and tough faces at the tire. I challenge the tire to show that it's tough.

"Most of my commercials show my tough, mean Steeler image. For instance, I'm doing a commercial for a company that makes bread. I go into a restaurant and order a sandwich made with this bread. I look very stern. I have a deadpan kind of stare. But when the sandwich comes I smile, and the announcer says, 'See, he's smiling.'

"I'm not trying to fight that image, either. It's helped me. When people greet me as 'Mean Joe' and little kids call me mean, I don't mind. It's a commercial thing. I don't think the image depicts my personality. I think I'm a lot more —well, I'm not mean. No, no, no. I'm a lot more easy-going than that. I'm a quiet kind of guy. I'm even shy."

He may be, but the other Steelers certainly aren't. They all push commercials of some sort. Lynn Swann promotes a department store; John Stallworth, pizza; Jack Ham, a bank; Franco Harris, spaghetti; Rocky Bleier, contact lenses; and Mike Kruczek, shaving lotion.

Meanwhile ticket scalpers were pushing Super Bowl tickets at prices from $200 to $250, a considerable mark up from the $30 specified on the ticket. But, after all, each team had won two Super Bowls and one of them would be the first to win three. The game also represented the first rematch in Super Bowl history. Despite the inflated prices, tickets were hard to find.

Joe Greene and the Steel Curtain were on top of Staubach all day, sacking him five times.

John Stallworth moves downfield with his 75-yard touchdown reception.

As the days began to dwindle, the talk centered on the game. The Steelers were earlier established as favorites from three to four and a half points. It appeared an accurate assessment. The teams were evenly matched. Roger Staubach was the NFL's top passer, and Bradshaw was ranked second. That fact alone gave every promise that this would be the most exciting Super Bowl of all.

Pittsburgh and Dallas had similar strengths. Each had an explosive offense and an overpowering defense. The Cowboys, with their flex defense, led the NFL against the run, yielding just 107.6 yards a game. The Steelers were right behind, topping the AFC by allowing only 110.9 yards. Remarkably, in winning their last seven games, Pittsburgh's famed Steel Curtain hadn't allowed over 100 yards on the ground in any one game. They were primed.

Most experts felt the Steelers had a slight edge on defense because of linebackers Jack Ham and Jack Lambert. Ham is like a matador; nobody can drop back or come up more quickly, and he is extremely intelligent. No middle linebacker in the NFL has better lateral pursuit than Lambert. Ham and Lambert influence opposing offenses more than any two players around.

On offense the Steelers also appeared slightly stronger. Harris, with his big game potential, offset the speedy Tony Dorsett. It was, however, the Steelers' excellent wide receivers, Swann and Stallworth, who rated an edge over the Cowboys' Drew Pearson and Tony Hill. In any case both the Steelers and the Cowboys were stronger than they had been when they had met each other for the first time three years ago.

It appeared that the Steelers would rely to a great extent on Bradshaw's strong arm and the speedy legs of Swann and Stallworth. The three had been the NFL's deadliest passing combination all season long.

Pittsburgh center Mike Webster intimated how important the Steelers' air attack was to the offense. "Teams have geared themselves to stop our running all year long because they know our backs don't have great speed," he said.

Certainly Harris would face a strong challenge in Dallas' flex defense. It's a staggering defense that isn't vulnerable to trap plays. Instead, the linemen up front take a split second to read a play before committing themselves, usually blocking the running lanes in the process. Yet Harris enjoyed his biggest day as a pro against Dallas in 1977, when he rumbled for 179 yards. And Franco still owned the Super Bowl record for rushing, 158 yards against Minnesota in 1975.

The early morning hours of Super Sunday were bleak. A heavy, wind-swept rain brought dismay to early risers. Yet the weather was no problem for Bradshaw. He hadn't slept well and because of all the noise and telephone calls had changed his room in the middle of the night. Bradshaw wouldn't have been upset if it had rained all day. He seems to excel while playing in bad weather.

There's a time-worn saying in Miami that if you don't like the weather just wait a little while and it will change. The 79,641 fans who were holding tickets in the open Orange Bowl certainly hoped so, especially those with the $200 ones. It rained hard all morning. A half hour before the four o'clock kickoff, however, the rain stopped. Incredibly, despite the heavy rains, the field was in excellent shape. There were no water spots or muddy underfooting.

The Steelers' offensive unit was scheduled to be introduced first. As the Pittsburgh defensive team came trotting out to the sidelines Donnie Shell was so emotionally charged he leaped high into the arms of Greene. It didn't appear as if he would ever come down. The adrenalin was flowing, all right.

It was carrying the offense, too. Swann came running out waving a yellow towel and encouraging the loyal Pittsburgh partisans to stand and flip theirs. In sharp contrast the Cowboys were methodically introduced to the crowd of 78,656. (Nine hundred eighty-five ticketholders didn't show up.) The mood was set. Only the coin toss was left.

George Halas, who had started all this professional football mania in the 1920's, had the honor of flipping the coin. For the occasion the venerable eighty-one-year-old owner of the Chicago Bears had purchased a $320 gold piece. He arrived on the field in style, in the front seat of an antique car. Dallas won the toss and elected to receive, but a happy Lambert raced off the field clutching the valuable gold piece.

The excitement of the opening kickoff roared through the stands as Roy Gerela booted the

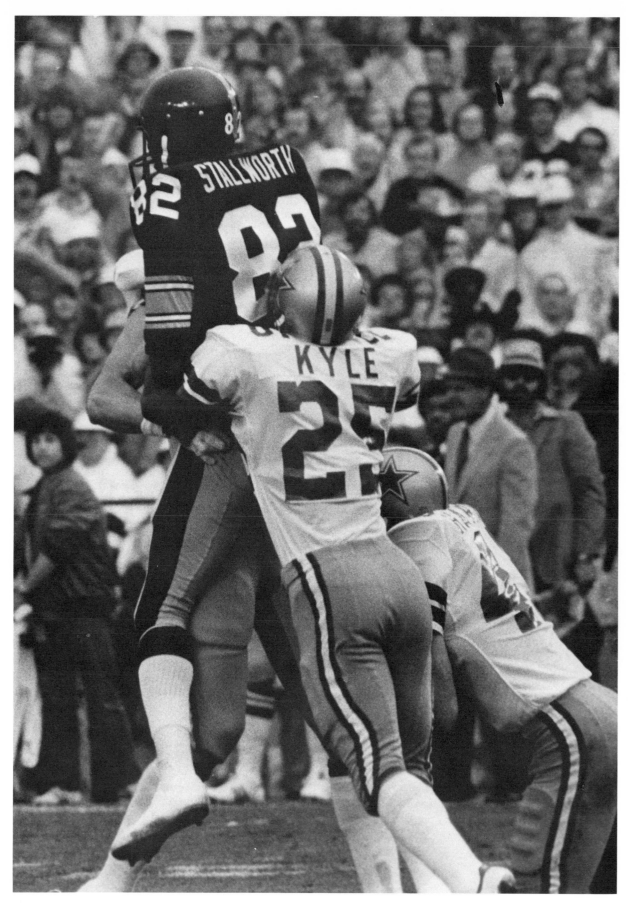

Despite the swarm of Dallas defenders Stallworth holds on for one of his three catches.

ball to Dallas' Butch Johnson. The swift wide receiver caught the ball on the 5-yard line and streaked his way for twenty-three yards before being dropped on the 28-yard line. As Staubach led the Dallas offense onto the field the Cowboy fans made their presence known.

On the first play of the game Staubach pitched out to Dorsett, who swept wide to his left for a nine-yard gain. Staubach called Dorsett's number again, and the speedy Dorsett burst through the middle for sixteen yards to Pittsburgh's 47-yard line. After Robert Newhouse was stopped for no gain Staubach went back to Dorsett. He took a pitchout, this time on the right side, and sped for thirteen yards and another first down on the Steelers' 34. Suddenly the Cowboys were threatening. Dorsett had carried the ball three times and found holes in the Steel Curtain for thirty-eight yards!

Dallas wanted a quick score. Disdaining crisp, straight-ahead football, they turned to a gimmick play, but it backfired. On an attempted double reverse wide receiver Drew Pearson fumbled. Defensive end John Banaszak opportunistically pounced on the loose football on the 47-yard line. The snappy Dallas drive was quickly aborted.

Now it was Bradshaw's turn. He hustled onto the field. He had good field position, yet he didn't want to be too anxious. On the first play, as Staubach had done, he pitched out to Franco Harris. Charlie Waters had anticipated the play and dropped Harris for a yard loss. Then Bradshaw tried the middle, where Harris could only get two yards. On third and nine Bradshaw expected a blitz. He was right. Nevertheless he quickly tossed a 12-yard pass to Stallworth over the middle. The Steelers had a first down on the Cowboys' 40.

Bradshaw then went back to Stallworth, this time down the left sideline. The rangy wide receiver caught the ball but was out of bounds. After Bleier gained only two yards Bradshaw was again faced with a big third down play. He delivered. He hooked up with Grossman for ten yards and a first down on the Dallas 28. The Steelers were in scoring range.

The gutsy Bradshaw didn't wait. He lobbed a soft 28-yard pass to Stallworth in the left corner of the end zone. Stallworth reached up and pulled the ball down for the game's first touchdown. Roy Gerela's kick made it 7–0, with 9:47 remaining.

After the Cowboys reached the Pittsburgh 39 following the kickoff, the Steel Curtain took command. On second and seven, Steve Furness broke loose to pin Staubach for a 12-yard loss. Then Dwight White charged through and dropped the Dallas quarterback for a 10-yard loss. The Cowboys were shoved back to their own 39 and forced to punt.

It appeared as if the Steelers would score again. On a third down play Bradshaw sent Harris over the middle and hit him with a 22-yard pass to the Dallas 42. Then Bradshaw connected with Swann on a 12-yard strike down the right sideline for another first down on the 30. Then Bradshaw made a mistake. He sent Stallworth wide left and stared him down the field. Linebacker D. D. Lewis, seeing Bradshaw's gaze, reacted. He moved in front of Stallworth and picked off Bradshaw's throw.

Near the end of the first quarter Bradshaw was victimized again. On a third down play he was sacked for a two-yard loss by Harvey Martin and fumbled the football. Ed "Too Tall" Jones quickly pounced on the ball on the Steeler 41-yard line with just a minute remaining. Dallas had a chance to strike back.

Newhouse moved for only two yards on first down. Staubach sent Pearson deep into the end zone, but Shell jumped and deflected the possible game-tying touchdown pass. With only six seconds left Dallas went into the shotgun formation on third down. Staubach found Tony Hill open on the 26-yard line. Hill ran by Shell down the left sideline, past Mel Blount who was shielded by Drew Pearson, and into the end zone. It was the only touchdown scored in the first quarter against Pittsburgh all season. With no time remaining on the clock Rafael Septien kicked the tying point.

After the ensuing kickoff Bradshaw fell prey to yet a third mistake. Confronted with a third and ten on his own 48-yard line, Bradshaw dropped back to pass. The Cowboys called a double linebacker blitz. Henderson locked Bradshaw in his arms and stripped the ball. Mike Hegman picked it up and before anyone realized what had happened ran thirty-seven yards for a touchdown. Septien's kick was accurate, and suddenly Dallas led, 14–7.

Franco breaks through the line on his touchdown ramble.

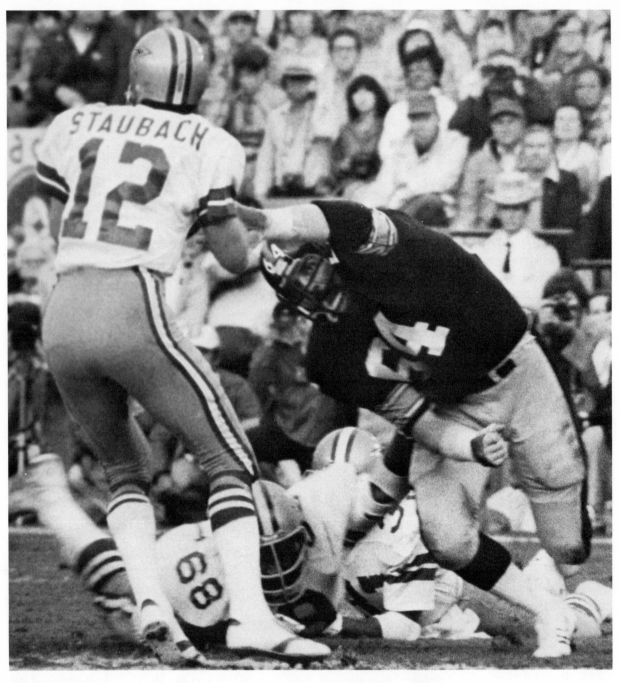

Steve Furness leaves two Dallas defenders in his wake and heads for Staubach.

What was worse, Bradshaw had hurt himself, unbeknownst to the crowd. Luckily, his left shoulder, not his right, was injured, and he had it checked on the sidelines after the fumble. Although Bradshaw was in pain he nevertheless returned to the lineup after the kickoff.

He didn't attempt to pass right away. Instead he gave the ball to Harris twice. Both times Harris tried the left side and managed a total of five yards. Bradshaw was in an obvious passing situation on third down and five from his own 25-yard line.

Bradshaw sent Swann on a deep post, but he attracted too many defenders. He looked at his secondary receiver and discovered that Stallworth was wide open on the 35. Stallworth sped past Aaron Kyle and then outran every other defender straining to catch him. He ran sixty-five yards to complete a 75-yard touchdown play. Gerela's kick tied the game at 14–14.

With five minutes left in the first half the Steelers tried to break the deadlock. On third down and eight from the Dallas 23, Hegman blitzed Bradshaw and dropped him for an 11-yard loss. Gerela was sent out to attempt a 51-yard field goal. Though Dallas was wary of a fake, Gerela followed through with his attempt. The ball traveled far but wasn't quite long enough; it hit the crossbar to the moans of the crowd.

Dallas began to drive. In five plays Staubach led the Cowboys from their own 34 to the Steelers' 32. On first down Staubach called a pass. Mel Blount guessed that Staubach would throw. He cut in front of Drew Pearson on the 16-yard line and ran thirteen yards with the interception.

Bradshaw reasoned he had enough time to get on the board again, especially after Dallas was penalized fifteen yards on the interception. He put the ball in play on his own 44-yard line. A holding penalty set the Steelers back to the 34. Bradshaw looked up at the clock; there was only 1:44 left in the half. Then he looked down the right sideline and found Swann for a 29-yard pass to the Dallas 37. He went back to Swann on the next play for twenty-one more yards to the Cowboy 16.

A pass failed. There were forty seconds left. On second down Bradshaw went with the run, and Harris broke free for nine yards. Now it was third and one on the seven. Bradshaw had the Cowboys guessing. Would he go for the first down? Bradshaw alertly called a pass-run option to his right. Dallas defended against the run. Bradshaw reacted immediately. He lofted a high pass to Bleier in the end zone. The doughty back leaped and with his legs stretched open clutched the ball between his hands. It was a fine effort. Gerela's kick pushed Pittsburgh's margin to 21–14 just before the first half concluded.

Two things were certain during halftime. One was that the halftime entertainment would be long, much longer than in any regular season game. The other was that the fans in the Orange

Bowl and the millions watching on television were witnessing an exciting game spiced with big plays. The Steelers and the Cowboys had already totaled thirty-five points!

Bradshaw had already enjoyed a big game. He had completed eleven of eighteen passes for three touchdowns and 253 yards and was nearing Super Bowl records in those categories. He had control of the air like a pilot about to shatter the sound barrier. His critics were mute now. Bradshaw was picking Dallas apart.

The Pittsburgh faithful anxiously awaited the second half kickoff. The Steelers were to receive. The fans thought that Bradshaw would pick up where he had left off in the first half and turn the game into a rout. He certainly had shown a hot hand. If Bradshaw could get another quick touchdown, the Cowboys would definitely be in trouble.

Yet the first two times the Steelers had the ball in the third period they couldn't even produce a first down. Bradshaw completed only one of the three passes he attempted. It looked as if the Steelers were playing cautiously. That Stallworth left the game with severe leg cramps might have caused Bradshaw to pull back somewhat.

After fielding a punt midway through the quarter, the Cowboys had excellent field position. They had a first down on the Pittsburgh 42-yard line. Staubach tried a surprise play. He handed the ball to Dorsett, who faked going through the line, then stopped, turned, and lateraled the ball back to Staubach. Hill sped down the sidelines. Staubach threw deep into the end zone but rookie cornerback Ron Johnson knocked the ball down.

Dorsett took a pitchout and gained four yards. On third down, Staubach kept the drive alive by hitting Preston Pearson with an eight-yard pass for a first down on the Steelers' 30. Dorsett then got a yard, Scott Laidlaw seven, and then Dorsett gained another five yards and a first down on the 17. The Cowboys were riding in for a score.

Staubach tried to get it all on first down. He sent his tight end Billy Joe Dupree down the right sideline but overthrew him. He then sent Dorsett up the middle, and the second-year star burst for seven yards before Shell stopped him on the 10-yard line. Dallas had a third and three

Steve Courson (77) and Sam Davis (57) give Bradshaw plenty of time on this one.

and called time out. Staubach went over to the sidelines and conferred with coach Tom Landry about the next play. When the game resumed, the Cowboys lined up with two tight ends. The 38-year-old veteran Jackie Smith came into the lineup. Staubach bent over the center. He analyzed the Steeler defense and began to bark his signals. Lambert sensed a pass and blitzed. Staubach got his pass off, however, a soft throw to Smith, who was all by himself in the end zone. He reached back, slipped, and the pass hit him on his chest. Smith fell over backwards and the ball bounced on the ground. A certain touchdown was lost.

The Cowboys had to settle for a field goal. There was some slight confusion when Septien ran onto the field as some of the Dallas players felt they should try for a touchdown or at least a first down. But Septien calmly booted a 27-yard field goal to trim Pittsburgh's advantage to 21–17, with 2:36 left in the period.

When Bradshaw hit Stallworth's replacement, Theo Bell, with a 12-yard pass for a first down on the Steeler 44, it appeared that he had the offense moving again. He suffered a couple of bad breaks, however, on his next two passes to Swann. Swann juggled the first pass and then dropped it. Bradshaw came right back to him on the same sideline pattern, but the reliable receiver dropped the ball as he was hit by cornerback Benny Barnes. When Bradshaw was blitzed for a three-yard loss on third down, Pittsburgh's drive fizzled as the quarter neared its end.

When the final period began, the Steelers still clung to a 21–17 edge. After the Cowboys failed to mount a scoring threat they punted deep into Pittsburgh's territory. Bradshaw put the ball in play on his 15-yard line. Harris managed only two yards on a pitchout. On second down linebacker Bob Breunig exerted pressure on Bradshaw and caused him to underthrow Bell on the left side.

Bradshaw was now confronted with an important third down play. If he didn't convert it, Craig Colquitt would have to punt from deep in Steeler territory. It would offer the Cowboys an excellent opportunity to secure prime field position. Bradshaw had to execute whatever play he called perfectly. He did, with one yard

to spare. He zipped a nine-yard pass to Grossman that provided a first down on the 26.

Bradshaw now had a little more room. He turned to Swann. This time Swann grabbed a 13-yard pass for another first down on the 39. Harris picked up five yards to move the ball to the 44. Bradshaw decided to pass on second down. He dispatched Swann down the right side on a post pattern.

Barnes kept alongside Swann, however. It was a foot race. The two bumped, and Barnes fell down on the Dallas 23-yard line. As Swann was about to make his cut, he fell, too. He reached out and tried vainly to catch the ball. Swann looked for a referee's flag. He saw field judge Fred Swearingen drop his and signal a tripping penalty on Barnes.

The Cowboys fumed, but to no avail. The Steelers had a first down on the 23-yard line. A short pass to Swann gained four yards. Harris leaned forward for two yards and the Steelers looked at third and four on the 17. Pittsburgh was assessed a five-yard penalty for taking too much time that put the ball back to the 22.

It was now third and nine. Bradshaw reasoned that the Cowboys would blitz again as they had done on the penalty down. He called a trap over left tackle. It was Harris' play and it worked perfectly. Harris burst through the line with the speed of a halfback and ran untouched into the end zone. Gerela's kick gave the Steelers a 28–17 lead with 7:10 left in the game.

Gerela's kickoff was short. Tackle Randy White, who had a fractured left hand that was heavily wrapped, couldn't control the ball on the 24-yard line. It rolled loose to the 18, where Dennis Winston recovered it for the Steelers. Pittsburgh had a golden opportunity.

Bradshaw didn't hesitate. He called Swann's number deep. Bradshaw uncorked a long pass toward the back line of the end zone. It looked too long for Swann to reach, but the gifted receiver, who has a flair for circus catches, ran hard, jumped, reached out as far as he could, and pulled the ball down. It was the most dramatic catch of the day. When Gerela added the extra point, Pittsburgh's margin ballooned to 35–17, with only 6:51 showing on the clock.

Yet Dallas never quit. Staubach, who had

Furness holds aloft a single finger that says it all — Number One.

been in tough spots before, led the Cowboys back. He drove them eighty-nine yards in just eight plays, hitting Dupree with a seven-yard touchdown pass. Septien's conversion cut Pittsburgh's adanvtage to 35–24, with only 2:23 remaining.

But time was Dallas' enemy now. Still, the Cowboys pressed, ever hopeful. Their hopes rose when Tony Dungy fumbled Septien's onside kickoff. Rookie Dennis Thurman recovered for Dallas on the Cowboys' 48-yard line. The clock showed 2:19 left.

Immediately Staubach went to the pass. He had to throw and throw and hope for a quick touchdown. There was an incomplete pass, then a completion, then a sack. But Staubach kept throwing, even when he was confronted with a fourth down and eighteen on the Steelers' 38. A 25-yard completion to Drew Pearson gave him life. Then on the four-yard line he drilled a pass to Butch Johnson in the end zone for a touchdown. Septien's conversion pulled Dallas to within four points, 35–31, but time was the biggest barrier. There were just twenty-two seconds remaining.

Another onside kick was evident. The Steelers placed some extra players on the first line. They were ready for the kick. They couldn't afford another mistake now. Septien aimed his short kick. It went toward Bleier. He carefully fell on the ball to clinch the victory. The Steelers became the first team in the history of the NFL to win three Super Bowls. The night was theirs.

The swarm of press made it practically impossible to reach the victorious Steeler dressing room. Access was delayed while Commissioner Pete Rozell presented the Super Bowl trophy in front of a television camera to Art Rooney and his sons, Dan and Art Jr. The dour owner showed controlled joy. For forty-two years his team had never won anything. Now, in five years, the Steelers had won three Super Bowls. No other team could equal that.

After the doors to the dressing room finally opened, the horde of writers sought out Bradshaw. They were directed to a large interview area in another section underneath the stands. Bradshaw, calm and relaxed, stood on a platform, leaning against a steel girder. He propped one leg against the pillar and held a paper cup in his left hand to spit tobacco juice. The only

thing that disturbed him about the game he had just won was the early jubilation on the sidelines by his teammates.

"Guys were celebrating with six minutes left," said Bradshaw. "They were slapping hands, shaking hands, saying how great it was. But I remembered the last time we played the Cowboys. I said, 'Hey, it's not so great. The game isn't over.'

"Boys, you can't say anything bad about this game. This son of a gun was fun. Both teams played their game. I want all you guys to say, 'By God, this was an exciting game.' It was just that we were a little flat when the second half began. We weren't coming off the ball real well. I didn't call plays that well, and they got some pressure on us.

"I threw more passes today than any time in my life because I was having success. I don't think I had anything to prove except I never did play well against Dallas. I guess I always tried too hard not to lose to Dallas. I was very conservative. But this year I learned that you don't play well unless you relax and let your abilities go to work for you. I was going to play my game today, play-action passes, mixing it up, just throwing the ball, baby. I wasn't going to let the Super Bowl dictate to me. I was going with what got us here. Win or lose, I didn't give a hoot.

"Our offensive line did a hell of a job. They don't set up. They fire out on pass protection and then recoil. It slows down the pass rush. If I had really been passing I would have done more the second half. I don't think I had fifty yards in the second half. The second half the Cowboys blitzed, zoned, mixed it up. We tried to run more. We came out flat, not really with it. I think we were wishing the game was over.

"I was never looking to be a superstar. I was always in the back seat and I liked it. Franco and Lynn got all the publicity, and that took the pressure off me. Now all of a sudden I'm so great, so smart. I'm just not ready for it."

Neither were the Cowboys. For the first time in his nine-year career Bradshaw had passed for over 300 yards. He established three Super Bowl records: most yards passing, 318; most touchdown passes, four; and longest scoring pass, seventy-five yards to John Stallworth.

"Terry is just fantastic," exclaimed Stallworth. "He did what a quarterback has to do. He's a super quarterback. He read the zones. He deserves whatever comes his way, like the MVP. Nothing we accomplished out there surprised me. We got into the playoffs on our passing. There was no reason not to stick with it."

Stallworth's buddy, Swann, was right alongside. He wore a baseball cap and was ready to open a magnum of champagne. He was interrupted by the writers, who wanted to know about the pass interference call in the fourth period.

"Definitely pass interference," claimed Swann. "As a receiver all I was interested in doing was watching the ball. I really didn't see Barnes, but he did kick my leg. It felt like he got me twice. I don't think it was intentional, but you never know. All I was looking for was a flag. Franco's run after the penalty was the greatest run I've ever seen.

"You know, Terry had an awful lot to do with us playing so well. He played a great game. His play selection was good, and he was confident and relaxed. That was a big thing with him. When we came into the locker room at halftime he told us we were a great team, but we should go back out there, play football, have fun, and this team would make history.

"This is the greatest sense of satisfaction I've ever had. This is the best team that ever came to Pittsburgh. We now have an outstanding leader in Terry Bradshaw."

In the solemn Cowboy dressing room the players dressed quietly. Even Henderson. Reflecting on the loss, coach Tom Landry felt that the key to his team's defeat was the interference penalty called on Barnes.

"I'd say it was the ball game for Pittsburgh," Landry said with a sigh. "Obviously it was the key play. A tight game became lopsided quickly. When you have an alley-oop pass and Swann jumps all over you, it's hard to call interference. It looked like both went for the ball and collided. I don't think interference should be called unless it was pushing.

"That dropped pass hurt, too. Jackie Smith was so wide open that Roger wanted to be conservative. He threw so soft he wouldn't miss it, but he came in short, and Jackie's feet slipped as he went for it. We were running well then and had a chance to turn the momentum our way."

Above the din of the noisy Steeler dressing room Chuck Noll cut a quiet figure. He's like that. He never displays any emotion. He analyzes a victory in the same manner he would a defeat. Somehow one had the feeling that he expected to win.

"Our veteran players wanted to win this very badly, guys like Joe Greene, Terry Bradshaw, L. C. Greenwood, Franco Harris, Lynn Swann, John Stallworth, and especially our offensive line," remarked Noll. "The line gave Terry great pass protection against Dallas' great pass rush. I wasn't surprised at our passing success. We think we can do anything we set our mind to. They gave us a lot of man coverage. We didn't think they could cover us man-to-man, and we still don't think so.

"Do I think Terry proved himself? Terry had nothing to prove. After all, he has won three Super Bowls, and nobody else did that. I told the football team as we came off the field, I don't think this team has peaked yet."

He was already looking forward to next year.

SUPER BOWL XIII

PITTSBURGH	7	14	0	14	35
DALLAS	7	7	3	14	31

Pittsburgh: 5:13, first period—Stallworth, 28-yard pass from Bradshaw (Gerela, kick).

Dallas: 15:00, first period—Hill, 39-yard pass from Staubach (Septien, kick).

Dallas: 2:52, second period—Hegman, 27-yard run on fumble recovery (Septien, kick).

Pittsburgh: 4:35, second period—Stallworth, 75-yard pass from Bradshaw (Gerela, kick).

Pittsburgh: 14:34, second period—Bleier, 7-yard pass from Bradshaw (Gerela, kick).

Dallas: 12:24, third period—Septien, 27-yard field goal.

Pittsburgh: 7:50, fourth period—Harris, 22-yard run (Gerela, kick).

Pittsburgh: 8:09, fourth period—Swann, 18-yard pass from Bradshaw (Gerela, kick).

Dallas: 12:37, fourth period—Dupree, 7-yard pass from Staubach (Septien, kick).

Dallas: 14:38, fourth period—Johnson, 4-yard pass from Staubach (Septien, kick).

Appendix

RESULTS AND ATTENDANCE

Steelers 28 at Buffalo 17	(W, 1–0)	64,147
Steelers 21—Seattle 10	(W, 2–0)	48,277
Steelers 28 at Cincinnati 3	(W, 3–0)	50,260
Steelers 15—Cleveland 9*	(W, 4–0)	49,513
Steelers 28 at N.Y. Jets 17	(W, 5–0)	52,058
Steelers 31—Atlanta 7	(W, 6–0)	48,202
Steelers 34 at Cleveland 14	(W, 7–0)	81,302
Steelers 17—Houston 24	(L, 7–1)	48,021
Steelers 27—Kansas City 24	(W, 8–1)	48,185
Steelers 20—New Orleans 14	(W, 9–1)	48,525
Steelers 7 at Los Angeles 10	(L, 9–2)	63,089
Steelers 7—Cincinnati 6	(W, 10–2)	47,578
Steelers 24 at San Francisco 7	(W, 11–2)	51,657
Steelers 13 at Houston 3	(W, 12–2)	54,261
Steelers 35—Baltimore 13	(W, 13–2)	41,957
Steelers 21 at Denver 17	(W, 14–2)	74,104

* overtime

1978 TEAM STATISTICS

	Steelers	Opponents
TOTAL FIRST DOWNS	316	264
Rushing	133	105
Passing	149	119
Penalty	34	40
Third Down: Made/Att.	112–233	90–231
Third Down Efficiency	48.1	39.0
TOTAL NET YARDS	4987	4168
Avg. Per Game	311.7	260.5
Total Plays	1046	999
Avg. Per Play	4.8	4.2
NET YARDS RUSHING	2297	1774
Avg. Per Game	143.6	110.9
Total Rushes	641	513
NET YARDS PASSING	2690	2394
Avg. Per Game	168.1	149.6
Tackled/Yards Lost	25–271	44–361
Gross Yards	2961	2755
Attempts/Completions	380–212	442–221
Pct. of Completions	55.8	50.0
Had Intercepted	22	27
PUNTS/AVERAGE	66–40.0	82–39.4
NET PUNTING AVERAGE	35.2	32.4
PENALTIES/YARDS	108–943	106–954
FUMBLES/BALL LOST	35–17	33–21
TOUCHDOWNS	46	22
Rushing	16	11
Passing	28	10
Returns	2	1
TOTAL POINTS	356	195

1978 SCORING BY PERIODS

	1	2	3	4	OT	Total
STEELERS	63	135	76	76	6	356
Opp. Total	6	63	57	69	0	195

1978 SCORING

	TDR	TDP	TDRT	PAT	FG	SAF	TP
GERELA	—	—	—	45–44	26–12	—	80
SWANN	0	11	0	—	—	—	66
STALLWORTH	0	9	0	—	—	—	54
HARRIS	8	0	0	—	—	—	48
BLEIER	5	1	0	—	—	—	36
THORNTON	2	1	0	—	—	—	18
CUNNINGHAM	0	2	0	—	—	—	12
SMITH	0	2	0	—	—	—	12
BRADSHAW	1	0	0	—	—	—	6
BELL	0	1	0	—	—	—	6
L. ANDERSON	0	0	1	—	—	—	6
SHELL	0	0	1	—	—	—	6
GROSSMAN	0	1	0	—	—	—	6
STEELERS TOTAL	16	28	2	45–44	26–12	—	356
Opp. Total	11	10	1	22–21	26–14	—	195

1978 RUSHING

	No.	Yds.	Avg.	LG	TD
HARRIS	310	1082	3.5	37	8
BLEIER	165	633	3.8	24	5
THORNTON	71	264	3.7	27	2
MOSER	42	153	3.6	15	0
BRADSHAW	32	93	2.9	17	1
DELOPLAINE	11	49	4.5	19	0
MAXSON*	4	9	2.3	7	0
SWANN	1	7	7.0	7	0
KRUCZEK	5	7	1.4	8	0
STEELERS TOTAL	641	2297	3.6	37	16
Opp. Total	513	1774	3.5	30	11

1978 RECEIVING

	No.	Yds.	Avg.	LG	TD
SWANN	61	880	14.4	62	11
STALLWORTH	41	798	19.5	70	9
GROSSMAN	37	448	12.1	26	1
HARRIS	22	144	6.5	15	0
BLEIER	17	168	9.9	32	1
CUNNINGHAM	16	321	20.1	48	2
SMITH	6	83	13.8	29t†	2
BELL	6	53	8.8	15t	1
THORNTON	5	66	13.2	24	1
MOSER	1	−1	−1.0	−1	0
BRADSHAW	0	1	—	1	0
STEELERS TOTAL	212	2961	14.0	70	28
Opp. Total	221	2755	12.5	49	10

1978 INTERCEPTIONS

	No.	Yds.	Avg.	LG	TD
DUNGY	6	95	15.8	65	0
BLOUNT	4	55	13.8	35	0
LAMBERT	4	41	10.3	24	0
JOHNSON	4	24	6.0	21	0
SHELL	3	21	7.0	20	0
HAM	3	7	2.3	7	0
WAGNER	2	34	17.0	20	0
TOEWS	1	12	12.0	12	0
STEELERS TOTAL	27	289	10.7	65	0
Opp. Total	22	212	9.6	31	0

1978 PUNTING

	No.	Yds.	Avg.	TB	In 20	LG	Blk.
COLQUITT	66	2642	40.0	4	14	58	0
STEELERS TOTAL	66	2642	40.0	4	14	58	0
Opp. Total	82	3228	39.4	6	18	60	0

1978 PUNT RETURNS

	No.	FC	Yds.	Avg.	LG	TD
TERRY*	7	0	80	11.4	24	0
REUTERSHAN**	20	0	148	7.4	18	0
BELL	21	2	152	7.2	18	0
SMITH	9	0	65	7.2	13	0
SHELL	1	0	6	6.0	6	0
STEELERS TOTAL	58	2	451	7.8	24	0
Opp. Total	38	9	239	6.3	42	0

1978 KICKOFF RETURNS

	No.	Yds.	Avg.	LG	TD
THORNTON	1	37	37.0	37	0
L. ANDERSON	37	930	25.1	95t	1
DELOPLAINE	1	19	19.0	19	0
MAXSON*	2	33	16.5	21	0
SMITH	1	16	16.0	16	0
MOSER	1	8	8.0	8	0
MULLINS	1	0	0.0	0	0
STEELERS TOTAL	44	1043	23.7	95t	1
Opp. Total	60	1336	22.3	40	0

1978 FIELD GOALS

Yards	1–19	20–29	30–39	40–49	50+	Total
GERELA	1–1	6–5	8–3	9–3	2–0	26–12
Opp. Total	0–0	4–3	10–6	9–5	3–0	26–14

1978 PASSING

	Att.	Comp.	Yards	Pct.	Avg./Att.	TD
BRADSHAW	368	207	2915	56.3	7.92	28
KRUCZEK	11	5	46	45.5	4.18	0
HARRIS	1	0	0	00.0	0.00	0
STEELERS TOTAL	380	212	2961	55.8	7.79	28
Opp. Total	442	221	2755	50.0	6.23	10

1978 PASSING

	Pct. TD	Int.	Pct. Int.	LG	Yds. Lost No. of Att.	Rating
BRADSHAW	7.6	20	5.4	70	21–222	84.8
KRUCZEK	0.0	2	18.2	21	4–49	—
HARRIS	0.0	0	0.0	0	0–0	—
STEELERS TOTAL	7.4	22	5.8	70	25–271	81.6
Opp. Total	2.3	27	6.1	49	44–361	52.0

* No longer with team
** On injured reserve
† Touchdown

1978 DEFENSIVE STATISTICS

Player	Tac/Asst/Total
Lambert	125/59/184
Wagner	73/30/103
Ham	70/24/94
Shell	62/25/87
Toews	57/21/78
Greene	38/32/70
Greenwood	42/26/68
Johnson	48/12/60
Banaszak	39/19/58
White	40/15/55
Cole	43/11/54
Blount	30/10/40
Winston	26/8/34
Furness	17/9/26
Dungy	18/4/22
Beasley	13/8/21
L. Anderson	17/1/18
Dunn	12/4/16
Moser	9/3/12
Reutershan	11/1/12
Deloplaine	7/0/7
Oldham	4/1/5
Thornton	5/0/5
Webster	5/0/5
F. Anderson	3/1/4
Bell	4/0/4
Swann	4/0/4

1978 FUMBLES/LOST

Bradshaw 9–6; Bleier 6–4; Stallworth 2–2; Harris 4–1; Thornton 3–1; Moser 3–1; Maxson 2–1; Cunningham 1–1; L. Anderson 2–0; Kruczek 1–0; Grossman 1–0; Smith 1–0.

1978 OPPONENTS' FUMBLES RECOVERED

Shell 5; Greene 5; Lambert 2; Ham 2; Dungy 2; Dunn 1; Greenwood 1; Furness 1; White 1; Johnson 1.

1978 SACKS

Greenwood 9; Toews 4½; Greene 4½; Ham 4; Lambert 3½; Dunn 3½; Shell 3; Banaszak 3; Wagner 2; White 2; Cole 2; Winston 1; Oldham 1; Beasley 1.

1978 PUNTS BLOCKED

F. Anderson 1.

1978 BEST INDIVIDUAL SINGLE-GAME PERFORMANCES

Yards Rushing   —104, Franco Harris vs. Atlanta (10–8)
Rushing Attempts— 27, Franco Harris vs. Buffalo (9–3) & Houston (12–3)
TDs Rushing   — 2, Rocky Bleier vs. Atlanta (10–8) & Franco Harris vs. Kansas City (10–29)
Yards Passing   —242, Terry Bradshaw vs. Cincinnati (9–17)
Passing Attempts — 33, Terry Bradshaw vs. Seattle (9–10) & Houston (10–23)
Passes Completed— 17, Terry Bradshaw vs. Seattle (9–10) & Houston (10–23)
TDs Passing   — 3, Terry Bradshaw vs. Jets (10–1), San Francisco (11–27) & Baltimore (12–9)
Yards Receiving —134, Lynn Swann vs. San Francisco (11–27)
Receptions   — 9, Randy Grossman vs. Houston (10–23)
TDs Receiving   — 2, Lynn Swann vs. N.Y. Jets (10–1), Houston (10–23) & San Francisco (11–27)
Interceptions   — 2, Blount vs. Cincinnati (11–19), Ham vs. San Francisco (11–27) & Lambert vs. Houston (12–3)
Longest Punt   — 58, Craig Colquitt vs. Denver (12–16)

THE LAST TIME . . .

PUNT RETURNED FOR TD

By Steelers—Lynn Swann (69 yards) vs. New Orleans, 11–25–74
By Opponents—Rick Upchurch (87 yards), Denver, 11–6–77

KICKOFF RETURNED FOR TD

By Steelers—Larry Anderson (95 yards) vs. Cleveland, 10–15–78
By Opponents—Larry Krause (100 yards), Green Bay, 12–6–70

INTERCEPTED PASS RETURNED FOR TD

By Steelers—Mel Blount (52 yards) vs. Philadelphia, 11–3–74
By Opponents—Lamar Parish (47 yards), Cincinnati, 12–10–77

FUMBLE RETURNED FOR TD

By Steelers—J. T. Thomas (21 yards, lateral from Jack Lambert) vs. Cincinnati, 12–13–75
By Opponents—Willie Miller (17 yards), Cleveland, 12–7–75

PUNT BLOCKED FOR TD

By Steelers—Henry Davis (5 yards) vs. Oakland, 9–17–72
By Opponents—Reggie Williams (end zone), Cincinnati, 10–17–77

FIELD GOAL BLOCKED FOR TD

By Steelers—Bob O'Neil (73 yards) vs. Chicago Cards, 10–13–57
By Opponents—Ray Renfro (79 yards), Cleveland, 11–8–53

SAFETY SCORED

By Steelers—vs. Houston, 11–21–76 (Loren Toews blocked a punt which bounced out of the end zone)
By Opponents—Houston, 1–7–79 (Washington tackled Rocky Bleier in end zone)

SHUTOUT

By Steelers—Pittsburgh 27, San Francisco 0, 9–19–77
By Opponents—Oakland 17, Pittsburgh 0, 9–29–74

SEASON BY SEASON STEELER LEADERS

RUSHING

Year	Player	Att.	Yardage	Avg.
1934	Warren Heller	132	528	4.0
1935	Art Strutt	92	323	3.5
1936	Warren Heller	106	322	3.0
1937	John Karcis	128	511	4.0
1938	Byron White	152	567	3.7
1939	Boyd Brumbaugh	111	343	3.1
1940	Lou Tomasetti	68	246	3.6
1941	Dick Riffle	109	388	3.6
1942	Bill Dudley	162	696	4.2
1943	Jack Hinkle	116	571	4.9
1944	John Grigas	185	610	3.2
1945	Buist Warren	96	285	3.0
1946	Bill Dudley	146	604	4.1
1947	Johnny Clement	129	670	5.2
1948	Bob Cifers	112	361	3.2
1949	Jerry Nuzum	139	611	4.4
1950	Joe Geri	188	705	3.8
1951	Frank Rogel	109	385	3.5
1952	Ray Mathews	66	315	4.7
1953	Frank Rogel	137	527	3.8
1954	Frank Rogel	111	415	3.8
1955	Frank Rogel	168	588	3.5
1956	Frank Rogel	131	476	3.6
1957	Billy Wells	154	532	3.5
1958	Tom Tracy	169	714	4.2
1959	Tom Tracy	199	794	4.0
1960	Tom Tracy	192	680	3.4
1961	John Henry Johnson	213	787	3.9
1962	John Henry Johnson	251	1141	4.5
1963	John Henry Johnson	186	775	4.2
1964	John Henry Johnson	235	1048	4.7
1965	Dick Hoak	131	426	3.2
1966	Bill Asbury	169	544	3.3
1967	Don Shy	99	341	3.4
1968	Dick Hoak	175	858	4.9
1969	Dick Hoak	151	531	3.5
1970	John Fuqua	138	691	5.0
1971	John Fuqua	155	625	4.0
1972	Franco Harris	188	1055	5.6*
1973	Franco Harris	188	698	3.7
1974	Franco Harris	208	1006	4.8
1975	Franco Harris	262	1246*	4.8
1976	Franco Harris	289	1128	3.9
1977	Franco Harris	300	1162	3.9
1978	Franco Harris	310*	1082	3.5

* Team Record

SCORING

Year	Player	TD	PAT	FG	TP
1935	Armand Niccolai	0	10	6	28
1936	Armand Niccolai	0	7	7	28
1937	Johnny "Blood" McNally	5	0	0	30
1938	Byron White	4	0	0	24
	Bill Sortet	4	0	0	24
1939	Armand Niccolai	0	15	3	24
1940	Armand Niccolai	0	6	6	24
1941	Art Jones	5	0	0	30
1942	Bill Dudley	6	0	0	36
1943	Ernie Steele	6	0	0	36
	Bob Thurbon	6	0	0	36
1944	Bob Thurbon	5	0	0	30
1945	Bill Dudley	3	2	0	20
1946	Bill Dudley	5	12	2	48
1947	Steve Lach	9	0	.0	54
1948	Joe Glamp	3	26	4	56
1949	Joe Geri	5	12	1	45
1950	Joe Geri	3	22	8	64
1951	Joe Geri	4	22	7	67
1952	Elbie Nickel	9	0	0	54
1953	Nick Bolkovac	1	27	4	45
	Ray Mathews	8	0	0	48
1954	Ray Mathews	7	0	0	42
1955	Ray Mathews	5	0	0	30
1956	Elbie Nickel	5	0	0	30
	Lynn Chandnois	5	0	0	30
1957	Earl Girard	4	2	1	29
1958	Tom Miner	0	31	14	73
1959	Bobby Layne	2	32	11	77
1960	Tom Tracy	9	0	3	63
1961	Buddy Dial	12	0	0	72
1962	Lou Michaels	0	32	26	110
1963	Lou Michaels	0	32	21	95
1964	Mike Clark	0	28	13	67
1965	Mike Clark	0	19	11	52
1966	Mike Clark	0	34	21	97
1967	Mike Clark	0	35	12	71
1968	Roy Jefferson	12	0	0	72
1969	Gene Mingo	0	26	12	62
1970	John Fuqua	9	0	0	54
1971	Roy Gerela	0	27	17	78
1972	Roy Gerela	0	35	28	119
1973	Roy Gerela	0	36	29*	123*
1974	Roy Gerela	0	33	20	93
1975	Roy Gerela	0	44*	17	95
1976	Franco Harris	14*	0	0	84
1977	Franco Harris	11	0	0	66
1978	Roy Gerela	0	44	12	80

* Team Record

PASSING

Year	Player	Att.	Comp.	Yards
1934	Warren Heller	112	31	511
1935	Warren Heller	41	9	88
1936	Ed Matesic	138	64	850
1937	Ed Fiske	43	17	318
1938	Frank Filchok	101	41	469
1939	Hugh McCullough	100	32	443
1940	Bill Patterson	117	34	529
1941	Boyd Brumbaugh	41	13	260
1942	Bill Dudley	94	35	438
1943	Roy Zimmerman	124	43	846
1944	Johnny Grigas	131	50	690
1945	Buist Warren	92	36	368
1946	Bill Dudley	90	32	452
1947	Johnny Clement	123	52	1004
1948	Ray Evans	137	64	924
1949	Joe Geri	77	31	554
1950	Joe Geri	113	41	866
1951	Chuck Ortmann	139	56	671
1952	Jim Finks	336	158	2307
1953	Jim Finks	292	131	1484
1954	Jim Finks	306	164	2003
1955	Jim Finks	344	165	2270
1956	Ted Marchibroda	275	124	1585
1957	Earl Morrall	289	139	1900
1958	Bobby Layne	268	133	2339
1959	Bobby Layne	297	142	1986
1960	Bobby Layne	209	103	1814
1961	Rudy Bukich	156	89	1253
1962	Bobby Layne	233	116	1686
1963	Ed Brown	362	168	2982*
1964	Ed Brown	272	121	1990
1965	Bill Nelsen	270	121	1917
1966	Ron Smith	181	79	1249
1967	Kent Nix	268	136	1587
1968	Dick Shiner	304	148	1856
1969	Dick Shiner	209	97	1422
1970	Terry Bradshaw	218	83	1410
1971	Terry Bradshaw	373*	203	2259
1972	Terry Bradshaw	308	147	1887
1973	Terry Bradshaw	180	89	1183
1974	Joe Gilliam	212	96	1274
	Terry Bradshaw	148	67	785
1975	Terry Bradshaw	286	165	2055
1976	Terry Bradshaw	192	92	1177
1977	Terry Bradshaw	314	162	2523
1978	Terry Bradshaw	368	207*	2915

* Team Record

PASS RECEIVING

Year	Player	Number	Yardage	LG	TD
1934	Ben Smith	12	190	—	0
1935	Jim Levey	11	112	—	2
1936	Wilbur Sortet	14	197	—	1
1937	Johnny "Blood" McNally	10	168	—	44
1938	Bill Davidson	12	229	—	0
1939	Sam Boyd	21	423	—	2
1940	George Platukis	15	290	—	2
1941	Don Looney	10	186	66	1
1942	Walt Kichefski	15	189	26	0
1943	Tony Bova	17	419	51	5
1944	Ed Rucinski	22	284	40	1
1945	Tony Bova	15	220	52	0
1946	Val Jansante	10	136	34	1
	Charley Mehelich	10	116	35	0
1947	Val Jansante	35	599	46	5
1948	Val Jansante	39	623	48	3
1949	Val Jansante	29	445	47	4
	Elbie Nickel	26	633	52	3
1950	Val Jansante	26	353	40	0
1951	Hank Minarik	35	459	37	1
1952	Elbie Nickel	55	884	54	9
1953	Elbie Nickel	62	743	40	4
1954	Ray Mathews	44	652	78	6
1955	Ray Mathews	42	762	61	6
1956	Ray Mathews	31	540	64	5
1957	Jack McClairen	46	630	48	2
1958	Jimmy Orr	33	910	78	7
1959	Jimmy Orr	35	604	43	5
1960	Buddy Dial	40	972	70	9
1961	Buddy Dial	53	1047	88*	12*

Year	Player	Number	Yardage	LG	TD
1962	Buddy Dial	50	981	62	6
1963	Buddy Dial	60	1295*	83	9
1964	Gary Ballman	47	935	47	7
1965	Gary Ballman	40	849	88	5
1966	John Hilton	46	603	32	4
1967	J. R. Wilburn	51	767	66	5
1968	Roy Jefferson	58	1074	62	11
1969	Roy Jefferson	67*	1079	63	9
1970	Ron Shanklin	30	691	81	4
	Dave Smith	30	458	87	2
1971	Ron Shanklin	49	652	42	6
	John Fuqua	49	669	57	3
1972	Ron Shanklin	38	669	57	3
1973	Ron Shanklin	30	711	67	10
1974	Frank Lewis	30	365	31	4
1975	Lynn Swann	49	781	43	11
1976	Lynn Swann	28	576	47	3
1977	Lynn Swann	50	789	47	7
1978	Lynn Swann	61	880	62	11

* Team Record

STEELERS ALL TIME LEADERS

RUSHING

Player	Yrs.	Atts.	Yds.	Avg.	LG	TDs
Franco Harris	1972–78	1745	7377	4.2	75	61
John Henry Johnson	1960–65	1025	4383	4.3	87	26
Dick Hoak	1961–70	1132	3965	3.5	77	25
Fran Rogel	1950–57	900	3271	3.6	51	17
Rocky Bleier	1968, 1970–78	766	3105	4.1	28	18
John Fuqua	1970–76	699	2942	4.2	85	21
Tom Tracy	1958–63	727	2712	3.7	64	15
Preston Pearson	1970–74	573	2243	3.9	47	8
Lynn Chandnois	1950–56	593	1934	3.2	34	12
Terry Bradshaw	1970–78	340	1888	5.6	39	28
Bill Dudley	1942, 1945–46	343	1505	4.4	42	14
Joe Geri	1949–51	411	1500	3.6	45	10

PASSING (Based on total yardage)

Player-Years	Atts.	Comps.	Yds.	Pct.	LG	TD	Ints.	Rtg.
Terry Bradshaw (1970–78)	2387	1215	16,194	50.9	70	121	138	65.6
Bobby Layne (1958–62)	1156	569	8983	49.2	78	67	67	70.7
Jim Finks (1949–55)	1382	661	8854	47.8	78	55	88	48.5
Ed Brown (1962–65)	736	339	5821	44.7	87	30	50	57.7
Bill Nelsen (1964–67)	589	274	4440	46.5	87	28	30	67.0
Kent Nix (1967–69)	451	217	2597	48.1	66	14	33	46.1
Terry Hanratty (1969–75)	417	159	2428	38.1	72	24	34	42.6
Dick Shiner (1968–69)	513	245	2278	47.8	63	25	27	54.7
Earl Morrall (1957–58)	335	145	2175	43.3	66	12	19	53.9
Joe Gilliam (1972–75)	331	147	2103	44.4	61t	9	17	53.3
Ted Marchibroda (1953, 1955–56)	340	157	1931	46.2	75	15	24	29.3
Rudy Bukich (1960–1961)	207	114	1611	57.1	88	13	19	81.4

PASS RECEIVING

Player	Yrs.	No.	Yds.	Avg.	LG	TDs
Elbie Nickel	1947–57	329	5133	15.6	77	37
Ray Mathews	1951–59	230	3919	16.1	77	34
Buddy Dial	1959–63	229	4723	20.6	88	42
Roy Jefferson	1965–69	199	3671	18.4	84	29
Lynn Swann	1974–78	199	3174	15.9	62	34
Ron Shanklin	1970–74	166	3047	18.4	81	24
Lynn Chandnois	1950–56	163	2062	12.6	55	8
Gary Ballman	1962–66	154	2949	19.2	88	22
Fran Rogel	1950–57	150	1087	7.2	64	2
Dick Hoak	1961–70	146	1552	10.6	48	10
Val Jansante	1946–51	144	2214	15.4	66	13

SCORING

Player	Yrs.	Tot TD	TD-R	TD-P	Pat	FG	TP
Roy Gerela	1971–78	0	0	0	293	146	731
Franco Harris	1972–78	64	61	3	0	0	384
Mike Clark	1964–67	0	0	0	116	57	287
Lou Michaels	1961–63	0	0	0	91	62	277
Ray Mathews	1951–59	43	13	30	1	0	261*
Buddy Dial	1959–63	42	0	42	0	0	252
Elbie Nickel	1947–57	37	0	37	0	0	222
Lynn Swann	1974–78	35	0	34	0	0	210
Dick Hoak	1961–70	33	25	8	0	0	198
John Henry Johnson	1960–65	32	26	6	0	0	192
Tom Tracy	1958–63	29	18	11	4	3	187
Roy Jefferson	1965–69	30	1	29	0	0	180
Armand Niccolai	1934–42	0	0	0	59	40	179

* Includes one safety

FORTY-SIX YEARS WITH THE STEELERS: 1933–1978

1978

CHUCK NOLL, Head Coach

Steelers		Opp.	
28	at Buffalo	17	(W)
21	Seattle	10	(W)
28	at Cincinnati	3	(W)
15	Cleveland*	9	(W)
28	at New York Jets	17	(W)
31	Atlanta	7	(W)
34	at Cleveland	14	(W)
17	Houston	24	(L)
27	Kansas City	24	(W)
20	New Orleans	14	(W)
7	at Los Angeles	10	(L)
7	Cincinnati	6	(W)
24	at San Francisco	7	(W)
13	at Houston	3	(W)
35	Baltimore	13	(W)
21	at Denver	17	(W)

14-2-0

356	*Won 14, Lost 2*	195

* overtime

AFC Playoff Game

33	Denver	10	(W)

AFC Championship

34	Houston	5	(W)

SUPER BOWL XIII

35	Dallas	31	(W)

1977
CHUCK NOLL, Head Coach

Steelers		Opp.
27	San Francisco	0 (W)
7	Oakland	16 (L)
28	at Cleveland	14 (W)
10	at Houston	27 (L)
20	Cincinnati	14 (W)
27	Houston	10 (W)
21	at Baltimore	31 (L)
7	at Denver	21 (L)
35	Cleveland	31 (W)
28	Dallas	13 (W)
23	at New York Jets	20 (W)
30	Seattle	20 (W)
10	at Cincinnati	17 (L)
10	at San Diego	9 (W)

9-5-0

283	*Won 9, Lost 5*	243
	AFC Playoff Game	
21	at Denver	34 (L)

1976
CHUCK NOLL, Head Coach

Steelers		Opp.
28	at Oakland	31 (L)
31	Cleveland	14 (W)
27	New England	30 (L)
6	at Minnesota	17 (L)
16	at Cleveland	18 (L)
23	Cincinnati	6 (W)
27	at New York Giants	0 (W)
23	San Diego	0 (W)
45	at Kansas City	0 (W)
14	Miami	3 (W)
32	Houston	16 (W)
7	at Cincinnati	3 (W)
42	Tampa Bay	0 (W)
21	at Houston	0 (W)

10-4-0

342	*Won 10, Lost 4*	138
	AFC Playoff Game	
40	at Baltimore	14 (W)
	AFC Championship Game	
7	at Oakland	24 (L)

1975
CHUCK NOLL, Head Coach

Steelers		Opp.
37	at San Diego	0 (W)
21	Buffalo	30 (L)
42	at Cleveland	6 (W)
20	Denver	9 (W)
34	Chicago	3 (W)
16	at Green Bay	13 (W)
30	at Cincinnati	24 (W)
24	Houston	17 (W)
28	Kansas City	3 (W)
32	at Houston	9 (W)
20	at New York Jets	7 (W)
31	Cleveland	17 (W)
35	Cincinnati	14 (W)
3	at Los Angeles	10 (L)

12-2-0

373	*Won 12, Lost 2*	162
	AFC Playoff Game	
28	Baltimore	10 (W)
	AFC Championship Game	
16	Oakland	10 (W)
	SUPER BOWL X	
21	Dallas	17 (W)

1974
CHUCK NOLL, Head Coach

Steelers		Opp.
30	Baltimore	0 (W)
35	at Denver*	35 (T)
0	Oakland	17 (L)
13	at Houston	7 (W)
34	at Kansas City	24 (W)
20	Cleveland	16 (W)
24	Atlanta	17 (W)
27	Philadelphia	0 (W)
10	at Cincinnati	17 (L)
26	at Cleveland	16 (W)
28	at New Orleans	7 (W)
10	Houston	13 (L)
21	at New England	17 (W)
27	Cincinnati	3 (W)

10-3-1

305	*Won 10, Lost 3, Tied 1*	189
* overtime		
	AFC Playoff Game	
32	Buffalo	14 (W)
	AFC Championship Game	
24	at Oakland	13 (W)
	SUPER BOWL IX	
16	Minnesota	6 (W)

1973
CHUCK NOLL, Head Coach

Steelers		Opp.
24	Detroit	10 (W)
33	Cleveland	6 (W)
36	at Houston	7 (W)
38	San Diego	21 (W)
7	at Cincinnati	19 (L)
26	New York Jets	14 (W)
20	Cincinnati	13 (W)
21	Washington	16 (W)
17	at Oakland	9 (W)
13	Denver	23 (L)
16	at Cleveland	21 (L)
26	at Miami	30 (L)
33	Houston	7 (W)
37	at San Francisco	14 (W)

10-4-0

337	*Won 10, Lost 4*	210
	AFC Playoff Game	
14	at Oakland	33 (L)

1972
CHUCK NOLL, Head Coach

Steelers		Opp.
34	Oakland	28 (W)
10	at Cincinnati	15 (L)
25	at St. Louis	19 (W)
13	at Dallas	17 (L)
24	Houston	7 (W)
33	New England	3 (W)
38	at Buffalo	21 (W)
40	Cincinnati	17 (W)
16	Kansas City	7 (W)
24	at Cleveland	26 (L)
23	Minnesota	10 (W)
30	Cleveland	0 (W)
9	at Houston	3 (W)
24	at San Diego	2 (W)

11-3-0

343	*Won 11, Lost 3*	175
	AFC Playoff Game	
13	Oakland	7 (W)
	AFC Championship Game	
17	Miami	21 (L)

1971
CHUCK NOLL, Head Coach

Steelers		Opp.
15	at Chicago	17 (L)
21	Cincinnati	10 (W)
21	San Diego	17 (W)
17	at Cleveland	27 (L)
16	at Kansas City	38 (L)
23	Houston	16 (W)
21	at Baltimore	34 (L)
26	Cleveland	9 (W)
21	at Miami	24 (L)
17	New York Giants	13 (W)
10	Denver	22 (L)
3	at Houston	29 (L)
21	at Cincinnati	13 (W)
14	Los Angeles	23 (L)

6-8-0

246	*Won 6, Lost 8*	292

1970
CHUCK NOLL, Head Coach

Steelers		Opp.
7	Houston	19 (L)
13	at Denver	16 (L)
7	at Cleveland	15 (L)
23	Buffalo	10 (W)
7	at Houston	3 (W)
14	at Oakland	31 (L)
21	Cincinnati	10 (W)
21	New York	17 (W)
14	Kansas City	31 (L)
7	at Cincinnati	34 (L)
28	Cleveland	9 (W)
12	Green Bay	20 (L)
16	at Atlanta	27 (L)
20	at Philadelphia	30 (L)

5-9-0

210	*Won 5, Lost 9*	272

1969
CHUCK NOLL, Head Coach

Steelers		Opp.	
16	Detroit	13	(W)
27	at Philadelphia	41	(L)
14	St. Louis	27	(L)
7	at New York	10	(L)
31	at Cleveland	42	(L)
7	Washington	14	(L)
34	Green Bay	38	(L)
7	at Chicago	38	(L)
3	Cleveland	24	(L)
14	at Minnesota	52	(L)
10	at St. Louis	47	(L)
7	Dallas	10	(L)
17	New York	21	(L)
24	at New Orleans	27	(L)

218   *Won 1, Lost 13*   404

1968
BILL AUSTIN, Head Coach

Steelers		Opp.	
20	New York	34	(L)
10	at Los Angeles	45	(L)
7	Baltimore	41	(L)
24	at Cleveland	31	(L)
13	at Washington	16	(L)
12	New Orleans	16	(L)
6	Philadelphia	3	(W)
41	at Atlanta	21	(W)
28	at St. Louis	28	(T)
24	Cleveland	45	(L)
28	San Francisco	45	(L)
10	St. Louis	20	(L)
7	at Dallas	28	(L)
14	at New Orleans	24	(L)

244   *Won 2, Lost 11, Tied 1*   397

1967
BILL AUSTIN, Head Coach

Steelers		Opp.	
41	Chicago	13	(W)
14	St. Louis	28	(L)
24	at Philadelphia	34	(L)
10	at Cleveland	21	(L)
24	New York	27	(L)
21	Dallas	24	(L)
14	at New Orleans	10	(W)
14	Cleveland	34	(L)
		14	(T)
		28	(L)
	Minnesota	41	(L)
	at Detroit	14	(W)
10	Washington	15	(L)
24	at Green Bay	17	(W)

281   *Won 4, Lost 9, Tied 1*   320

1966
BILL AUSTIN, Head Coach

Steelers		Opp.	
34	New York	34	(T)
17	Detroit	3	(W)
27	Washington	33	(L)
10	at Washington	24	(L)
10	at Cleveland	41	(L)
14	Philadelphia	31	(L)
21	at Dallas	52	(L)
16	Cleveland	6	(W)
30	St. Louis	9	(W)
7	Dallas	20	(L)
3	at St. Louis	6	(L)
23	at Philadelphia	27	(L)
47	at New York	28	(W)
57	at Atlanta	33	(W)

316   *Won 5, Lost 8, Tied 1*   347

1965
MIKE NIXON, Head Coach

Steelers		Opp.	
9	Green Bay	41	(L)
17	at San Francisco	27	(L)
13	New York	23	(L)
19	at Cleveland	24	(L)
7	St. Louis	20	(L)
20	at Philadelphia	14	(W)
22	Dallas	13	(W)
17	at St. Louis	21	(L)
17	at Dallas	24	(L)
3	Washington	31	(L)
21	Cleveland	42	(L)
10	at New York	35	(L)
13	Philadelphia	47	(L)
14	at Washington	35	(L)

202   *Won 2, Lost 12*   397

1964
BUDDY PARKER, Head Coach

Steelers		Opp.	
14	Los Angeles	26	(L)
27	New York	24	(W)
23	Dallas	17	(W)
7	at Philadelphia	21	(L)
23	at Cleveland	7	(W)
10	at Minnesota	30	(L)
10	Philadelphia	34	(L)
17	Cleveland	30	(L)
30	at St. Louis	34	(L)
0	Washington	30	(L)
44	at New York	17	(W)
20	St. Louis	21	(L)
14	at Washington	7	(W)
14	at Dallas	17	(L)

253   *Won 5, Lost 9*   315

1963
BUDDY PARKER, Head Coach

Steelers		Opp.	
21	at Philadelphia	21	(T)
31	New York	0	(W)
23	St. Louis	10	(W)
23	at Cleveland	35	(L)
23	at St. Louis	24	(L)
38	Washington	27	(W)
27	Dallas	21	(W)
14	at Green Bay	33	(L)
9	Cleveland	7	(W)
34	at Washington	28	(W)
17	Chicago	17	(T)
20	Philadelphia	20	(L)
24	at Dallas	19	(W)
17	at New York	33	(L)

321   *Won 7, Lost 4, Tied 3*   295

1962
BUDDY PARKER, Head Coach

Steelers		Opp.	
7	at Detroit	45	(L)
30	at Dallas	28	(W)
27	New York	31	(L)
13	Philadelphia	7	(W)
20	at New York	17	(W)
27	Dallas	42	(L)
14	Cleveland	41	(L)
39	Minnesota	31	(W)
26	at St. Louis	17	(W)
23	Washington	21	(W)
14	at Cleveland	35	(L)
19	St. Louis	7	(W)
26	at Philadelphia	17	(W)
27	at Washington	24	(W)

312   *Won 9, Lost 5*   363

Playoff Bowl in Miami

10	Detroit	17	(L)

1961
BUDDY PARKER, Head Coach

Steelers		Opp.	
24	at Dallas	27	(L)
14	New York	17	(L)
14	at Los Angeles	24	(L)
16	at Philadelphia	21	(L)
20	Washington	0	(W)
28	Cleveland	30	(L)
20	San Francisco	10	(W)
17	at Cleveland	13	(W)
37	Dallas	7	(W)
21	at New York	42	(L)
30	St. Louis	27	(W)
24	Philadelphia	35	(L)
30	at Washington	14	(W)
0	at St. Louis	20	(L)

295   *Won 6, Lost 8*   287

1960
BUDDY PARKER, Head Coach

Steelers		Opp.	
35	at Dallas	28	(W)
20	at Cleveland	28	(L)
17	New York	19	(L)
27	St. Louis	14	(W)
27	at Washington	27	(T)

Steelers		Opp.	
13	Green Bay	19	(L)
7	at Philadelphia	34	(L)
24	at New York	27	(L)
14	Cleveland	10	(W)
22	Washington	10	(W)
27	Philadelphia	21	(W)
7	at St. Louis	38	(L)

240 *Won 5, Lost 6, Tied 1* 275

1959
BUDDY PARKER, Head Coach

Steelers		Opp.	
17	Cleveland	7	(W)
17	Washington	23	(L)
24	at Philadelphia	28	(L)
27	at Washington	6	(W)
16	New York	21	(L)
24	at Chicago Cards	45	(L)
10	Detroit	10	(T)
14	at New York	9	(W)
21	at Cleveland	20	(W)
31	Philadelphia	0	(W)
21	at Chicago Bears	27	(L)
35	Chicago Cards	20	(W)

257 *Won 6, Lost 5, Tied 1* 196

1958
BUDDY PARKER, Head Coach

Steelers		Opp.	
20	at San Francisco	23	(L)
12	Cleveland	45	(L)
24	Philadelphia	3	(W)
10	at Cleveland	27	(L)
6	at New York	17	(L)
24	Washington	16	(W)
31	at Philadelphia	24	(W)
31	New York	10	(W)
27	at Chicago Cards	20	(W)
24	Chicago Bears	10	(W)
14	at Washington	14	(T)
38	Chicago Cards	21	(W)

261 *Won 7, Lost 4, Tied 1* 230

1957
BUDDY PARKER, Head Coach

Steelers		Opp.	
28	Washington	7	(W)
12	Cleveland	23	(L)
29	Chicago Cards	20	(W)
0	at New York	35	(L)
6	Philadelphia	0	(W)
19	at Baltimore	13	(W)
0	at Cleveland	24	(L)
10	Green Bay	27	(L)
6	at Philadelphia	7	(L)

Steelers		Opp.	
21	New York	10	(W)
3	at Washington	10	(L)
27	at Chicago Cards	2	(W)

161 *Won 6, Lost 6* 178

1956
WALT KIESLING, Head Coach

Steelers		Opp.	
30	Washington	13	(W)
10	Cleveland	14	(L)
21	Philadelphia	35	(L)
10	at New York	38	(L)
24	at Cleveland	16	(W)
14	New York	17	(L)
7	at Philadelphia	14	(L)
14	Chicago Cards	7	(W)
27	at Chicago Cards	38	(L)
30	Los Angeles	13	(W)
7	at Detroit	45	(L)
23	at Washington	0	(W)

217 *Won 5, Lost 7* 250

1955
WALT KIESLING, Head Coach

Steelers		Opp.	
14	Chicago Cards	7	(W)
26	at Los Angeles	27	(L)
30	New York	23	(W)
13	Philadelphia	7	(W)
19	at New York	17	(W)
0	at Philadelphia	24	(L)
13	at Chicago Cards	27	(L)
28	Detroit	31	(L)
14	at Cleveland	41	(L)
14	Washington	23	(L)
7	Cleveland	30	(L)
17	at Washington	28	(L)

195 *Won 4, Lost 8* 285

1954
WALT KIESLING, Head Coach

Steelers		Opp.	
21	at Green Bay	20	(W)
37	Washington	7	(W)
22	at Philadelphia	24	(L)
55	Cleveland	27	(W)
17	Philadelphia	7	(W)
14	at Chicago Cards	17	(L)
6	New York	30	(L)
14	at Washington	17	(L)
3	San Francisco	31	(L)
20	Chicago Cards	17	**(W)**
3	at New York	24	(L)
7	at Cleveland	42	(L)

219 *Won 5, Lost 7* 263

1953
JOE BACH, Head Coach

Steelers		Opp.	
21	at Detroit	38	(L)
24	New York	14	(W)
31	Chicago Cards	28	(W)
7	at Philadelphia	23	(L)
31	Green Bay	14	(W)
7	Philadelphia	35	(L)
16	at Cleveland	34	(L)
14	at New York	10	(W)
16	Cleveland	20	(L)
9	Washington	17	(L)
21	at Chicago Cards	17	(W)
14	at Washington	13	(W)

211 *Won 6, Lost 6* 263

1952
JOE BACH, Head Coach

Steelers		Opp.	
25	Philadelphia	31	(L)
20	Cleveland	21	(L)
21	at Philadelphia	26	(L)
24	Washington	28	(L)
34	at Chicago Cards	28	(W)
24	at Washington	23	(W)
6	Detroit	31	(L)
28	at Cleveland	29	(L)
17	Chicago Cards	14	(W)
63	New York	7	(W)
24	at San Francisco	7	(W)
14	at Los Angeles	28	(L)

300 *Won 5, Lost 7* 245

1951
JOHN MICHELOSEN, Head Coach

Steelers		Opp.	
13	New York	13	(T)
33	at Green Bay	35	(L)
24	San Francisco	28	(L)
0	at Cleveland	17	(L)
28	at Chicago Cards	14	(W)
13	Philadelphia	34	(L)
28	Green Bay	7	(W)
7	Washington	22	(L)
17	at Philadelphia	13	(W)
0	at New York	14	(L)
0	Cleveland	28	(L)
20	at Washington	10	(W)

183 *Won 4, Lost 7, Tied 1* 235

1950
JOHN MICHELOSEN, Head Coach

Steelers		Opp.	
7	New York	18	(L)
7	at Detroit	10	(L)
26	at Washington	7	(W)
17	Cleveland	30	(L)
17	at New York	6	(W)
10	Philadelphia	17	(L)
7	at Cleveland	45	(L)

Steelers		Opp.
9	at Philadelphia	7 (W)
17	Baltimore	7 (W)
28	at Chicago Cards	17 (W)
7	Washington	24 (L)
28	Chicago Cards	7 (W)
180	Won 6, Lost 6	195

1949
JOHN MICHELOSEN, Head Coach

Steelers		Opp.
28	New York Giants	7 (W)
14	Washington	27 (L)
14	Detroit	7 (W)
21	at New York Giants	17 (W)
24	New York Bulldogs	13 (W)
7	Philadelphia	38 (L)
14	at Washington	27 (L)
7	Los Angeles	7 (T)
30	at Green Bay	7 (W)
17	at Philadelphia	34 (L)
21	at Chicago Bears	30 (L)
27	at New York Bulldogs	0 (W)
224	Won 6, Lost 5, Tied 1	214

1948
JOHN MICHELOSEN, Head Coach

Steelers		Opp.
14	at Washington	17 (L)
24	Boston	14 (W)
10	Washington	7 (W)
7	at Boston	13 (L)
27	at New York	34 (L)
7	Philadelphia	37 (L)
38	Green Bay	7 (W)
7	Chicago Cards	24 (L)
14	at Detroit	17 (L)
0	at Philadelphia	17 (L)
38	New York	28 (W)
14	at Los Angeles	31 (L)
200	Won 4, Lost 8	243

1947
JOCK SUTHERLAND, Head Coach

Steelers		Opp.
17	Detroit	10 (W)
7	Los Angeles	48 (L)
26	at Washington	27 (L)
30	at Boston	14 (W)
35	Philadelphia	24 (W)
38	at New York	21 (W)
18	at Green Bay	17 (W)
21	Washington	14 (W)
24	New York	7 (W)
7	at Chicago Bears	49 (L)
0	at Philadelphia	21 (L)
17	Boston	7 (W)
240	Won 8, Lost 4	259
	Eastern Division Playoff	
0	Philadelphia	21 (L)

1946
JOCK SUTHERLAND, Head Coach

Steelers		Opp.
14	Chicago Cards	7 (W)
14	at Washington	14 (T)
14	New York	17 (L)
16	Boston	7 (W)
7	at Green Bay	17 (L)
33	at Boston	7 (W)
14	Washington	7 (W)
7	at Detroit	17 (L)
10	Philadelphia	7 (W)
0	at New York	7 (L)
7	at Philadelphia	10 (L)
136	Won 5, Lost 5, Tied 1	117

1945
JIM LEONARD, Head Coach

Steelers		Opp.
7	at Boston	28 (L)
6	New York	34 (L)
0	Washington	14 (L)
21	at New York	7 (W)
6	Boston	10 (L)
3	Philadelphia	45 (L)
23	Chicago Cards	0 (W)
6	at Philadelphia	30 (L)
7	Chicago Bears	28 (L)
0	at Washington	24 (L)
82	Won 2, Lost 8	220

1944*
WALT KIESLING and
PHIL HANDLER, Head Coaches

Steelers		Opp.
28	Cleveland	30 (L)
7	Green Bay	34 (L)
7	at Chicago Bears	34 (L)
0	at New York	23 (L)
20	at Washington	42 (L)
6	Detroit	27 (L)
7	at Detroit	21 (L)
6	**Cleveland	33 (L)
20	**Green Bay	35 (L)
7	Chicago Bears	49 (L)
108	Won 0, Lost 10	328

*Combined with Chicago Cards
**Home game played in Chicago

1943*
WALT KIESLING and
GREASY NEALE, Head Coaches

Steelers		Opp.
17	**Brooklyn	0 (W)
28	**New York	14 (W)
21	at Chicago Bears	48 (L)
14	at New York	42 (L)
34	Chicago Cards	3 (W)
14	**Washington	14 (T)
7	at Brooklyn	13 (L)

Steelers		Opp.
35	at Detroit	34 (W)
27	at Washington	14 (W)
28	**Green Bay	38 (L)
225	Won 5, Lost 4, Tied 1	220

*Combined with Philadelphia
Eagles
**Home game played in
Philadelphia

1942
WALT KIESLING, Head Coach

Steelers		Opp.
14	Philadelphia	24 (L)
14	at Washington	24 (L)
13	New York	10 (W)
7	at Brooklyn	0 (W)
14	at Philadelphia	0 (W)
0	Washington	14 (L)
17	at New York	9 (W)
35	at Detroit	7 (W)
19	Chicago Cards	3 (W)
13	Brooklyn	0 (W)
21	at Green Bay	24 (L)
167	Won 7, Lost 4	119

1941
BERT BELL, ALDO DONELLI
and WALT KIESLING,
Head Coaches

Steelers		Opp.
14	at Cleveland	17 (L)
7	Philadelphia	10 (L)
10	New York	37 (L)
20	Washington	24 (L)
7	at New York	28 (L)
7	at Chicago Bears	34 (L)
3	at Washington	23 (L)
7	at Philadelphia	7 (T)
14	Brooklyn	7 (W)
7	Green Bay	54 (L)
7	at Brooklyn	35 (L)
103	Won 1, Lost 9, Tied 1	276

1940
WALT KIESLING, Head Coach

Steelers		Opp.
7	Chicago Cards	7 (T)
10	New York	10 (T)
10	at Detroit	7 (W)
3	Brooklyn	10 (L)
10	Washington	40 (L)
0	at Brooklyn	21 (L)
0	at New York	12 (L)
3	at Green Bay	24 (L)
10	at Washington	37 (L)
7	Philadelphia	3 (W)
0	at Philadelphia	7 (L)
60	Won 2, Lost 7, Tied 2	178

1939

**WALT KIESLING and
JOHN "BLOOD" McNALLY,
Head Coaches**

Steelers		Opp.
7	at Brooklyn	12 (L)
0	Chicago Cards	10 (L)
0	Chicago Bears	32 (L)
7	New York	14 (L)
14	at Washington	44 (L)
14	Washington	21 (L)
14	at Cleveland	14 (T)
13	at Brooklyn	17 (L)
7	at New York	23 (L)
14	at Philadelphia	17 (L)
24	Philadelphia	12 (W)

| 114 | *Won 1, Lost 9, Tied 1* | 216 |

1938

**JOHN "BLOOD" McNALLY,
Head Coach**

Steelers		Opp.
7	at Detroit	16 (L)
14	New York	27 (L)
7	at Philadelphia	27 (L)
17	at Brooklyn	3 (W)
13	at New York	10 (W)
7	Brooklyn	17 (L)
0	at Green Bay	20 (L)
0	Washington	7 (L)
7	at Philadelphia	14 (L)
0	at Washington	15 (L)
7	at Cleveland	13 (L)

| 79 | *Won 2, Lost 9* | 169 |

1937

**JOHN "BLOOD" McNALLY,
Head Coach**

Steelers		Opp.
27	Philadelphia	14 (W)
21	at Brooklyn	0 (W)
7	New York	10 (L)
0	Chicago Bears	7 (L)
3	at Detroit	7 (L)
20	at Washington	34 (L)
7	Chicago Cards	13 (L)
16	at Philadelphia	7 (W)
0	at New York	17 (L)
21	Washington	13 (W)
0	Brooklyn	23 (L)

| 122 | *Won 4, Lost 7* | 145 |

1936

JOE BACH, Head Coach

Steelers		Opp.
10	Boston	0 (W)
10	at Brooklyn	6 (W)
10	New York	7 (W)
9	Chicago Bears	27 (L)
17	Philadelphia	0 (W)
6	at Chicago Bears	26 (L)
10	at Green Bay	42 (L)
10	Brooklyn	7 (W)
6	at Philadelphia	0 (W)
3	at Detroit	28 (L)
6	at Chicago Cards	14 (L)
0	at Boston	30 (L)

| 97 | *Won 6, Lost 6* | 187 |

1935

JOE BACH, Head Coach

Steelers		Opp.
17	at Philadelphia	7 (W)
7	New York	42 (L)
7	Chicago Bears	23 (L)
0	at Green Bay	27 (L)
6	Philadelphia	17 (L)

Steelers		Opp.
17	Chicago Cards	13 (W)
6	Boston	0 (W)
7	Brooklyn	13 (L)
16	at Brooklyn	7 (W)
14	Green Bay	34 (L)
3	at Boston	13 (L)
0	at New York	13 (L)

| 100 | *Won 4, Lost 8* | 209 |

1934

LUBY DiMEOLO, Head Coach

Steelers		Opp.
13	Cincinnati	0 (W)
0	Boston	7 (L)
0	Philadelphia	17 (L)
12	New York	14 (L)
9	at Philadelphia	7 (W)
0	Chicago Bears	28 (L)
0	at Boston	39 (L)
7	at New York	17 (L)
3	at Brooklyn	21 (L)
7	at Detroit	40 (L)
0	at St. Louis	6 (L)
0	Brooklyn	10 (L)

| 51 | *Won 2, Lost 10* | 206 |

1933

JAP DOUDS, Head Coach

Steelers		Opp.
17	Cincinnati	0 (W)
2	New York	23 (L)
14	Chicago Cardinals	13 (W)
6	Boston	21 (L)
0	at Green Bay	47 (L)
0	at Cincinnati	0 (T)
16	at Boston	14 (L)
3	at Brooklyn	3 (T)
0	Brooklyn	32 (L)
6	at Philadelphia	25 (L)
3	at New York	27 (L)

| 67 | *Won 3, Lost 6, Tied 2* | 205 |

STEELERS VS. NFL OPPONENTS

STEELERS vs. ATLANTA FALCONS

	Steelers	Falcons		Steelers	Falcons
1966	57	33	1970	16	27
1968	41	21	1974h	24	17
			1978h	31	7

Steelers won 4, lost 1

STEELERS vs. BALTIMORE COLTS

	Steelers	Colts		Steelers	Colts
1950h	17	7	1975h	28	10
1957	19	13	(AFC Playoffs)		
1968h	7	41	1976	40	14
1971	21	34	(AFC Playoffs)		
1974h	30	0	1977	21	31
			1978h	35	13

Steelers won 6, lost 3

STEELERS vs. BOSTON YANKS

	Steelers	Yanks		Steelers	Yanks
1945	7	28	1947	30	14
1945h	6	10	1947h	17	7
1946h	16	7	1948h	24	14
1946	33	7	1948	7	13

Steelers won 5, lost 3

STEELERS vs. BROOKLYN DODGERS

	Steelers	Dodgers		Steelers	Dodgers
1933	3	3	1937	21	0
1933	0	32	1937h	0	23
1934	3	21	1938	17	3
1934h	0	10	1938h	7	17
1935h	7	13	1939	7	12
1935	16	7	1939	13	17
1936	10	6	1940h	3	10
1936h	10	7	1940	0	21

	Steelers	Dodgers		Steelers	Dodgers
1941h	14	7	1942h	13	0
1941	7	35	1943h	17	0
1942	7	0	1943	7	13

Steelers won 9, lost 12, tied 1

STEELERS vs. BUFFALO BILLS

	Steelers	Bills		Steelers	Bills
1970h	23	10	(AFC Playoffs)		
1972	38	21	1975h	21	30
1974h	32	14	1978	28	17

Steelers won 4, lost 1

STEELERS vs. CHICAGO BEARS

	Steelers	Bears		Steelers	Bears
1934h	0	28	1945h	7	28
1935h	7	23	1947	7	49
1936h	9	27	1949	21	30
1936	7	26	1958h	24	10
1937h	0	7	1959	21	27
1939h	0	32	1963h	17	17
1941	7	34	1967h	13	41
1943	21	48	1969	7	38
1944	7	34	1971	15	17
1944h	7	39	1975h	34	3

Steelers won 2, lost 17, tied 1

STEELERS vs. CINCINNATI BENGALS

	Steelers	Bengals		Steelers	Bengals
1970h	21	10	1974h	27	3
1970	7	34	1975	30	24
1971h	21	10	1975h	35	14
1971	21	13	1976h	23	6
1972	10	15	1976	7	3
1972h	40	17	1977h	20	14
1973	7	19	1977	10	17
1973h	20	13	1978	28	3
1974	10	17	1978h	7	6

Steelers won 13, lost 5

STEELERS vs. CINCINNATI REDS

	Steelers	Reds		Steelers	Reds
1933	17	0	1934h	13	0
1933	0	0	1934	0	13*

Steelers won 2, lost 1, tied 1

* Franchise transferred to St. Louis during 1934 season.

STEELERS vs. CLEVELAND BROWNS

	Steelers	Browns		Steelers	Browns
1950h	17	30	1954	7	42
1950	7	45	1955	14	41
1951	0	17	1955h	7	30
1951h	0	28	1956h	10	14
1952h	20	21	1956	24	16
1952	28	29	1957h	12	23
1953h	16	20	1957	0	24
1953	16	34	1958h	12	45
1954h	55	27	1958	10	27

	Steelers	Browns		Steelers	Browns
1959h	17	7	1969	31	42
1959	21	20	1969h	3	24
1960	20	28	1970	7	15
1960h	14	10	1970h	28	9
1961h	28	30	1971	17	27
1961	17	13	1971h	26	9
1962h	14	41	1972	24	26
1962	14	35	1972h	30	0
1963	23	35	1973h	33	6
1963h	9	7	1973	16	21
1964	23	7	1974h	20	16
1964h	17	30	1974	26	16
1965	19	24	1975	42	6
1965h	21	42	1975h	31	17
1966	14	41	1976	16	18
1966h	16	6	1976h	31	14
1967	10	21	1977	28	14
1967h	14	34	1977h	35	31
1968	24	31	1978h	15	9
1968h	24	45	1978	34	14

Steelers won 22, lost 36

STEELERS vs. DALLAS COWBOYS

	Steelers	Cowboys		Steelers	Cowboys
1960	35	28	1966	21	52
1961	24	27	1966h	7	20
1961h	37	7	1967h	21	24
1962	30	28	1968	7	28
1962h	27	42	1969h	7	10
1963h	27	21	1972	13	17
1963	24	19	1975	21	17
1964h	23	17	(Super Bowl X)		
1964	14	17	1977h	28	13
1965h	22	13	1978	35	31
1965	17	24	(Super Bowl XIII)		

Steelers won 10, lost 10

STEELERS vs. DENVER BRONCOS

	Steelers	Broncos		Steelers	Broncos
1970	13	16	1977	7	21
1971h	10	22	1977	21	34
1973h	13	23	(AFC Playoff)		
1974	35	35	1978	21	17
(Overtime)			1978	33	10
1975h	20	9	(AFC Playoff)		

Steelers won 3, lost 5, tied 1

STEELERS vs. DETROIT LIONS

	Steelers	Lions		Steelers	Lions
1934	7	40	1949h	14	7
1936	3	28	1950	7	10
1937	3	7	1952h	6	31
1938	7	16	1953	21	38
1940	10	7	1955h	28	31
1942	35	7	1956	7	45
1943h	35	34	1959h	10	10
1944h	6	27	1962	7	45
1944	7	21	1966h	17	3
1946	7	17	1967	24	14
1947h	17	10	1969h	16	13
1948	14	17	1973h	24	10

Steelers won 9, lost 14, tied 1

STEELERS VS. NFL OPPONENTS (continued)

STEELERS vs. GREEN BAY PACKERS

	Steelers	Packers		Steelers	Packers
1933	0	47	1949	30	7
1935	0	27	1951	33	35
1935h	14	34	1951h	28	7
1936	10	42	1953h	31	14
1938	0	20	1954	21	20
1940	3	24	1957h	10	27
1941h	7	54	1960h	13	19
1942	21	24	1963	14	33
1943h	28	38	1965h	9	41
1944	7	34	1967	24	17
1944h	20	35	1969h	34	38
1946	7	17	1970h	12	20
1947	18	17	1975	16	13
1948h	38	7			

Steelers won 8, lost 19

STEELERS vs. HOUSTON OILERS

	Steelers	Oilers		Steelers	Oilers
1970h	7	19	1975h	24	17
1970	7	3	1975	32	9
1971h	23	16	1976h	32	16
1971	3	29	1976	21	0
1972h	24	7	1977	10	27
1972	9	3	1977h	27	10
1973	36	7	1978h	17	24
1973h	33	7	1978	13	3
1974	13	7	1978	34	5
1974h	10	13	(AFC Championship)		

Steelers won 14, lost 5

STEELERS vs. KANSAS CITY CHIEFS

	Steelers	Chiefs		Steelers	Chiefs
1970h	14	31	1975h	28	3
1971	16	38	1976	45	0
1972h	16	7	1978h	27	24
1974	34	24			

Steelers won 5, lost 2

STEELERS vs. LOS ANGELES RAMS

	Steelers	Rams		Steelers	Rams
1938	7	13	1955	26	27
1939	14	14	1956h	30	13
1941	14	17	1961	14	24
1944h	28	30	1964h	14	26
1944h	6	33	1968	10	45
1947*h	7	48	1971h	14	23
1948	14	31	1975	3	10
1949h	7	7	1978	7	10
1952	14	28			

Steelers won 1, lost 14, tied 2

* Franchise transferred from Cleveland to Los Angeles after 1945 season.

STEELERS vs. MIAMI DOLPHINS

	Steelers	Dolphins		Steelers	Dolphins
1971	21	24	1973	26	30
1972	17	21	1976h	14	3
(AFC Championship)					

Steelers won 1, lost 3

STEELERS vs. MINNESOTA VIKINGS

	Steelers	Vikings		Steelers	Vikings
1962h	39	31	1972h	23	10
1964	10	30	1975	16	6
1967h	27	41	(Super Bowl IX)		
1969	14	52	1976	6	17

Steelers won 3, lost 4

STEELERS vs. NEW ENGLAND PATRIOTS

	Steelers	Patriots		Steelers	Patriots
1972h	33	3	1976h	27	30
1974	21	17			

Steelers won 2, lost 1

STEELERS vs. NEW ORLEANS SAINTS

	Steelers	Saints		Steelers	Saints
1967	14	10	1969	24	27
1968h	12	16	1974	28	7
1968	14	24	1978h	20	14

Steelers won 3, lost 3

STEELERS vs. NEW YORK BULLDOGS

	Steelers	Bulldogs		Steelers	Bulldogs
1949h	24	13	1949	27	0

Steelers won 2, lost 0

STEELERS vs. NEW YORK GIANTS

	Steelers	Giants		Steelers	Giants
1933	2	23	1949h	28	7
1933	3	27	1949	21	17
1934h	12	14	1950h	7	18
1934	7	17	1950	17	6
1935h	7	42	1951h	13	13
1935	0	13	1951	0	14
1936h	10	7	1952h	63	7
1937h	7	10	1953	14	10
1937	0	17	1954h	12	14
1938h	14	27	1954	3	24
1938	13	10	1955h	30	23
1939h	7	14	1955	19	17
1939	7	23	1956	10	38
1940h	10	10	1956h	14	17
1940	0	12	1957	0	35
1941h	10	37	1957h	21	10
1941	7	28	1958	31	10
1942h	13	10	1958h	6	17
1942	17	9	1959h	16	21
1943h	28	14	1959	14	9
1943	14	42	1960h	17	19
1944	0	23	1960	24	27
1945h	6	34	1961h	14	17
1945	21	7	1961	21	42
1946h	14	17	1962h	27	31
1946	0	7	1962	20	17
1947	38	21	1963h	31	0
1947h	24	7	1963	17	33
1948	38	28	1964h	27	24
1948h	27	34	1964	44	17

	Steelers	Giants		Steelers	Giants
1965h	13	23	1968h	20	34
1965	10	35	1969	7	10
1966h	34	34	1969h	17	21
1966h	47	28	1971	17	13
1967h	24	27	1976	27	0
1967	20	28			

Steelers won 26, lost 42, tied 3

STEELERS vs. NEW YORK JETS

	Steelers	Jets		Steelers	Jets
1970h	21	17	1977	23	20
1973h	26	14	1978	28	17
1975	20	7			

Steelers won 5, lost 0

STEELERS vs. OAKLAND RAIDERS

	Steelers	Raiders		Steelers	Raiders
1970	14	31	1974	24	13
1972h	34	28	(AFC Championship)		
1972h	13	7	1975h	16	10
(AFC Playoffs)			(AFC Championship)		
1973	17	9	1976	28	31
1973	14	33	1976	7	24
(AFC Playoffs)			(AFC Championship)		
1974h	0	17	1977h	7	16

Steelers won 5, lost 6

STEELERS vs. PHILADELPHIA EAGLES

	Steelers	Eagles		Steelers	Eagles
1933	6	25	1952h	25	31
1934h	0	17	1952	21	26
1934	9	7	1953	7	23
1935	17	0	1953h	7	35
1935h	6	17	1954	17	7
1936h	17	0	1954h	22	24
1936	6	0	1955h	13	7
1936*	27	14	1955	0	24
1937**	16	7	1956h	21	35
1938h	7	27	1956	7	14
1938	7	14	1957h	6	0
1939	14	17	1957	6	7
1939h	24	12	1958h	24	3
1940h	7	3	1958h	31	24
1940	0	7	1959	31	0
1941h	7	10	1959h	24	28
1941	7	7	1960	21	34
1942h	14	24	1960h	27	21
1942	14	0	1961	16	21
1945h	3	45	1961h	24	35
1945	6	30	1962h	13	7
1946h	10	7	1962	26	17
1946	7	10	1963	21	21
1947h	35	24	1963h	20	20
1947	0	21	1964	7	21
1947h	0	21	1964h	10	34
(Eastern Conference Playoff)			1965	20	14
1948h	7	34	1965h	13	47
1948	0	17	1966h	14	31
1949h	7	38	1966	23	27
1949	17	34	1967	24	34
1950h	10	17	1968h	6	3
1950	9	7	1969	27	41
1951h	13	34	1970	20	30
1951	17	13	1974h	27	0

Steelers won 25, lost 41, tied 3

* Buffalo, N.Y.   ** Charleston, W. Va.

STEELERS vs. ST. LOUIS CARDINALS

	Steelers	Cardinals		Steelers	Cardinals
1933	14	13	1958	27	20
1935h	17	13	1958h	28	21
1936	14	6	1959*	35	20
1937h	7	13	1959	24	45
1939h	0	10	1960h	27	14
1940h	7	7	1960	7	38
1942h	19	3	1961h	30	27
1943h	34	13	1961	0	20
1945h	23	0	1962	26	17
1946h	14	7	1962h	19	7
1948h	7	24	1963h	23	10
1950	28	17	1963	23	24
1950h	28	7	1964	30	34
1951	28	14	1964h	20	21
1952	17	14	1965h	7	20
1952h	34	28	1965	17	21
1953h	31	28	1966h	30	9
1953	21	17	1966	3	6
1954	14	17	1967h	14	28
1954h	20	17	1967	14	14
1955h	14	7	1968	28	28
1956h	14	7	1968h	10	20
1956	27	38	1969h	14	27
1957h	29	20	1969	10	47
1957	27	2	1972	25	19

Steelers won 28, lost 20, tied 3

* Franchise transferred from Chicago to St. Louis after 1959 season.

STEELERS vs. SAN DIEGO CHARGERS

	Steelers	Chargers		Steelers	Chargers
1971h	21	17	1975	37	0
1972	24	2	1976h	23	0
1973h	38	21	1977	10	9

Steelers won 6, lost 0

STEELERS vs. SAN FRANCISCO 49ERS

	Steelers	49ers		Steelers	49ers
1951h	24	28	1965	17	27
1952	24	7	1968h	28	45
1954	3	31	1973	37	14
1958	20	23	1977h	27	0
1961h	20	10			

Steelers won 4, lost 5

STEELERS vs. SEATTLE SEAHAWKS

	Steelers	Seahawks		Steelers	Seahawks
1977h	30	20	1978	21	10

Steelers won 2, lost 0

STEELERS vs. TAMPA BAY BUCCANEERS

	Steelers	Bucs
1976h	42	0

Steelers won 1, lost 0

STEELERS vs. WASHINGTON REDSKINS

	Steelers	Redskins		Steelers	Redskins
1933	0	21	1936h	10	0
1933	16	14	1936	0	30
1934h	0	7	1937*	20	34
1934	0	39	1937h	21	13
1935h	6	0	1938h	0	7
1935	3	13	1938	0	15

	Steelers	Redskins		Steelers	Redskins
1939	14	44	1954	14	17
1939h	14	21	1955h	14	23
1940h	10	40	1955	17	28
1940	10	37	1956h	30	13
1941h	20	24	1956	23	0
1941	3	23	1957h	28	7
1942	14	24	1957	3	10
1942h	0	14	1958h	24	16
1943h	14	14	1958	14	14
1943	27	14	1959h	17	23
1944	20	42	1959	27	6
1945h	0	14	1960	22	10
1945	0	24	1960h	27	27
1946	14	14	1961h	20	0
1946h	14	7	1961	30	14
1947	26	27	1962h	23	21
1947h	21	14	1962	27	24
1948	14	17	1963h	38	27
1948h	10	7	1963	34	28
1949h	14	27	1964h	0	30
1949	14	27	1964	14	7
1950	7	24	1965h	3	31
1950h	26	7	1965	14	35
1951h	7	22	1966h	27	33
1951	20	10	1966	10	24
1952h	24	28	1967h	10	15
1952	24	23	1968	13	16
1953h	9	17	1969h	7	14
1953	14	13	1973h	21	16
1954h	37	7			

Steelers won 27, lost 40, tied 4

* Franchise transferred from Boston to Washington after 1936 season.

STEELER PLAYER DRAFTS: THE NOLL YEARS

1978

1. Johnson, Ron (CB), Eastern Michigan 2. Fry, Willie (DE), Notre Dame 3. Craig Colquitt (P), Tennessee 4. Anderson, Larry (CB), Louisiana Tech 5. Choice traded to Green Bay for Dave Pureifory 6. Reutershan, Randy (WR), Pitt 7. Dufresne, Mark (TE), Nebraska 8-a. Moser, Rick (RB), Rhode Island (choice from St. Louis for Marv Kellum) 8-b. Keys, Andre (WR), California Poly 9. Reynolds, Lance (OT), Brigham Young 10-a. Becker, Doug (LB), Notre Dame 10-b. Jurich, Tom (PK), Northern Arizona (choice from Tampa Bay for Ernie Holmes) 11-a. Terry, Nat (CB), Florida State (choice from Tampa Bay for Ernie Holmes) 11-b. Brzoza, Tom (C), Pitt 12. Carr, Brad (LB), Maryland.

1977

1. Cole, Robin (LB), New Mexico 2. Thornton, Sidney (RB), Northwestern Louisiana 3-a. Beasley, Tom (DT), Virginia Tech (choice from New York Jets) 3-b. Smith, Jim (WR), Michigan 4-a. Petersen, Ted (C), Eastern Illinois (choice from Green Bay) 4-b. Smith, Laverne (RB), Kansas (choice from Chicago) 4-c. Audick, Dan (G), Hawaii 5-a. Stoudt, Cliff (QB), Youngstown State (choice from Kansas City) 5-b. Courson, Steve (G), South Carolina (choice from Detroit) 5-c. Winston, Dennis (LB), Arkansas 6. Harris, Paul (LB), Alabama 7. Frisch, Randy (DT), Missouri 8. August, Phil (WR), Miami (Fla.) 9. Kelly, Roosevelt (TE), Eastern Kentucky 10-a. Cowans, Alvin (DB), Florida (choice from Buffalo) 10-b. LaCrosse,

Dave (LB), Wake Forest 11. West, Lou (DB), Cincinnati 12. Stephens, Jimmy (TE), Florida.

1976

1. Cunningham, Bennie (TE), Clemson 2-a. Pinney, Ray (C), Washington (choice from Chicago) 2-b. Kruczek, Mike (QB), Boston College (choice from Baltimore) 2-c. Files, James (G-C), McNeese State 3-a. Coder, Ron (DT), Penn State (choice from Green Bay) 3-b. Pough, Ernest (WR), Texas Southern 4-a. Monds, Wonder (S), Nebraska (choice from Baltimore) 4-lb. Bell, Theo (WR), Arizona 5. Norton, Rodney (LB), Rice 6-a. Dunn, Gary (DT), Miami (Fla), (choice from St. Louis) 6-b. Deloplaine, Jack (RB, Salem (W. Va.) 7. Burton, Barry (TE), Vanderbilt 8. McAleney, Ed (DE), Massachusetts 9. Gaines, Wentford (CB), Cincinnati 10. Campbell, Gary (LB), Colorado 11. Fuchs, Rolland (RB), Arkansas 12. Carroll, Bill (WR), East Texas State 13. Kain, Larry (LB), Ohio State 14. Fields, Wayne (DB), Florida 15. Davis, Mel (DE), North Texas State 16. Butts, Randy (RB), Kearney State 17. Kirk, Kelvin (WR), Dayton.

1975

1. Brown, Dave (DB), Michigan 2. Barber, Bob (DE), Grambling 3. White, Walter (TE), Maryland 4. Evans, Harold (LB), Houston 5. Sexton, Brent (DB), Elon 6. Crenshaw, Marvin (OT), Nebraska 7. Mattingly, Wayne (OT), Colorado 8. Kropp, Tom (LB), Kearney St. (choice from Kansas City) 8-a. Humphrey, Al (DE), Tulsa 9. Clark, Eugene (G), UCLA (choice from New England) 9-a. Reimer, Bruce (RB), No. Dakota St. 10. Heyer, Kirk (DT), Kearney St. (choice from New England) 10-a. Gray, Archie (WR), Wyoming 11. Little, Randy (TE), W. Liberty St. (W. Va.) 12. Murphy, Greg (DE), Penn. St. 13. Gaddis, Robert (WR), Mississippi Valley 14. Collier, Mike (RB), Morgan St. 15. Thatcher, Jim (WR), Langston (choice from Kansas City) 15-a. Smith, Marty (DT), Louisville 16. Bassler, Miller (TE), Houston 17. Hegener, Stan (G), Nebraska.

1974

1. Swann, Lynn (WR), So. California 2. Lambert, Jack (LB), Kent St. 3. Choice to Oakland 4-a. Stallworth, John (WR), Alabama A. & M. (choice from New England) 4-b. Allen, Jim (DB), UCLA 5. Webster, Mike (C), Wisconsin 6-a. Wolf, James (DE), Prairie View (choice from Denver) 6-b. Druschel, Rick (OT), No. Carolina St. 7-a. Sitterle, Allen (OT), No. Carolina St. (choice from New England) 7-b. Garske, Scott (TE), Eastern Washington St. 8. Gefert, Mark (LB), Purdue 9-a. Reamon, Tom (RB), Missouri (choice from Denver) 9-b. Davis, Charlie (DT), Texas Christian 10-a Kregel, Jim (G), Ohio St. (choice from New England) 10-b. Atkinson, Dave (DB), Brigham Young 11. Morton, Dickey (RB), Arkansas 12. Lickiss, Hugh (LB), Simpson (Iowa) 13. Kolch, Frank (QB), Eastern Michigan 14. Henley, Bruce (DB), Rice 15. Hunt, Larry (DT), Iowa St. 16. Morgan, Octavus (LB), Illinois 17. Moore, Larry (DE), Angelo St. (Tex.)

1973

1. Thomas, James (DB), Florida St. 2. Phares, Ken (DB), Mississippi St. 3. Bernhardt, Roger (G), Kansas 4. Clark, Gail (LB), Michigan St. 5. Reavis, David (DE), Arkansas (choice from New Orleans) 5-a. Clark, Larry (LB), No. Illinois 6. Bell, Ron (RB), Illinois St. 7. Dorsey, Nate (DE), Mississippi Valley 8. Toews, Loren (LB), California (choice from Denver) 9. Bon-

ham, Bracy (G), No. Carolina Central 10. Wunderly, Don (DT), Arkansas 11. White, Bob (DB), Arizona 12. Lee, Willie (RB), Indiana St. 13. Fergerson, Rick (WR), Kansas St. 14. Cowan, Roger (DT), Stanford 15. Cross, Charles (DB), Iowa 16. Nardi, Glen (DT), Navy 17. Shannon, Mike (DT), Oregon St.

1972

1. Harris, Franco (RB), Penn State 2. Gravelle, Gordon (OT), Brigham Young 3. McMakin, John (TE), Clemson 4. Brinkley, Lorenzo (DB), Missouri (choice from NY Giants) 4-a. Bradley, Ed (LB), Wake Forest 5. Furness, Steve (DE), Rhode Island 6. Meyer, Dennis (DB), Arkansas St. 7. Colquitt, Joe (DE), Kansas St. (choice from NY Giants) 8. Vincent, Stahle (RB), Rice 9. Kelley, Don (DB), Clemson 10. Brown, Bob (DT), Tampa 11. Gilliam, Joe (QB), Tennessee St. 12. Curl, Ron (OT), Michigan St. 13. Messmer, Ernie (DT), Villanova 14. Durrance, Tom (RB), Florida 15. Hulecki, John (G), Massachusetts (choice from Houston) 15-a. Harrington, Charles (G), Wichita 16. Hawkins, Nate (WR), Nevada-Las Vegas 17. Linehan, Ron (B), Idaho.

1971

1. Lewis, Frank (WR), Grambling 2. Ham, Jack (LB), Penn St. 3. Davis, Steve (RB), Delaware St. 4. Mullins, Gerry (G), So. California 4-a. White, Dwight (DE), E. Texas St. (choice from Baltimore) 5. Brown, Larry (TE), Kansas (choice from New Orleans) 5-a. Holmes, Melvin (OT), No. Car. A&T 5-b. Anderson, Ralph (DB), W. Texas St. (choice from Miami) 5-c. Brister, Fred (LB), Mississippi (choice from Minnesota) 6. Hanneman, Craig (G), Oregon St. 7. McClure, Worthy (OT-G), Mississippi 8. Crowe, Larry (RB), Texas Southern (choice from New Orleans) 8-a. Rogers, Paul (K), Nebraska 8-b. Holmes, Ernie (DT), Texas Southern (choice from Miami) 9. Anderson, Mike (LB), Louisiana St. 10. O'Shea, Jim (LB), Boston College 11. Wagner, Mike (DB), Western Illinois 12. Choice to Baltimore 13. Young, Alfred (WR), So. Car. St. 14. Evans, McKinney (DB), New Mex. Highlands 15. Makin, Ray (G), Kentucky 16. Huntley, Walter (DB), Trinity (Tex.) 17. Ehle, Dan (RB), Howard Payne.

1970

1. Bradshaw, Terry (QB), Louisiana Tech 2. Shanklin, Ron (WR), North Texas St. 3. Blount, Mel (DB), Southern 4. George, Ed (OT), Wake Forest 4-a. Evenson, Jim (RB), Oregon (choice from New York Giants) 5. Staggers, Jon (WR), Missouri 6. Barrera, Manuel (LB), Kansas State 6-a. Kegler, Clarence (OT), So. Carolina St. 7. Griffin, Danny (RB), Texas-Arlington 8. Smith, Dave (WR), Indiana (Pa.) 9. Crennel, Carl (LB), West Virginia 10. Brown, Isiah (DB), Stanford 11. Hunt, Calvin (C), Baylor 12. Sharp, Rick (OT), Washington 13. Main, Billy (RB), Oregon St. 14. Askson Burt (LB), Texas Southern 15. Keppy, Glen (DT), Platteville (Wis.) 16. Yanossy, Frank (DT), Tennessee 17. Key, Harry (TE), Mississippi Valley.

1969

1. Greene, Joe (DT), No. Texas St. 2. Hanratty, Terry (QB), Notre Dame 2-a. Bankston, Warren (RB), Tulane (choice from San Francisco) 3. Kolb, Jon (C),

Oklahoma St. 4. Campbell, Bob (RB), Penn St. 5. Choice to St. Louis 6. Choice to Green Bay 7. Beatty, Charles (DB), No. Texas St. 7-a. Brown, Chadwick (OT), E. Texas St. 8. Cooper, Joe (WR), Tennessee St. 9 Sodaski, John (DB), Villanova 10. Greenwood, L.C. (DE), Arkansas AM & N 11. Washington, Clarence (DT), Arkansas AM & N 12. Fisher, Doug (LB), San Diego St. 13. Lynch, John (LB), Drake 14. Houmard, Bob (RB), Ohio U. 15. Liberto, Ken (WR), Louisiana Tech 16. Mosley, Dock (WR), Alcorn A & M 17. Eppright, Bill (K), Kent St.

ALL TIME STEELER ROSTER: 1933–78

A

Adamchik, Ed (T), Pitt	1967
Adams, Bob (TE), Pacific	1969–71
Adams, Paul (C), Morehead Teachers	1947
Agajanian, Ben (K), New Mexico	1945
Alban, Dick (E), Northwestern	1956–59
Alberghini, Tom (G), Holy Cross	1945
Albrecht, Art (C-OT), Wisconsin	1942
Alderton, John (E), Maryland	1953
Allen, Charles (LB), Washington	1965
Allen, Chuck (LB), Washington	1970–71
Allen, Jim (DB), UCLA	1974–77
Allen, Lou (T), Duke	1950–51
Alley, Don (WR), Adams State	1969
Anadabaker, Rudy (G), Pitt	1952, 1954
Anderson, Art (T), Idaho	1963
Anderson, Chet (E), Minnesota	1967
Anderson, Fred (DE-DT) Prairie View A & M	1978
Anderson, Larry (CB), Louisiana Tech	1978
Anderson, Ralph (DB), West Texas State	1971–72
Arndt, Al (G), South Dakota State	1935
Arndt, Dick (T), Idaho	1967–70
Arnold, Jay (QB), Texas	1941
Artman, Corwan (T), Stanford	1933
Asbury, Willie (B), Kent State	1966–68
Askson, Burth (DE), Texas Southern	1971
Atkinson, Frank (T), Stanford	1963
Augusterfer, Gene (B), Catholic U.	1935
Austin, Ocie (DB), Utah State	1970–71

B

Badar, Rich (QB), North Carolina	1967
Baker, Conway (T), Centenary	1944**
Baker, John (E), North Carolina College	1963–67
Baldacci, Lou (B), Michigan	1956
Ballman, Gary (B), Michigan State	1962–66
Balog, Bob (C), Denver	1949–50
Banaszak, John (DE), Eastern Michigan	1975–78
Banonis, Vince (C), Detroit	1944
Bankston, Warren (RB), Tulane	1969–72
Barbolak, Pete (T), Purdue	1949
Barker, Ed (E), Washington State	1953
Barnett, Tom (B), Purdue	1959–60
Barry, Fred (DB), Boston College	1970
Bartlett, Earl (B), Centre	1939
Bartaanen, Jim (C), Michigan	1938
Basrak, Mike (C), Duquesne	1937–38
Bassi, Dick (G), Santa Clara	1941

ALL TIME STEELERS ROSTER: 1933–78
(continued)

Beams, Byron (T), Notre Dame	1959–60
Beasley, Tom (DT), Virginia Tech	1978
Beatty, Charles (DB), North Texas State	1969–72
Beatty, Ed (C), Mississippi	1957–61
Becker, Wayland (E), Marquette	1939
Bell, Theo (WR), Arizona	1976, 1978
Bernet, Ed (E), SMU	1955
Bettis, Tom (LB), Purdue	1962
Billock, Frank (G), St. Mary's of Minnesota	1937
Binotto, John (B), Duquesne	1942
Bishop, Don (B), Los Angeles College	1958–59
Bivins, Charles (B), Morris Brown	1967
Blankenship, Greg (LB), California State (Hay.)	1976
Bleier, Rocky (B), Notre Dame	1968, 1970–78
Blount, Mel (DB), Southern	1970–78
Bolkovac, Nick (T), Pitt	1953–54
Bond, Randall (QB), Washington	1939
Bonelli, Ernie (B), Pitt	1946
Booth, Clarence (B), SMU	1944**
Boyle, Shorty (E)	1934
Bova, Tony (E), St. Francis	1942, 1943*, 1944**, 1945–47
Bowman, Bill (B), William & Mary	1957
Boyd, Sam (E), Baylor	1939–40
Bradley, Ed (LB), Wake Forest	1972–75
Bradshaw, Charles (T), Baylor	1961–66
Bradshaw, Jim (B), Chattanooga	1963–67
Bradshaw, Terry (QB), Louisiana Tech	1970–78
Brady, Pat (B), Nevada	1952–54
Brandau, Art (C), Tennessee	1945–46
Brandt, Jim (B), St. Thomas	1952–54
Bray, Maurice (T), SMU	1935–36
Breedlove, Rod (LB), Maryland	1965–68
Breedon, Bill (B), Oklahoma	1937
Breen, Gene (LB), Virginia Tech	1965–66
Brett, Ed (E), Washington State	1936–37
Brewster, Pete (E), Purdue	1959–60
Broussard, Fred (C), Texas A & M	1955
Brovelli, Angelo (QB), St. Mary's of California	1933–34
Brown, Dave (DB), Michigan	1975
Brown, Ed (QB), San Francisco	1962–65
Brown, John (T), Syracuse	1967–72
Brown, Larry (TE-OT), Kansas	1971–76, 1978
Brown, Tom (E), William & Mary	1942
Brown, William (QB), Texas Tech	1945
Browning, Greg (E), Denver	1947
Bruder, Henry (QB), Northwestern	1940
Brumbaugh, Boyd (B), Duquesne	1939–41
Brumfield, Jim (RB), Indiana State (Ind.)	1971
Brundage, Dewey (E), Brigham Young	1954
Bruney, Fred (B), Ohio State	1956–57
Bryant, Hubie (WR), Minnesota	1970
Bucek, Felix (G), Texas A & M	1946
Buda, Carl (G), Tulsa	1945
Bukich, Rudy (QB), Southern California	1960–61
Bulger, Chester (T), Auburn	1944**
Bullocks, Amos (B), Southern Illinois	1966
Burleson, John (G), SMU	1933

Burnett, Len (DB), Oregon	1961
Burnette, Tom (B), North Carolina	1938
Burrell, John (E), Rice	1962–64
Butler, Jack (B), St. Bonaventure	1951–59
Butler, Jim (B), Edward Waters	1965–67
Butler, John (B), Tennessee	1943–44
Bykowski, Frank (G), Purdue	1940

C

Cabrelli, Larry (E), Colgate	1943*
Calcagni, Ralph (T), Pennsylvania	1947
Call, John (B), Colgate	1959
Calland, Lee (DB), Louisville	1969–72
Calvin, Tom (B), Alabama	1952–54
Cameron, Paul (B), UCLA	1954
Campbell, Bob (RB), Penn State	1969
Campbell, Don (T), Carnegie Tech	1939–41
Campbell, Glenn (E), Emporia State	1935
Campbell, John (LB), Minnesota	1965–69
Campbell, Leon (B), Arkansas	1955
Campbell, Ray (LB), Marquette	1958–60
Canale, Rocco (G), Boston College	1943*
Capp, Dick (E), Boston College	1968
Cara, Dom (E), North Carolina State	1937–38
Cardwell, Joe (T), Duke	1937–38
Carpenter, Preston (E), Arkansas	1960–63
Casper, Charles (QB), TCU	1935
Cenci, John (C), Pitt	1956
Chamberlain, Garth (G), Brigham Young	1945
Chandnois, Lynn (B), Michigan State	1950–56
Cheatham, Ernest (T), Loyola	1954
Cherry, Edgar (B), Hardin-Simmons	1939
Cherundolo, Chuck (C), Penn State	1941–42, 1945–48
Christy, Dick (B), North Carolina State	1958
Cibulas, Joe (T), Duquesne	1945
Ciccone, Ben (C), Duquesne	1934–35
Cichowski, Gene (B), Indiana	1957
Cifelli, Gus (T), Notre Dame	1954
Cifers, Bob (QB), Tennessee	1947–48
Clack, Jim (C-G), Wake Forest	1971–77
Clark, Jim (B), Pitt	1933–34
Clark, Mike (K), Texas A & M	1964–67
Clement, Henry (E), North Carolina	1961
Clement, John (B), SMU	1946–48*
Cole, Robin (LB), New Mexico	1977–78
Cole, Terry (B), Indiana	1970
Collier, Mike (RB), Morgan State	1975
Colquitt, Craig (P), Tennessee	1978
Compagno, Tony (B), St. Mary's of California	1946–48
Compton, Dick (E), McMurry	1967–68
Condit, Merlyn (B), Carnegie Tech	1940, 1946
Conn, Dick (DB), Georgia	1974
Connelly, Mike (C), Utah State	1968
Conti, Enio (G), Bucknell	1943*
Coomer, Joe (T), Austin	1941, 1945–46
Cooper, Sam (T), Geneva	1933
Cordileone, Lou (G), Clemson	1962–63
Coronado, Bob (E), Pacific	1961
Cotton, Russell (B), Texas Mines	1942
Courson, Steve (G), South Carolina	1978
Cousino, Brad (LB), Miami (O.)	1977
Craft, Russ (B), Alabama	1954

Cregar, William (G), Holy Cross	1947–48	
Crennel, Carl (LB), West Virginia	1970	
Critchfield, Larry (G), Grove City	1933	
Croft, Winfield (G), Utah	1936	
Cropper, Marshall (E), Maryland	1967–69	
Cunningham, Bennie (TE), Clemson	1976–78	
Currivan, Don (E), Boston College	1944**	
Curry, Roy (B), Jackson State	1963	

D

Dailey, Ted (E), Pitt	1933
Daniel, Willie (B), Mississippi State	1961–66
Davidson, Bill (B), Temple	1937–39
Davis, Art (B), Mississippi State	1956
Davis, Charlie (DT), TCU	1974
Davis, Dave (WR), Tennessee State	1973
Davis, Henry (LB), Grambling	1970–73
Davis, Paul (QB), Otterbein	1947–48
Davis, Robert (E), Penn State	1946–50
Davis, Sam (G), Allen	1967–78
Davis, Steve (RB), Delaware State	1972–74
Dawson, Len (QB), Purdue	1957–59
DeCarbo, Nick (G), Duquesne	1933
DeCarlo, Art (B), Georgia	1953
Deloplaine, Jack (RB), Salem (W. Va.)	1976–78
Demko, George (T), Appalachian State	1961
Dempsey, John (T), Bucknell	1934
DePascal, Carmine (E), Wichita	1945
DePaul, Henry (G), Duquesne	1945
Derby, Dean (B), Washington	1957–61
Dess, Darrell (G), North Carolina State	1958
Dial, Buddy (E), Rice	1959–63
Dicus, Chuck (WR), Arkansas	1973
Dockery, John (DB), Harvard	1972–73
Dodril, Dale (G), Colorado A & M	1951–59
Dodson, Les (B), Mississippi	1941
Doehring, John (B)	1935
Dolly, Dick (E), West Virginia	1941–45
Doloway, Cliff (E), Carnegie Tech	1935
Donelli, Allan (B), Duquesne	1941–42
Douds, Forrest (T), W & J	1933–35
Dougherty, Bob (LB), Kentucky	1958
Douglas, Bob (B), Kansas State	1938
Doyle, Dick (B), Ohio State	1955
Doyle, Ted (T), Nebraska	1938–42, 1943*, 1944**
Drulis, Al (B), Temple	1947
Druschel, Rick (G-OT), North Carolina State	1974
Dudley, Bill (B), Virginia	1942, 1945–46
Dugan, Len (C), Wichita	1939
Duggan, Gil (T), Oklahoma	1944**
Duhart, Paul (B), Florida	1945
Dungy, Tony (DB), Minnesota	1977–78
Dunn, Gary (DT), Miami (Fla.)	1976–78
Dutton, Bill (B), Pitt	1946

E

Eaton, Vic (QB), Missouri	1955
Edwards, Glen (DB), Florida A & M	1971–78
Elliott, Jim (K), Presbyterian	1967
Ellstrom, Marv (B), Oklahoma	1935
Elter, Leo (B), Duquesne and Villanova	1953–54, 1958–59
Engebretsen, Paul (G) Northwestern	1933

Engles, Rick (P), Tulsa	1977
Evans, Jon (E), Oklahoma A & M	1958
Evans, Ray (QB), Kansas	1948

F

Farrar, Venice (B), North Carolina State	1938–39
Farrell, Ed (B), Muhlenberg	1938
Farroh, Shipley (G), Iowa	1938
Feher, Nick (G), Georgia	1955
Feniello, Garry (G), Wake Forest	1947
Ferguson, Bob (B), Ohio State	1962–63
Ferry, Lou (T), Villanova	1952–55
Fife, Ralph (C), Pitt	1946
Filchock, Frank (QB), Indiana	1938
Finks, Jim (QB), Tulsa	1949–55
Fisher, Doug (LB), San Diego State	1969–70
Fisher, Everett (B), Santa Clara	1940
Fisher, Ray (T), Eastern Illinois	1959
Fiske, Max (B), DePaul	1936–39
Flanagan, Dick (G), Ohio State	1953–55
Folkins, Lee (E), Washington	1965
Foltz, Vernon (C), St. Vincent	1945
Ford, Henry (B), Pitt	1956
Foruria, John (B), Idaho	1967–68
Fournet, Sid (G), LSU	1957
Francis, Sam (B), Nebraska	1939
Frank, Joe (T), Georgetown	1943*
Frketich, Len (T), Penn State	1945
Fugler, Dick (T), Tulane	1952
Fullerton, Ed (B), Maryland	1953
Fuqua, John (B), Morgan State	1970–76
Furness, Steve (DT), Rhode Island	1972–78

G

Gage, Bob (B), Clemson	1949–50
Gagner, Larry (G), Florida	1966–69
Gaona, Bob (T), Wake Forest	1953–56
Garnaas, Wilford (B), Minnesota	1946–48
Garrett, Reggie (WR), Eastern Michigan	1974–75
Gasparella, Joe (QB), Notre Dame	1948, 1950–51
Gauer, Charles (E), Colgate	1943*
Gentry, Byron (G), Southern California	1937–39
Gerela, Roy (PK), New Mexico State	1973–78
Geri, Joe (B), Georgia	1949–51
Gildea, John (QB), St. Bonaventure	1935–37
Gilliam, Joe (QB), Tennessee State	1972–75
Girard, Earl (B), Wisconsin	1957
Glamp, Joe (B), LSU	1947–49
Glass, Glenn (B), Tennessee	1962–63
Glass, Park (C), Westminster	1947
Glatz, Fred (E), Pitt	1967
Glick, Gary (B), Colorado A & M	1956–59
Goff, Clark (T), Florida	1940
Goldsmith, Bill (C), Emporia Teachers	1947
Gonda, George (B), Duquesne	1942
Gorinski, Walt (B), LSU	1946
Graff, Neil (QB), Wisconsin	1976–77
Graham, Ken (DB), Washington State	1970
Gravette, Gordon (OT), Brigham Young	1972–76
Graves, Ray (C), Tennessee	1943*
Gray, Sam (E), Tulsa	1946–47
Green, Bob (K), Florida	1960–61
Greene, Joe (DT), North Texas State	1969–78

ALL TIME STEELERS ROSTER: 1933–78
(continued)

Greeney, Norm (G), Notre Dame	1934–35
Greenwood, L. C. (DE),	
Arkansas AM & N	1969–78
Grigas, John (B), Holy Cross	1944**
Gros, Earl (B), LSU	1967–69
Grossman, Randy (TE), Temple	1974–78
Gunderman, Bob (B), Virginia	1957
Gunnels, Riley (T), Georgia	1965–66

H

Hackney, Elmer (B),	
Kansas State	1941
Haggerty, Mike (G), Miami	1967–70
Haines, Byron (B), Washington	1937
Haley, Dick (B), Pitt	1961–64
Hall, Ron (B), Missouri Valley	1959
Ham, Jack (LB), Penn State	1971–78
Hanlon, Bob (B), Loras	1949
Hanneman, Craig (DE),	
Oregon State	1972–73
Hanratty, Terry (QB),	
Notre Dame	1969–75
Hanson, Tom (B), Temple	1938
Harkey, Lem (B), Emporia	1955
Harper, Maurice (C), Austin	1941
Harris, Bill (E),	
Hardin-Simmons	1937
Harris, Franco (RB), Penn State	1972–78
Harris, Lou (B), Kent State	1968
Harrison, Reggie (RB), Cincinnati	1974–77
Harrison, Richard (E),	
Boston College	1964
Harrison, Robert (LB), Oklahoma	1964
Hartley, Howard (B), Duke	1949–52
Hayduk, Henry (G),	
Washington State	1935
Hayes, Dick (LB), Clemson	1959–60, 1962
Hays, George (E), St. Bonaventure	1950–52
Hebert, Ken (E & K), Houston	1968
Hegarty, Bill (T), Villanova	1953
Held, Paul (QB), San Jose State	1954
Heller, Warren (B), Pitt	1934–36
Henderson, Jon (B), Colorado State	1968–69
Hendley, Dick (QB), Clemson	1951
Henry, Mike (LB),	
Southern California	1959–61
Henry, Urban (T), Georgia Tech	1964
Hensley, Dick (E), Kentucky	1952
Henson, Ken (C), TCU	1965
Hewitt, Bill (E), Michigan	1943*
Hickey, Howard (E), Arkansas	1941
Hill, Harlon (E), Florence State	1962
Hill, Jim (B), Tennessee	1955
Hillebrand, Jerry (LB), Colorado	1968–70
Hilton, John (E), Richmond	1965–69
Hines, Glen Ray (OT), Arkansas	1973
Hinkle, John (B), Syracuse	1943*
Hinte, Hale (E), Pitt	1942
Hinton, Chuck (T),	
North Carolina College	1964–71
Hipps, Claude (B), Georgia	1952–53
Hoague, Joe (B), Colgate	1941–42, 1946
Hoak, Dick (B), Penn State	1961–70
Hoel, Bob (G), Minnesota	1935
Hogan, Darrell (G), Trinity-Texas	1949–53
Hohn, Bob (B), Nebraska	1965–69
Holcomb, Bill (T), Texas Tech	1937
Holler, Ed (LB), South Carolina	1964

Hollingsworth, Joe (B),	
East Kentucky State	1949–51
Holm, Bernard (B), Alabama	1933
Holmer, Walt (B), Northwestern	1933
Holmes, Ernie (DT),	
Texas Southern	1972–77
Holmes, Mel (OT),	
North Carolina A & T	1971–73
Hood, Frank (B), Pitt	1933
Hornick, Bill (T), Tulane	1947
Hubbard, Cal (T), Geneva	
and Centenary	1936
Hubka, Gene (B), Bucknell	1947
Hughes, Dennis (TE), Georgia	1970–71
Hughes, Dick (B), Tulsa	1957
Hughes, George (G),	
William & Mary	1950–54
Hunter, Art (C), Notre Dame	1965

I

Itzel, John (B), Pitt	1945
Ivy, Frank (E), Oklahoma	1940
Izo, George (QB), Notre Dame	1966

J

James, Dan (T), Ohio State	1960–66
Janecek, Clarence (G), Purdue	1933, 1935
Jansante, Val (E), Duquesne	1946–51
Jarvi, Toimi (B), Northern Illinois	1945
Jecha, Ralph (G), Northwestern	1956
Jefferson, Roy (E), Utah	1965–69
Jelley, Tom (E), Miami	1951
Jenkins, Ralph (C), Clemson	1947
Jeter, Tony (E), Nebraska	1966, 1968
Johnson, John Henry (B),	
St. Mary's of California and	
Arizona State	1960–65
Johnson, Ron (CB),	
Eastern Michigan	1978
Johnston, Chet (B), Elmhurst	
and Marquette	1939–40
Johnston, Rex (B),	
Southern California	1960
Jones, Art (B), Richmond	1941, 1945

K

Kahler, Royal (T), Nebraska	1941
Kakasic, George (G), Duquesne	1936–39
Kalina, Dave (WR), Miami (Fla.)	1970
Kapele, John (T), Brigham Young	1960–62
Kaplan, Phil (G), Miami (Fla.)	1947
Karcis, John (B), Carnegie Tech	1936–38
Karets, Joe ( ),	———
Karpowich, Ed (T), Catholic U.	1936–39
Karras, Ted (T), Indiana	1958–59
Kase, George (G), Duquesne	1939
Kavel, George (B), Carnegie Tech	1934
Keating, Tom (DT), Michigan	1973
Kellum, Marv (LB), Wichita State	1974–76
Kelley, Jim (E), Notre Dame	1964
Kelsch, Mose (B), Christian	1933–34
Kemp, Jack (QB), Occidental	1957
Kemp, Ray (T), Duquesne	1933
Kenerson, John (G),	
Kentucky State	1962
Kerkorian, Gary (QB), Stanford	1952
Keys, Brady (B), Colorado State	1961–67
Kichefski, Walt (E), Miami	1940–42, 1944**
Kielbasa, Max (B), Duquesne	1946
Kiesling, Walt (G), St. Thomas	1937–38
Kiick, George (B), Bucknell	1940, 1945
Killorin, Pat (C), Syracuse	1966

Kilroy, Frank (T), Temple	1943*
Kimble, Frank (E),	
West Virginia	1945
King, Phil (B), Vanderbilt	1964
Kirk, Ken (LB), Mississippi	1960
Kish, Ben (B), Pitt	1943*
Kissell, Ed (B), Wake Forest	1952–54
Klapstein, Earl (T), Pacific	1946
Klein, Dick (T), Iowa	1961
Klumb, John (E), Washington State	1940
Kolb, Jon (OT), Oklahoma State	1969–78
Kolberg, Elmer (E), Oregon State	1941
Kondria, John (T), St. Vincent's	1945
Kortas, Ken (T), Louisville	1965–68
Kosanovich, Bronco (C), Penn State	1947
Koshlap, Jules (B), Georgetown	1945
Kotite, Dick (TE), Wagner	1968
Kottler, Martin (B), Centre	1933
Kresky, Joe (G), Wisconsin	1935
Krisher, Bill (G), Oklahoma	1958
Kruczek, Mike (QB),	
Boston College	1976–78
Krupa, Joe (DT), Purdue	1956–64
Kurrasch, Roy (E), UCLA	1948
Kvaternik, Cvonimir (G), Kansas	1934

L

Lach, Steve (B), Duke	1946–47
LaCrosse, Dave (LB), Wake Forest	1977–78
Ladygo, Pete (G), Maryland	1952, 1954
Lajousky, Bill (G), Catholic U.	1936
Lamas, Joe (G), Mount St. Mary's	1942
Lambert, Jack (LB), Kent State	1974–78
Lambert, Frank (K), Mississippi	1965–66
Lantz, Montgomery (C),	
Grove City	1933
Larose, Dan (T), Missouri	1964
Lassahn, Lou (E), Western	
Maryland	1938
Lasse, Dick (LB), Syracuse	1958–59
Lattner, John (B), Notre Dame	1954
Laux, Ted (B), St. Joseph of	
Pennsylvania	1943*
Law, Hubbard (C), Sam Houston	1942, 1945
Layne, Bobby (QB), Texas	1958–62
Lea, Paul (T), Tulane	1951
Leahy, Bob (QB), Emporia State	1971
Leahy, Gerald (B), Colorado	1957
Lee, Bernard (B), Villanova	1938
Lee, Herman (T), Florida A & M	1957
Lee, John (B), Carnegie Tech	1939
Leftridge, Dick (B), West Virginia	1966
Lemek, Ray (G), Notre Dame	1962–65
Letsinger, Jim (T), Purdue	1933
Levanti, Lou (G), Illinois	1951–52
Levey, Jim (B)	1934–36
Lewis, Frank (WR), Grambling	1971–77
Lewis, Joe (T), Compton Junior	1958–60
Liddick, Dave (T), George	
Washington	1957
Lind, Mike (B), Notre Dame	1965–66
Lipscomb, Gene (T)	1961–62
Littlefield, Carl (B),	
Washington State	1939
Logan, Charles (E), Northeastern	1964
Long, Bill (E), Oklahoma A & M	1949–50
Longnecker, Ken (T),	
Lebanon Valley	1960
Looney, Don (E), TCU	1941–42
Lowther, Russ (B), Detroit	1945
Lucente, John (B), West Virginia	1945

Luna, Bob (B), Alabama	1959
Lusteg, Booth (K), Connecticut	1968

M

Mack, Red (B), Notre Dame	1952–63, 1965
Mackrides, Bill (QB), Nevada	1953
Magac, Mike (G), Missouri	1965–66
Magulick, George (B), St. Francis	1944**
Maher, Francis (B), Toledo	1941
Malkovich, Joe (C), Duquesne	1935
Mallick, Francis (T)	1965
Mandich, Jim (TE)	1978
Mansfield, Ray (C), Washington	1964–76
Manske, Edgar (E), Northwestern	1938
Maples, Bob (C), Baylor	1971
Marion, Jerry (B), Wyoming	1967
Maras, Joe (C), Duquesne	1938–40
Marchi, Basilio (C), NYU	1934
Marchibroda, Ted (QB),	
St. Bonaventure and Detroit	1953, 1955–56
Marker, Henry (B), West Virginia	1934
Marotti, Lou (G), Toledo	1944**
Martha, Paul (B), Pitt	1964–69
Martin, John (B), Oklahoma	1944
Martin, Vernon (B), Texas	1942, 1944**
Masters, Bob (B), Baylor	1939, 1943*
Masters, Walt (B), Penn	1944**
Mastrangelo, John (G),	
Notre Dame	1947–48
Matesic, Ed (B), Pitt	1936
Matesic, Joe (T), Arizona State	1954
Mathews, Ray (B), Clemson	1951–59
Mattioli, Fran (G), Pitt	1946
Matuszak, Marv (LB), Tulsa	1953, 1955–56
Maxson, Alvin (RB), SMU	1977
May, Ray (LB), Southern	
California	1967–69
Mayhew, Hayden (G), Texas Mines	1936–38
Mazzanti, Jerry (E), Arkansas	1967
McCabe, Richie (B), Pitt	1955, 1957–58
McCaffray, Art (T), Pacific	1946
McCall, Don (RB), Southern	
California	1969
McCarthy, John (B), St. Francis	1944**
McClairen, Jack (E),	
Bethune-Cookman	1955–60
McClung, Willie (T), Florida A & M	1955–57
McConnell, Dewey (E), Wyoming	1954
McCullough, Hugh (B), Okla.	1939, 1943*
McDade, Karl (C), Portland	1938
McDonald, Ed (B), Duquesne	1936
McDonough, Coley (QB), Day	1939–41, 1944**
McDonough, Paul (E), Utah	1938
McFadden, Marv (G),	
Michigan State	1952, 1956
McGee, Ben (E), Jackson State	1964–72
McMakin, John (TE), Clemson	1972–74
McNally, John "Blood" (B),	
St. John of Minnesota	1934, 1937–39
McNamara, Ed (T), Holy Cross	1945
McPeak, Bill (E), Pitt	1949–57
McWilliams, Tom (B),	
Mississippi State	1950
Meadows, Ed (E), Duke	1955
Meeks, Bryant (C), South Carolina	1947–48
Mehelech, Chuck (E), Duquesne	1946–51
Meilinger, Steve (E), Kentucky	1961
Merkovsky, Elmer (T), Pitt	1944**, 1945–46
Messner, Max (LB), Cincinnati	1964–65
Meyer, Dennis (DB),	
Arkansas State	1973

ALL TIME STEELERS ROSTER: 1933–78
(continued)

Meyer, Ron (QB), South Dakota State	1966
Michael, Bill (G), Ohio State	1957
Michaels, Ed (G), Villanova	1943*
Michaels, Lou (R), Kentucky	1961–63
Michalik, Art (G), St. Ambrose	1955–56
Midler, Lou (G), Minnesota	1939
Miller, Tom (E), Hampden Sydney	1943*
Minarik, Henry (E), Michigan State	1951
Miner, Tom (E), Tulsa	1958
Mingo, Gene (K)	1969–70
Minini, Frank (B), San Jose State	1949
Modzelewski, Dick (T), Maryland	1955
Modzelewski, Ed (B), Maryland	1952
Moegle, Dick (B), Rice	1960
Momson, Tony (C), Michigan	1951
Moore, Bill (B), Loyola of New Orleans	1933
Moore, Red (G), Penn State	1947–49
Morales, Gonzales (B), St. Mary's of California	1947–48
Morgan, Bob (B), New Mexico	1967–68
Morrall, Earl (QB), Michigan State	1957–58
Morris, John (B), Oregon	1960
Moser, Rick (RB), Rhode Island	1978
Mosher, Clure (B), Louisville	1942
Mosley, Norm (B), Alabama	1948
Moss, Paul (E), Purdue	1933
Motley, Marion (B), Nevada	1955
Mott, Norm (B), Georgia	1934
Mulleneaux, Lee (C), Utah State	1935–36
Mullins, Gerry (G-OT), Southern California	1971–78
Murley, Dick (T), Purdue	1956
Murray, Earl (G), Purdue	1952
Musulin, George, Pitt	1938

N

Nagler, Gern (E), Santa Clara	1959
Naiota, John (B), St. Francis	1942, 1945
Nardi, Dick (B), Ohio State	1939
Nelsen, Bill (QB), Southern California	1963–67
Nery, Carl (G), Duquesne	1940–41
Niccolai, Armand (T), Duquesne	1934–42
Nichols, Allen (B), Temple	1945
Nichols, Bob (T), Stanford	1965
Nickel, Elbie (E), Cincinnati	1947–57
Nicksich, George (G), St. Bonaventure	1950
Nisby, John (G), Pacific	1957–61
Nix, Kent (QB), TCU	1967–69
Nixon, Mike (B), Pitt	1935
Nobile, Leo (G), Penn State	1948–49
Nofsinger, Terry (QB), Utah	1961–64
Noppenberg, John (B), Miami	1940–41
Nosich, John (T), Duquesne	1938
Nutter, "Buzz" (C), VPI	1961–64
Nuzum, Jerry (B), New Mexico A & M	1948–51

O

O'Brien, Fran (T), Michigan State	1966–67
O'Brien, John (E), Florida	1954–56
O'Delli, Mel (B), Duquesne	1944**, 1945
Oehler, John (C), Purdue	1933–34
Oelerich, John (B), St. Ambrose	1938
Olejniczak, Stan (T), Pitt	1935
Oliver, Clarence (DB), San Diego State	1969–70
Olszewski, Al (E), Penn State and Pitt	1945
O'Malley, Joe (E), Georgia	1955–56
O'Neil, Bob (G), Notre Dame	1956–57
Oniskey, Dick (G), Chattanooga	1955
Orr, Jim (E), Georgia	1958–60
Ortman, Chuck (QB), Michigan	1951

P

Palmer, Tom (T), Wake Forest	1953–54
Papach, George (B), Purdue	1948–49
Pastin, Frank (G), Waynesburg	1942
Paschell, Bill (B)	1940
Pascka, Gordon (G), Minnesota	1943
Patrick, John (B), Penn State	1941, 1945–46
Patterson, Bill (QB), Baylor	1940
Pavia, Ralph (G), Dayton	1947
Pavkov, Stonko (G), Idaho	1939–40
Peaks, Clarence (B), Michigan State	1964–65
Pearson, Barry (WR), Northwestern	1972–73
Pearson, Preston (B), Illinois	1970–74
Pense, Leon (QB), Arkansas	1945
Perko, John (G), Duquesne	1937–40, 1944**, 1945–47
Perry, Lowell (B), Michigan	1956
Petchel, John (QB), Duquesne	1945
Petersen, Ted (OT-C), Eastern Illinois	1977–78
Petrella, John (B), Penn State	1945
Pierre, John (E), Pitt	1945
Pillath, Roger (T), Wisconsin	1966
Pine, Ed (LB), Utah	1965
Pinney, Ray (OT-C), Washington	1976–78
Pirro, Rocco (G), Catholic U.	1940–41
Pittman, Mel (C), Hardin-Simmons	1935
Platukas, George (C), Duquesne	1938–41
Popovich, John (B), St. Vincent	1944**, 1945
Postus, Al (B), Villanova	1945
Pottios, Myron (LB), Notre Dame	1963–65
Potts, Bill (B), Villanova	1934
Pough, Ernest (WR), Texas Southern	1976–77
Powell, Tim (E), Northwestern	1966
Powers, John (E), Notre Dame	1962–66
Priatko, Bill (LB), Pitt	1957

Q

Quatse, Hesse (T), Pitt	1933–34

R

Raborn, Carrol (C), SMU	1936–37
Rado, Alex (B), New River State	1934–35
Rado, George (G), Duquesne	1935–38
Radosevich, George (C), Pitt	1953
Ragunas, Vince (B), VMI	1949
Rajkovich, Pete (B), Detroit	1934
Randour, Hub, Pitt	1935
Rankin, Walt (B), Texas Tech	1944**
Raskowski, Leo (T), Ohio State	1933
Reavis, Dave (OT), Arkansas	1974–75
Rechichar, Bert (B), Tennessee	1960
Reger, John (LB), Pitt	1955–63

Renfro, Will (G), Memphis State	1960
Repko, Joe (T), Boston College	1946–47
Recutt, Ray (E), VMI	1943*
Reynolds, Billy (B), Pitt	1958
Reynolds, Jim (B),	
Oklahoma A & M	1946
Rhodes, Don (T), W & J	1933
Ribble, Loran (G),	
Hardin-Simmons	1934–35
Richards, Perry (E), Detroit	1957
Riffle, Dick (B), Albright	1941–42
Rizzo, Tony, Duquesne	1938
Roberts, John (B), Georgia	1934
Robinson, Gil (E), Catawba	1933
Robinson, Jack (T),	
N.E. Missouri State	1938
Robnett, Marshall (C), Texas A & M	1944**
Rodak, Mike (B), West Reserve	1942
Rogel, Fran (B), Penn State	1950–57
Rogers, Cullen (B), Texas A & M	1946
Rorison, Jim (T),	
Southern California	1938
Rosepink, Marty (G), Pitt	1947
Rowley, Bob (LB), Virginia	1957
Rowser, John (DB), Michigan	1970–73
Rozelle, Aubrey (LB), Delta State	1957
Rucinski, Ed (E), Indiana	1944**
Ruple, Ernie (T), Arkansas	1968–69
Russell, Andy (LB), Missouri	1963, 1966–76
Ryan, Ed (E), St. Mary's (Cal.)	1948

S

Sader, Steve (B)	1943*
Sample, John (B), Maryland State	1961–62
Samuel, Don (B), Oregon State	1949–50
Samuelson, Carl (T), Nebraska	1948–51
Sandberg, Sigurd (T),	
Iowa Wesleyan	1935–37
Sandefur, Wayne (B), Purdue	1936–37
Sanders, John (G), SMU	1940–42
Sandig, Curt (B), St. Mary of Texas	1942
Sandusky, Mike (T), Maryland	1957–65
Sapp, Theron (B), Georgia	1963–65
Saul, Bill (LB), Penn State	1964, 1966–68
Saumer, Sylvester (B), St. Olaf	1934
Scarbath, Jack (QB), Maryland	1956
Scales, Charles (B), Indiana	1960–61
Scherer, Bernard (E), Nebraska	1939
Schiechl, John (C), Santa Clara	1941–42
Schmidt, John (C), Carnegie Tech	1940
Schmitz, Bob (LB),	
Montana State	1961–66
Schnelker, Bob (E),	
Bowling Green	1961
Schuelke, Karl (B), Wisconsin	1939
Schultz, Eberle (G), Oregon State	1941–42
Schwartz, Elmer (B),	
Washington State	1933
Schweder, John (G), Penn	1951–55
Scolnik, Glenn (WR), Indiana	1973
Scot, Wilbert (LB), Indiana	1961
Scudero, Joe (B), San Francisco	1960
Seabright, Charles (QB),	
West Virginia	1946–50
Sears, Vic (T), Oregon State	1943*
Sebastian, Mike (B), Pitt	1935
Semes, Bernard (B), Duquesne	1944**
Seward, Dean (B)	—
Sexton, Brent (DB), Elon	1977
Shaffer, George (B), W & J	1933
Shanklin, Ron (WR),	
North Texas State	1970–75

Sharp, Rick (T), Washington	1970–71
Shell, Donnie (DB),	
South Carolina State	1974–78
Shepard, Charles (B),	
North Texas State	1956
Sheriff, Stan (LB), Cal Polytech	1954
Sherman, Alex (QB), Brooklyn	1943*
Sherman, Bob (B), Iowa	1964–65
Shields, Burrell (B), John Carroll	1954
Shiner, Dick (QB), Maryland	1968–69
Shipkey, Jerry (B), UCLA	1948–52
Shorter, Jim (B), Detroit	1969
Shurtz, Hubert (T), LSU	1948
Shy, Don (B), San Diego State	1967–68
Simerson, John (T), Purdue	1958
Simington, Milt (G), Arkansas	1942
Simmons, Jerry (B),	
Bethune-Cookman	1965–66
Simms, Bob (E), Rutgers	1962
Simpson, Jack (B), Florida	1961–62
Sinkovitz, Frank (C), Duke	1947–52
Sirochman, George (G), Duquesne	1942
Sites, Vince (E), Pitt	1936–37
Skladany, Joe (E), Pitt	1934
Skorich, Nick (G),	
Cincinnati	1946–48
Skoronski, Ed (E), Purdue	1935–36
Skulos, Mike (G), W & J	1938
Slater, Walter (B), Tennessee	1947
Smith, Ben (E), Alabama	1934–35
Smith, Billy Ray (T), Arkansas	1958–60
Smith, Bob (B),	
North Texas State	1966
Smith, Dave (WR), Indiana (Pa.)	1970–72
Smith, Jim (WR), Michigan	1977–78
Smith, Laverne (RB), Kansas	1977–78
Smith, Ron (QB), Richmond	1966
Smith, Steve (E), Michigan	1966
Smith, Stu (QB), Bucknell	1937–38
Smith, Truett (QB), Wyoming	
and Mississippi State	1950–51
Smith, Warren (T), Kansas	
Wesleyan	1948
Snyder, Bill (G), Ohio U.	1934–35
Sodaski, John (DB), Villanova	1970
Soleau, Bob (LB), William & Mary	1964
Somers, George (T), LaSalle	1941–42
Sorce, Ross (T), Georgetown	1945
Sortet, Wilbur (E), West Virginia	1933–40
Souchak, Frank (E), Pitt	1939
Spinks, Jack (G), Alcorn A & M	1952
Spizak, Charley (QB),	
Carnegie Tech	1938
Staggers, Jon (WR), Missouri	1970–71
Stallworth, John (WR),	
Alabama A & M	1974–78
Stanton, John (B),	
North Carolina State	1961
Starret, Ben (B),	
St. Mary's of California	1941
Stautner, Ernie (T),	
Boston College	1950–63
Steele, Ernie (B), Washington	1943*
Stehouwer, Ron (B),	
Colorado State	1960–64
Stenger, Brian (LB), Notre Dame	1969–72
Stenn, Paul (T), Villanova	1947
Steward, Denn (B), Ursinus	1943*
Stock, John (E), Pitt	1956
Stofko, Ed (B), St. Francis	1945
Stoudt, Cliff (QB),	
Youngstown State	1977–78

Stough, Glen (T), Duke — 1945
Strand, Eli (G),
  Iowa State College — 1966
Strugar, George (T), Washington — 1962
Strutt, Art (B), Duquesne — 1935–36
Stule, Ernie (B) — ——
Suhey, Steve (G), Penn State — 1948–49
Sulima, George (E), Boston U. — 1952–54
Sullivan, Frank (C), Loyola
  (New Orleans) — 1940
Sullivan, Robert (B),
  Holy Cross Iowa — 1947
Sutherin, Don (B), Ohio State — 1959–60
Swann, Lynn (WR),
  Southern California — 1974–78
Szot, Walter (T), Bucknell — 1949–50

T

Tanguay, Jim (B), NYU — 1933
Tarasovic, George (E), LSU — 1952–53, 1956–63
Tatum, Jesse (E),
  North Carolina State — 1938
Taylor, Mike (T),
  Southern California — 1968–69
Tepe, Lou (C), Duke — 1953–55
Tesser, Ray (E), Carnegie Tech — 1933–34
Thomas, Clendon (B), Oklahoma — 1962–68
Thomas, J. T. (DB), Florida State — 1973–77
Thompson, Clarence (B),
  Minnesota — 1937–38
Thompson, Tommy (QB), Tulsa — 1940
Thornton, Sidney (RB),
  Northwestern Louisiana — 1977–78
Thurbon, Bob (B), Pitt — 1943*, 1944**
Tiller, Morgan (E), Denver — 1945
Tinsley, Sid (B), Clemson — 1945
Titus, George (C), Holy Cross — 1946
Toews, Loren (LB), California — 1973–78
Tomasetti, Lou (B), Bucknell — 1939–40
Tomasic, Andy (B), Temple — 1942–46
Tomlinson, Dick (G), Kansas — 1950–51
Tommerson, Clarence (B),
  Wisconsin — 1938–39
Tosi, John (G), Niagara — 1939
Tracy, Tom (B), Tennessee — 1958–63
Tsoutsouvas, Lou (C), Stanford — 1938
Turley, John (QB), Ohio Wesleyan — 1935–36

V

Van Dyke, Bruce (G), Missouri — 1967–73
Varrichione, Frank (T),
  Notre Dame — 1955–60
Vaughan, John (QB),
  Indiana State (Pa.) — 1933–34
Vidoni, Vic (E), Duquesne — 1935–36
Voss, Lloyd (T), Nebraska — 1966–71

W

Wade, Bob (DB), Morgan State — 1968
Wade, Tom (QB), Texas — 1964–65
Wager, Clint (E), St. Mary's of
  Minnesota — 1944**
Wagner, Mike (DB),
  Western Illinois — 1971–78
Walden, Bob (P), Georgia — 1968–77
Walsh, Bill (C), Notre Dame — 1949–55
Warren, Buist (B), Tennessee — 1945
Washington, Clarence (DT),
  Arkansas AM & N — 1969–70

Watkins, Tom (B), Iowa State — 1968
Watson, Allen (K),
  Newport (Wales) — 1970
Watson, Sid (B), Northeastern — 1955–57
Webster, Georgia (LB),
  Michigan State — 1972–73
Webster, Mike (C-G), Wisconsin — 1974–78
Weed, Thurlow (K), Ohio State — 1955
Weinberg, Henry (G), Duquesne — 1934
Weinstock, Izzy (B), Pitt — 1937–38
Weisenbaugh, Henry (B), Pitt — 1935
Wells, Billy (B),
  Michigan State — 1957
Wendlick, Joe (E), Oregon State — 1941
Wenzel, Ralph (E), Tulane — 1942
Wenzel, Ralph (G),
  San Diego State — 1966–70
Westfall, Ed (B), Ohio Wesleyan — 1933
Wetzel, Damon (B), Ohio State — 1935
Whalen, Tom (B), Catholic U. — 1933
Wheeler, Ernie (B),
  North Dakota State — 1939
White, Byron (B), Colorado — 1938
White, Dwight (DE),
  East Texas State — 1971–78
White, Paul (B), Michigan — 1947
Wiehl, Joe (T), Duquesne — 1935
Wilburn, J. R. (WR),
  South Carolina — 1966–70
Wiley, Jack (T), Waynesburg — 1946–50
Williams, Dave (WR),
  Washington — 1973
Williams, Don (G), Texas — 1941
Williams, Erwin (WR), Maryland State — 1969
Williams, Joe (B), Ohio State — 1939
Williams, Sidney (LB), Southern — 1969
Williamson, Fred (B),
  Northwestern — 1960
Wilson, Bill (E), Gonzaga — 1938
Winfrey, Carl (LB), Wisconsin — 1972
Winston, Dennis (LB), Arkansas — 1977–78
Wolf, Jim (DE), Prairie View — 1974
Womack, Joe (B),
  Los Angeles State — 1962
Woodson, Marv (B), Indiana — 1964–69
Woudenberg, John (T), Denver — 1940–42
Wren, Lowe (B), Missouri — 1960
Wukits, Al (C), Duquesne — 1943*, 1944**, 1945
Wydo, Frank (T), Cornell — 1947–51

Y

Young, Al (WR),
  South Carolina State — 1971–72
Young, Dick (B), Chattanooga — 1957
Younger, Paul (B), Grambling — 1958
Yurchey, John (B), Duquesne — 1940

Z

Zaninelli, Silvio (B), Duquesne — 1934–37
Zimmerman, Leroy (QB),
  San Jose State — 1943*
Zombek, Joe (E), Pitt — 1954
Zopetti, Frank (B), Duquesne — 1941

  * Steelers combined with Philadelphia Eagles.
  ** Steelers combined with Chicago Cardinals.